Here's What Others Are Saying About *Notary Public Handbook: A Guide For New York* *By Alfred E. Piombino*

"A review of **Notary Public Handbook: A Guide for New York** *reveals a desperately needed and well written book on the subject of notaries public. It is an invaluable, informative, instructive, clearly written, easy to use reference guide and provides a comprehensive collection of information concerning the office of notary public."*

Judge Mario A. Procaccino
Former Comptroller, City of New York
Former Commissioner of Taxation & Finance, State of New York

"The book has features which make it valuable for the lay reader merely interested in the topic and very valuable for anyone facing the notary examination. It should be quite valuable to libraries in New York, and to candidates taking the examination. The text is easily understood by a lay reader. I liked the enthusiasm shown for the subject by the author and his personal approach to the reader."

Dr. Michael Pope
Director of the Library
Dutchess Community College

"We have a number of notaries public here in City Hall. They are a vital part of municipal government. I will bring this important book to their attention."

The Honorable Edward I. Koch
Mayor, City of New York

"An excellent resource on the topic. It explains all aspects of the office in language that is clear and concise. The notary public performs a valuable service for citizens from all walks of life and this book meets a long-standing need for information on the office."

Ms. Ethel Mueller
Head, Reference Department
Adriance Memorial Library

"The notary public provides an essential task in society requiring integrity and good judgment. Notaries public should be proud to serve their citizenry, and in turn, the citizenry should be knowledgeable of, and show the office its merited respect. ***Notary Public Handbook: A Guide for New York*** *is a clear, understandable presentation of the notary's duties . . . a valuable reference guide for current notaries public and the general public needing their assistance."*

The Honorable Hamilton Fish, Jr.
United States Congressman
Vice Chairman, Judiciary Committee, House of Representatives

NOTARY PUBLIC HANDBOOK:
A Guide for New York

FOURTH EDITION

Alfred E. Piombino

East Coast Publishing

First Printing, 1988
Second Printing, 1989 completely revised
Third Printing, 1990
Fourth Printing, 1990
Fifth Printing, 1991
Sixth Printing, 1992 revised
Seventh Printing, 1993 revised
Eighth Printing, 1994 revised
Ninth Printing, 1995 revised
Tenth Printing, 1995 revised
Eleventh Printing, 1995 revised
Twelfth Printing, 1996 revised
Thirteenth Printing, 1997 revised
Fourteenth Printing, 1997 revised
Fifteenth Printing, 1998 revised
Sixteenth Printing, 1999 revised
Seventeenth Printing, 2000 completely revised
Eighteenth Printing, 2002 revised
Nineteenth Printing, 2003
Twentieth Printing, 2004
Twenty-First Printing, 2011

Cover design: Charlotte Staub, New York, New York
Typography: Peirce Graphic Services, Inc., Stuart, Florida
Photography: Dave Makris, Poughkeepsie, New York
Printing and Binding: Bookmasters, Inc., Ashland, Ohio

Library of Congress Cataloging-in-Publication Data

Piombino, Alfred E. (Alfred Ernest), 1962–
Notary public handbook: a guide for New York / Alfred E. Piombino.—4th Ed.
p. cm.
Includes bibliographical references and index.
ISBN 0-944560-50-4
1. Notaries—New York (State) 2. Commissioners of Deeds—New York (State)
I. Title.
KFN5985.N6P66 2011
347.747'016—dc20
[347.470716] CIP

Printed in the United States of America

About the Author

Recognized as the "Dean" of American notaries, independent scholar Alfred E. Piombino is a notary law, practice and ethics authority. As a speaker on the national lecture circuit, Piombino's dynamic style and rare humor place him behind lecterns addressing scores of prestigious groups including the National Association of Secretaries of State, the International Association of Clerks, Recorders, Election Officials and Treasurers, International Institute of Municipal Clerks, and the Center for Financial Training.

Piombino is the author of nine legal books, a courtroom expert witness and litigation consultant and is listed in *Who's Who in American Law*. When notarial-legal issues arise, he is a sought-after commentator, quoted by news media including *The New York Times*, *The Wall Street Journal* and *USA Today*.

His public office dossier includes government duty in numerous professional, public administration posts, including Civil Service Commissioner and Fair Hearing Officer for the City of Portland, Maine. He held the state constitutional office of Register of Probate for the County of Cumberland, Maine, serving as Chief Clerk, Magistrate and Surrogate of the Probate Court and Registry of Probate. He holds a life term as a Maine State Dedimus Justice.

He is a member of the American Bar Association Information Security Committee and a contributor to American Bar Association *Model Digital Signature Guidelines* concerning electronic signatures, encryption, and electronic legal documents.

Mr. Piombino received his Bachelor of Science Degree and a Master of Public Administration Degree from Marist College in New York. He is a Harvard Law School trained mediator and is past State University of New York (SUNY) college business law faculty.

He was born in the Hudson River Valley Region of New York, near Hyde Park in Dutchess County.

NOTARY PUBLIC HANDBOOK:
A Guide for New York

FOURTH EDITION

This book is dedicated to my grandmother,
Madeline Elmendorf,
and my grandfather,
Alfonso Piombino.

"The study of the law qualifies a man to be useful to himself, to his neighbors, and to the public."

Thomas Jefferson, 1790

Acknowledgments

The project of writing a book demands countless hours of research, drafting and editing. Throughout each of these phases, I was fortunate to receive the assistance and cooperation of numerous individuals, agencies and institutions.

I would like to recognize Nicholas A. Tulve, Jr., of Newburgh, recipient of the 2000 "Notary of the Year" Award from the American Society of Notaries, for his guidance, helpful suggestions and professional encouragement.

Thanks are given to the following people for extending their cooperation, professional courtesy and friendship: Hon. Thomas G. Clingan, Albany Co. Clerk; Hon. Joseph Presutti, Allegany Co. Clerk; Hon. Hector L. Diaz, Bronx Co. Clerk; Hon. Barbara J. Fiala, Broome Co. Clerk; Hon. James K. Griffith, Cattaraugus Co. Clerk; Hon. Joseph R. Marshall, Cayuga Co. Clerk; Hon. Sandra Sopak, Chautauqua Co. Clerk; Hon. Catherine K. Hughes, Chemung Co. Clerk; Hon. Mary C. Weidman, Chenango Co. Clerk; Hon. John H. Zurlo, Clinton Co. Clerk; Hon. Lisa Lewicki, Columbia Co. Clerk; Hon. Judith F. Riehlman, Cortland Co. Clerk; Hon. Gary L. Cady; Delaware Co. Clerk; Hon. Richard M. Anderson, Dutchess Co. Clerk; Hon. David J. Swarts, Erie Co. Clerk; Hon. Joseph A. Provoncha, Essex Co. Clerk; Hon. Wanda D. Murtagh, Franklin Co. Clerk; Hon. William E. Eschler, Fulton Co. Clerk; Hon. Don M. Read, Genesee Co. Clerk; Hon. Mary Ann Kordich, Greene Co. Clerk; Hon. Jane S. Zarecki, Hamilton Co. Clerk; Hon. Sylvia M. Rowan, Herkimer; Hon. Jo Ann M. Wilder, Jefferson Co. Clerk; Hon. Wilbur Levin, Kings Co. Clerk; Hon. Douglas Hanno, Lewis Co. Clerk; Hon. James Culbertson, Livingston Co. Clerk; Hon. O. Perry Tooker, III, Madison Co. Clerk; Hon. Maggie Brooks, Monroe Co. Clerk; Hon. Helen A. Bartone, Montgomery

Co. Clerk; Hon. Karen V. Murphy, Nassau Co. Clerk; Hon. Norman Goodman, New York Co. Clerk; Hon. Wayne F. Jagow, Niagara Co. Clerk; Hon. A. Sandra Caruso, Oneida Co. Clerk; M. Ann Ciarpelli, Onondaga Co. Clerk; Hon. John H. Cooley, Ontario Co. Clerk; Hon. Donna L. Benson, Orange Co. Clerk; Hon. Carol R. Lonnen, Orleans Co. Clerk; Hon. George J. Williams, Oswego Co. Clerk; Brian F. Carso, Otsego Co. Clerk; Hon. Joseph L. Peloso, Jr., Putnam Co. Clerk; Hon. Gloria D'Amico, Queens Co. Clerk; Hon. Frank J. Merola, Rensselaer Co. Clerk; Hon. Mario J. Esposito, Richmond Co. Clerk; Hon. Edward Gorman, Rockland Co. Clerk; Hon. Patricia Ritchie, St. Lawrence Co. Clerk; Hon. Kathleen A. Marchione, Saratoga Co. Clerk; Hon. John Woodward, Schenectady Co. Clerk; Hon. E. David Hallock, Schoharie Co. Clerk; Hon. Linda M. Compton, Schuyler Co. Clerk; Hon. Christina Louise Lotz, Seneca Co. Clerk; Hon. Judith M. Hunter, Steuben Co. Clerk; Hon. Edward P. Romaine, Suffolk Co. Clerk; Hon. George L. Cooke, Sullivan Co. Clerk; Hon. Carole LaPlante, Tioga Co. Clerk; Hon. Aurora Valenti, Tompkins Co. Clerk; Hon. Albert Spada, Ulster Co. Clerk; Hon. Caryl M. Clark, Warren Co. Clerk; Hon. Donald J. Stewart, Washington Co. Clerk; Hon. Leonard N. Spano, Westchester Co. Clerk; Hon. Janet Coveny, Wyoming Co. Clerk, and Hon. Julie Betts, Yates Co. Clerk.

I would like to extend my appreciation to the librarians at the following libraries for their reference assistance: Adriance Memorial Library, Poughkeepsie; Dutchess Community College, Poughkeepsie; Marist College, Poughkeepsie; New York Public Library, 42nd Street, Manhattan; and Vassar College, Poughkeepsie.

In addition, special thanks go to: Joan House and Yvonne Smith, New York State Library, Albany; Duncan McCollum and Roger Ritzmann, New York State Archives; Richard Arnold, MacDonald Dewitt Library at Ulster (County) Community College, Stone Ridge; and Catherine A. Maher, New York State Supreme Court–John F. Barnard Memorial Law Library at Poughkeepsie.

I am grateful for assistance from Judge Mario C. Procaccino; Hon. Hamilton Fish Jr., U.S. Congressman, 21st District; Hon. Edward I. Koch, Mayor of the City of New York; Scott L. Volkman, Esq.; Dr. Michael Pope, Dutchess Community College; Ethel Mueller, Adriance Memorial Library; Hon. Jay P. Rolison

Jr., N.Y. State Senator, 41st District; Hon. Stephen Saland, N.Y. Member of Assembly, 97th District; Hon. Melvin N. Zimmer, N.Y. Member of Assembly, 120th District; Joseph Amello, New York State Department of State; Mary Ann Burnhans, Theresa Gilgert and Dottie Fitchett.

I wish to gratefully acknowledge the contributions of Francis J. Serbaroli, Esq., for his considerable efforts, suggestions, ideas and insights.

I owe a special debt of thanks to my editor, Kathleen K. Makris, whose help and management efforts were priceless. Through her patient and meticulous review of each draft, the manuscript was refined into a polished book.

Finally, I am thankful for the suggestions received from the many individuals not previously mentioned. The support and encouragement of my colleagues, students, friends, and especially my parents, Barbara Jean and Alfred R. Piombino, have helped to make this challenging project most invigorating and enjoyable.

Table of Contents

Preface

After teaching hundreds of notary public orientation and refresher seminars, it was quite surprising to discover how little is known about notarial powers and duties, particularly among commissioned notaries public. Amazingly, virtually all the attendees at these classes thought the function of a notary public was to merely verify signatures and nothing else! At one class in particular, a commissioned notary public candidly admitted before his peers that he "wanted to learn what [he] should have been doing for the past twelve years." These experiences made me question how effectively all the notaries public were performing their duties as required by law. This information is only one symptom of a much greater ailment.

The New York State Association of Notaries Public, Inc., (NYSANP), designed and conducted a comprehensive, statewide study of notary public performance. The sample consisted of 220 randomly selected notaries in 22 cities, utilizing a common affidavit, which was presented to the notary public for "notarization". The final results were shocking. Some of the more negligent actions included: 91.7% failed to administer an oath of any form; 82.5% failed to adequately identify the affiant; 97.7% failed to indicate the correct venue on the affidavit; and 46.5% of the rubber stamps used were not in legal conformity. It was reported that the overwhelming majority of the acts were performed in a cavalier manner, and in many cases, the entire process was merely the notary applying his stamp impression and official signature to the affidavit.

The special investigation was the first formal audit of this nature on notarial activity in United States history.

These and other results of the study are evidence of the advanced stage of decay and neglect that the office of notary public has suffered. As an integral component of the state's legal/judicial system, these implications hold grave consequences. For example, the courts depend heavily upon the affidavits and depositions presented as evidence, and rely upon the notary public to administer an oath or affirmation to the affiant/deponent. The introduction of unsworn affidavits and depositions could potentially jeopardize the integrity of the entire justice system.

The national attention that has resulted from the release of this landmark investigation has caused many states to launch their own probes of the competence and integrity of their notaries public.

One of the major factors contributing to this chaos is that previously, the guidelines and regulations for notaries public were not found in one source. Instead, they were scattered among numerous separate volumes of state law, including Real Property Law, General Construction Law, Executive Law, Public Officers Law, Uniform Commercial Code, Banking Law, Domestic Relations Law, Election Law, Penal Law, Judicial Law, Civil Practice Law and Rules, and the Constitution of the State of New York. The Common Law and the decisions of many court cases also have a direct impact upon the powers, duties and procedures of notaries public.

The only resource the state provides for notaries public or those preparing for the required exam is a skimpy 12 page booklet. It contains a hodgepodge of laws and definitions, brimming with paragraph-long sentences of "legalese." This disarray of information is a far cry from a clearly written, easy-to-use reference guide. Rather than stimulating enthusiasm and a desire to learn more about the office, this booklet instills unnecessary apprehension, confusion and fails to impart a clear understanding of notarial duties and responsibilities. It simply does not contain all of the information a notary public *needs* to correctly perform his duties, nor does it explain why certain legal procedures *must* be performed properly.

Because of the lack of knowledge conveyed during the seminars and the shocking results of the study, I was determined to write this book, providing a single, comprehensive collection concerning the office of notary public. This book is filled with helpful suggestions gained from actual situations experienced by notaries public working in a variety of fields. Confusing laws, concepts and procedures are clarified in plain English. Many examples and sample documents are provided to illustrate situations that the notary public is likely to encounter. An emphasis is placed upon realistically and practically guiding the reader through the procedures.

The New York State Association of Notaries Public, Inc., (NYSANP), has been founded to support and represent New York notaries. This non-profit corporation is dedicated to the state-wide improvement of the office of notary public. It was formed to foster excellence, unity, and recognition of all New York notaries public, and improve the quality of notarial services provided to the public. NYSANP is leading the effort to restore the rightful dignity, deserved esteem and public trust of this honorable office. NYSANP will help strengthen the integrity of notaries public by providing them with the knowledge, confidence and support they need to properly perform their duties for the public who depend upon them.

While the results of the state-wide study bear serious consequences, the potential for restoring the esteem and trust of the office of notary public appears attainable, through a cohesive effort of notary public educational programs, coupled with the use of this reference guide, and the support of the New York State Association of Notaries Public.

The duties and responsibilities of the office of notary public should never be taken casually. After taking the oath of office, a citizen has "crossed the threshold" and assumed the duties and responsibilities as a public officer. When performing duties, notaries public should insist that their constituents seeking their official services show due respect for the office. Notaries public should proudly and honorably perform their duties, never compromising the standards of the office. Keeping these ideals in mind, serving their fellow citizens will be a rewarding and interesting experience.

A.E.P.

Chapter 1

The Office of Notary Public

With its origins in the judiciary, the office of notary public is a respected position in our society with an interesting history. It is not a right, but a privilege to receive an appointment as a notary public. A person admitted into the honorable class of officers has the right to be proud of this achievement.

The notary public holds a trusted role in our legal and commercial systems. As a government officer, the notary is typically involved in the initial stages of many critical as well as routine situations. Integrity and good judgment are vital qualities of an effective notary public.

Nature of the Office

The notary public is a sworn public officer with the power to perform a number of official legal acts. In most states, including New York, a notary public is a state officer. The office of notary public is technically classified as a ministerial office, meaning it does not involve significant judgment or discretion of the notarial acts being performed. It is not a judicial or legislative position.

Although the office has been categorized as ministerial, in many instances the prudent judgment of the notary public is reasonable and essential. For example, the law requires a notary public to refuse to officiate unless the parties are personally known or their identity has been satisfactorily proven. However, the state does not clearly define how to identify those individuals. The decision is left to the careful judgment of the notary public. Use of the office of notary public in other than the specific, step-by-step procedure required by law is viewed as a serious offense by the state.

In New York, notaries public are commissioned by the secretary of state. The appointment is based upon a favorable review of an application for appointment and acceptable results achieved on a written examination.

In 2000, New York had approximately 248,000 notaries public. The state's population at that time was 17,735,000 residents. The ratio equalled 14.0 notaries for every 1000 residents.

Origin and History of Notaries Public

The origin of public officers now called notaries public can be traced to the ancient Roman Republic, although their functions are now different. At the time of the Republic, *scribae* and *librarii* or public secretaries were found. The private secretaries (frequently slaves) were called *exceptores,* and *notarii* if they were shorthand writers. The paid public secretaries assisted authorities in their duties of office, similar to our contemporary secretaries.

The public secretaries increased both in number and importance. They worked in the cabinet of the Emperor in distinct departments under the supervision of a *magister scriniorum.* Other persons called *tabelliones* can be compared to our present notaries public. In the public marketplace or forum, scribes offered their services to persons who wanted to have their letters written or documents drawn. This class of persons was *tabelliones forenses* or *persona publicae.* They provided the services of drafting legal documents or *libelli,* which would be presented to the courts of law or other authorities of state. Fee schedules were established for them by the authorities.

The number of *tabelliones* grew rapidly. They formed into a guild or corporation called *schola,* under a presiding officer called *primicerius.* The state authorities began to watch over them, determining whether a person should be admitted into (or an unworthy person removed from) the guild. These persons prepared legal documents, but they still carried on their business in the public market place. Specific requirements were outlined which qualified a document as legal evidence.

Witnesses attested the papers drawn by these public scribes or *tabelliones.* It was later required by law that three witnesses should attest a document in cases where the principals could write; five witnesses if the parties could not write. It was further required that the notary public or *tabellio* be physically present at the drawing of the document and sign and date the execution.

Emperors and princes, needing documents drawn and countersigned, appointed and employed *notarii.* Additional notaries were appointed by popes, bishops and cloisters.

During the Middle Ages, a candidate had to undergo an examination. The study became formalized with rules and notarial schools were established.

Gradually, royal notaries were no longer recognized. Only notaries public appointed by the general government were given authority as public officers and recognized to perform notarial duties.

In England, the functions and powers of a notary public include drawing and preparing deeds relating to real and personal property, noting and protesting bills of exchange, preparing acts of honor and authenticating and certifying examined copies of documents. They prepare and attest documents going abroad, receive the affidavits or declarations of mariners and masters of ships and draft their protests, and perform all other notarial acts, including administer oaths, affirmations and affidavits.

In the United States, the duties and functions of notaries public resemble those of England. They are appointed by state/commonwealth governors or another state officer for a specific term and receive their powers from the government of the people through the laws of the state or commonwealth.

The Civil Law Notary

The historical origins of the civil law notary and the common law notary public are the same, but the two occupations have developed along very different lines. Our notary public is a person of very slight importance. The civil law notary is a person of considerable importance. The notary in the typical civil law country services three principal functions. First, he drafts important legal instruments, such as wills, corporate charters, conveyances, and contracts. Although advocates [akin to a common lawyer] sometimes get involved in drafting instruments, the notary continues to do most of this work in civil law nations. an spite of the notary's established position in this field, however, there is some tension between advocates and notaries over jurisdictional matters.) Second, the notary authenticates instruments. An authenticated instrument (called everywhere in the civil law world a "public act") has special evidentiary effects; it conclusively establishes that the instrument itself is genuine, and what it recites accurately represents what the parties said and what the notary saw and heard. Evidence that contradicts the statements in a public act is not admissible in an ordinary judicial proceeding. One who wishes to attack the authenticity of a public act must institute a special action for that purpose, and such an action is rarely brought. Third, the notary acts as a kind of public record office. He is required to retain a copy of every instrument he prepares and furnish authenticated copies on request. An authenticated copy usually has the same evidentiary value as an original.

Civil law notaries are usually given quasi-monopolies. A typical civil law nation will be divided into notarial districts, and in each district a limited number of notaries will have exclusive competence. Unlike advocates, who are free to refuse to serve a client, the notary must serve all comers. This, added to his functions as record office and his monopoly position, tends to make him a public as well as private functionary. Access to the profession of notary is difficult because the number of notarial offices is quite limited. Candidates for notarial positions must ordinarily be graduates of university law schools, and must serve an apprenticeship in a notary's office. Typically, aspirants for such positions will take a national examination, and if successful, will be appointed to a vacancy when it occurs. Ordinarily there will be a national notaries organization that will serve the same sort of functions for notaries as the national bar association serves for advocates and other organizations for judges, prosecutors, and government lawyers.

The civil law tradition is dominant in Western Europe, all of Latin America, and many parts of Asia, Africa, and the Middle East. It is also dominant in Quebec, Canada, as well as Louisiana and Puerto Rico in the United States.

Source: *The Civil Law Tradition: An Introduction to the Legal Systems of Western Europe and Latin America* by John Henry Merryman, Stanford University Press, Stanford, California, 1969.

Authorized Notarial Practice

A notary public is a public officer whose function is to:

1. administer *oaths* and *affirmations;*
2. attest and certify, by his signature and official seal, certain documents in order to make them legally acceptable outside of New York;

3. take and certify *acknowledgments* and *proofs of execution* of documents;
4. take and certify *affidavits;*
5. take and certify *depositions;*
6. perform certain official acts relating to commercial matters, such as the *protesting* of notes, bills and drafts; and
7. serve as an *official state witness* in connection with the forced opening of bank safe deposit boxes.

The notary public is authorized by the state or federal law to administer oaths and to attest (i.e. declare to be genuine) the authenticity of signatures. Notaries public are appointed by the state to assist citizens in performing certain official legal and business acts. This is accomplished by the officer attaching his name and official certificate to documents.

UNAUTHORIZED NOTARIAL PRACTICE

Unless a lawyer, a notary public cannot engage directly or indirectly in the practice of law. Violation could lead to removal from office, possible imprisonment, fines, or all three penalties. The following list represents forbidden activities involving the practice of law:

A notary public:

1. may *not* give advice on the law. He may not draw any legal papers, such as wills, deeds, bills of sale, mortgages, contracts, chattel mortgages, leases, offers, options, incorporation papers, releases, mechanic liens, powers of attorney, complaints, all legal pleadings, papers in summary proceedings to evict a tenant or in bankruptcy, or any paper which the courts have said are legal documents or papers;
2. may *not* ask for and/or receive legal business to send to a lawyer or lawyers with whom he has any business connection or from whom he receives any money or other consideration for sending the business;
3. may *not* divide or agree to divide his fees with a lawyer or accept any part of a lawyer's fee on any legal business; and
4. may *not* advertise, circulate or state that he has any powers or rights not given to a notary public.

Notaries Public Ex-Officio

A variety of officials, in addition to notaries public, may administer oaths and affirmations, take affidavits, depositions, and acknowledgments. The jurisdiction limitation depends on the office. An ex-officio notary is sometimes referred to as a notarial officer.

Acknowledgments and *proofs of execution* of a conveyance (or deed) of New York real property may be taken by the following officials under the conditions noted.

State supreme court justices, official examiners of title, official referees (and notaries public) may perform state-wide.

Judges of courts of record, court clerks, commissioners of deeds, city mayors and recorders, surrogate court judges, special surrogate court judges, special county judges, county clerks or other county recording officers may act within their official jurisdiction.

Justices of the peace, town councilmen, village police justices, or judges of courts of "inferior" (local) jurisdiction may act anywhere in the county containing the town, village or city in which they are authorized to perform their official duties.

Oaths and *affirmations* may be administered by any person authorized to take acknowledgments of deeds by the Real Property Law. Any person authorized by state law to receive evidence may administer an oath or affirmation for that purpose. Juror oaths may be administered by a court clerk and his deputies. However, this does not apply to any oath of office.

An *oath of office* may be administered by: a judge of the court of appeals; the state attorney general; any officer authorized to take (within the state) the acknowledgment of the execution of a real property deed; an officer in whose office the oath is legally required to be filed (or by his properly designated assistant); or the presiding officer or clerk (who have themselves taken an oath of office) of a body of officers.

A notary public has the power to administer *either* form of oath.

Secretary of State

Appointed by the governor, the secretary of state is responsible for the department of state. Responsibilities include being the depository of the original state laws, records, and filing certificates of assumed names and certificates of incorporation (other than those involving banking, insurance and education institutions). The department is the agent for process served upon New York corporations. The secretary of state records corporate dissolutions; authorizes foreign corporations to do business in the state; attests and records the issuance of commissions to state officers; may appoint and remove notaries public; appoints commissioners of deeds in other states and territories; and administers oaths of office to legislators and other state officers.

The secretary of state regulates and licenses real estate brokers and salespersons, barbers, cosmetologists and hairdressers, private investigators, billiard rooms, steamship ticket agents, hearing aid dealers, apartment referral agents, those involved in the renovation and sale of bedding and upholstered furniture, and motor vehicle manufacturers. The secretary of state also approves real estate courses offered to potential salespersons and brokers. In addition, the department registers trademarks and service marks, trading stamp companies and games of chance utilized in promoting retail sales (other than the New York State Lottery).

The department serves as a clearing house of information about the kinds of federal, state and private assistance available to local governments. In this regard, the secretary of state contracts and cooperates with the federal government in administering grants to the state and municipalities, metropolitan regional planning agencies, community action agencies and Indian tribal councils. The department of state administers and provides technical assistance for the following grant programs: the Low Income Home Energy Assistance Program; the Community Services Block Grant; the Coastal Energy Impact Program: the Coastal Zone Management Program; the Appalachian Regional Commission; and Department of Energy Weatherization Grants.

Through the office of fire prevention and control, the department administers the fire mobilization and mutual aid plan and the statewide fire incident reporting system. The department of state's codes division makes funds available to localities to help them implement the Uniform Fire Prevention and Building Code.

County Clerk

The county clerk is the chief recording officer of each county. He is elected in a general election in all state counties, except in the five counties of New York City, where he is appointed by the appellate division of the state supreme court in the judicial department in which the county is located.

He is the custodian of all "recordable" documents and records for a county. Property deeds and mortgages, business certificates (assumed business names), corporation papers, change of name documents, pistol permit records, oaths of office and signature files of notaries public, judgments, liens, foreclosures, as well as other documents including divorce papers, adoption records, powers of attorney, veteran's discharges, lis pendens and various other records are filed, deposited, and recorded in his office.

The county clerk processes applications for U.S. Passports and state hunting/fishing licenses, and operates the local offices of the state department of motor vehicles. In addition, he is the clerk of the local state supreme court and county courts.

Effective July 24, 1991, New York law requires each of the 62 county clerk's offices to provide notary services at no cost during normal office hours.

Commissioners in Other States

A commissioner of deeds possesses powers similar to a notary. This appointed public office was created by state statute in 1818 in an effort to supplement the number of notaries public. The scope of authority of a commissioner, however, is limited to taking oaths and affirmations, oaths of office, acknowledgments and proofs of execution. Unlike the notary public, a commissioner has no powers or functions by virtue of the common law.

A commissioner is limited in his authority to exercise his official powers to the boundaries of the jurisdiction (e.g. city) for which he is appointed. Although the eligibility requirements are essentially the same as applicants for notary public commissions, a commissioner must reside in New York, regardless if employed at a New York business address.

Commissioners are entitled to collect fees for services in accordance with the statutory fee schedule for notaries public. There is no difference in fee structure. No additional fees are permitted. Commissioners are subject to disciplinary action and removal from office for misconduct by the local government which granted their appointment. Terms of office are two years. Generally, the commissioner is required to perform his official notarial acts in a manner identical to a notary public.

Foreign commissioners of deeds are appointed by the secretary of state to assist New Yorkers in other states and countries. These commissioners reside in another state or country and, for example, take acknowledgments of deeds and other papers which are to be used as evidence or filed in New York.

Chapter 1 Questions

1. What is a notary public?
2. What is the nature of the office of notary public?
3. Briefly explain the origin and history of the office of notary public.
4. Who appoints and commissions a notary public?
5. How is a commission different than a license?
6. Explain the term "ministerial".
7. What is authorized notarial practice?
8. What is unauthorized notarial practice?
9. Explain the difference between the civil law and common law notary public. Which is the basis for the notary public in the United States? Which two U.S. jurisdictions are exceptions to this rule?
10. What are the three principal functions of a civil law notary public?
11. Who are ex-officio notaries public?
12. What is a commissioner of deeds?
13. What are the duties of commissioners of deeds? Explain the origin of this role.
14. Explain the difference between a notary public and a commissioner of deeds.
15. Explain the difference between a domestic and foreign commissioner of deeds.

Chapter 2

The Commissioning Process in New York

ELIGIBILITY AND QUALIFICATIONS

To be eligible for appointment to the office of notary public, New York Public Officers Law requires a minimum age of 18 years at the time of application. The applicant is required to be a resident of New York or otherwise have an office or place of business in the state. There is no minimum length of residency requirement. According to New York law, U.S. citizenship is required for appointment. Because of a ruling by the U.S. Supreme Court in 1984 which overturned a Texas requirement of U.S. citizenship, New York's Department of State is now disregarding the New York law. Therefore, the inconsistency is evident that while the U.S. Supreme Court has ruled that an appointment cannot be denied strictly on the basis that an applicant is an alien, New York law maintains that an alien is ineligible.

Unless the applicant is an attorney and counsellor at law admitted to practice in New York, the secretary of state requires separate verification that the applicant is of good moral character. The applicant must have the equivalent of a common school (sixth grade elementary school) education and be familiar with the duties and responsibilities of of a notary public. The applicant must also pass a written examination.

A proposed change of the Executive Law allowing an alien to be eligible for consideration of appointment was allowed to die (expire) at the end of the 1985–86 state legislative session.

Attorneys

A person admitted to practice as an attorney and counselor in the courts of New York (and who maintains an office for the practice of law is in New York) is eligible for appointment. He may retain his appointment although residing in or moving to an adjoining state. The attorney is considered a resident of the county where he maintains his law office. If an attorney desires appointment as a notary public, he must submit a completed application for appointment with the required application fee to the secretary of state. The written examination requirement is waived for lawyers admitted to the New York Bar.

Member of the State Legislature

A member of the state legislature may be appointed as a notary public. According to the New York Constitution, however, if a state legislator accepts appointment to any civil office under the Government of the United States, or the State of New York or any municipality (except state militia and U.S. military reserves), the member's legislative seat will become vacant (i.e. he loses his legislative position). This is because a person is generally not permitted to hold two public offices at the same time. The restriction does not apply to an appointment to any office in which the member will not receive compensation. Notaries public were previously approved by the senate (part of the legislative branch); they are now appointed by the secretary of state (executive branch). Therefore, a person can be a member of the state legislature and a notary public at the same time.

Commissioner/Inspector of Elections

Commissioners and inspectors of elections are also exceptions to the previously stated law. Although they may occupy two state offices at the same time (notary public and commissioner/inspector), the Election Law designates that they are eligible for appointment and would not have to give up one position for the other.

Ineligibility

An essential element of the office of notary public is integrity. Notaries public and applicants should be aware that any demonstration—criminal or otherwise—of dishonesty may lead to their disqualification. Further, the notary public may have his commission revoked (for due cause) at any time during his term of office. ***Moral turpitude*** is the phrase which refers to anything done contrary to justice, honesty, modesty or morality. It includes corrupted and perverted offenses concerning the duties which a person owes to another or to society, contrary to the accepted and customary rules between members of society. It implies something immoral in itself, regardless of whether it is punishable by law. Therefore, it excludes unintentional wrong or an improper act done without unlawful intent. It is usually restricted to the most serious offenses, consisting of felonies and crimes which are ***malum in se*** (a wrong in itself).

Crimes are distinguished into two classifications—misdemeanor and felony. A misdemeanor is a crime punishable by a prison term of less than one year. A felony is a crime punishable by a prison term of one year or more.

No one may be appointed as a notary public who has been convicted in New York or elsewhere, of a *felony* or any of the following offenses (which are misdemeanors and felonies):

A. illegally using, carrying or possessing a pistol or other dangerous weapon;
B. making or possessing burglar's instruments;
C. buying or receiving or criminally possessing stolen property;
D. unlawful entry of a building;
E. aiding escape from a prison;
F. unlawfully possessing or distributing habit forming narcotic drugs;
G. violations of the former Penal Law as in force and effect immediately prior to September 1, 1967:
   section 270 (practicing or appearing as attorney at law without being admitted and registered);
   270-a (soliciting business on behalf of an attorney);
   270-b (entering hospital to negotiate settlement or obtain release or statement);
   270-c (aiding, assisting or abetting the solicitation of persons or the procurement of a retainer for or on behalf of an attorney);
   271 (none but attorneys to practice in the state),
   275 (purchase of claims by corporations or collections agencies);
   276 (sharing of compensation by attorneys prohibited),

550 (sending letter or simulating document, when deemed complete); and
551-a (simulating documents);

H. violating section 722 of the former Penal Law as in force and effect immediately prior to September 1, 1967:
subsection 6 (jostling/swindling);
subsection 8 (loitering and soliciting men for purpose of committing a crime against nature or other lewdness);
subsection 10 (standing on sidewalk making insulting remarks to or about passing pedestrians or annoying pedestrians); and
subsection 11 (engaged in some illegal occupation or bearing an evil reputation and with an unlawful purpose consorting with thieves and criminals or frequenting unlawful resorts);

I. violations of Penal Law sections:
165.25 (jostling);
165.30 (fraudulent accosting);
240.30, subsection 1 (aggravated harassment in the second degree); and
240.35, subsection 3 (loitering involving deviate sexual behavior);

J. violations of Judiciary Law sections:
478 (practicing or appearing as an attorney at law without being admitted and registered);
479 (soliciting business on behalf of any attorney);
480 (entering hospital to negotiate settlement or obtain release or statement);
481 (aiding, assisting or abetting the solicitation of persons or the procurement of a retainer for or on behalf of any attorney);
489 (purchase of claims by corporations or collection agencies); and
491 (sharing of compensation by attorneys prohibited);

K. vagrancy or prostitution; and

L. violation of the United States Selective Draft Act of 1917 or the Selective Training and Service Act of 1940.

A convicted felon is eligible for appointment consideration if the felon has received a certificate of good conduct from the parole board or an executive pardon from the governor.

CERTIFICATE OF GOOD CONDUCT: A document, issued by the NYS board of parole, to an eligible convicted offender which removes civil disabilities, imposed by law, prohibiting certain types of employment and licenses for individuals who have been convicted of two or more felonies. It also *may* restore the right to hold public office. For consideration, certain minimum periods of good conduct in the community are necessary: one year for a misdemeanor; three years for a class c, d or e felony; five years for a class a or b felony.

CERTIFICATE OF RELIEF FROM DISABILITIES: Commonly referred to as a certificate of relief, it is a document, issued upon release from imprisonment (if any) by the sentencing court or NYS board of parole, to an eligible convicted offender which removes civil disabilities, imposed by law, prohibiting certain types of employment and licenses for individuals who have been convicted of misdemeanors or a maximum of one felony. It does *not* restore the right to hold public. A certificate applies only to one criminal incident, not an entire criminal history.

New York correction law outlines factors to be considered concerning a previous criminal conviction: (1) the public policy of the state to encourage the licensure of persons previously convicted of one or more criminal offenses; (2) the specific duties and responsibilities necessarily related to the license sought; (3) the bearing, if any, the criminal offense(s) for which the person was previoulsy convicted will have on his fitness or ability to perform one or more such duties or responsibilities; (4) the time which has elapsed since the occurrence of the criminal offense(s); the age of the person at the time of the occurrence of the criminal offense(s); the seriousness of the offense(s); (5) any information produced by the person, or produced on his behalf, in regard to his rehabilitation and good conduct; (6) the legitimate interest of the public agency in protecting property, and the safety and welfare of specific individuals or the general public.

In making a determination, the department of state will also give consideration to a certificate of relief from (civil) disabilities or a certificate of good conduct, issued to the applicant, which shall create a presumption of rehabilitation in regard to the specific offense(s) named in such certificates.

No person who has been removed from office as a commissioner of deeds for the City of New York is eligible for appointment to the office of notary public.

Sheriff

The Constitution of the State of New York prohibits sheriffs from holding another public office during their term as sheriff. Accordingly, a sheriff is not eligible for appointment as a notary public. However, a deputy sheriff is eligible for appointment.

Appointment Process

Prior to formally applying for appointment, New York requires that applicants be given a written test to determine the applicant's understanding of general legal and business terminology, and fundamental principles and procedures. Before April 1988, the applicant was entitled to receive a single test administration

Initial Appointment Process Summary*

NYS pre-appointment N.P. examination (walk-in basis) must be taken and passed with 70% or higher grade

$15 NYS N.P. examination fee–NYS Department of State

NYS application for appointment as N.P. (which includes sworn N.P. oath of office), original NYS N.P. examination results notice marked "pass", and application fee(s) must be filed with NYS DOS within two years of examination date

$60 check or money order–NYS Department of State (represents $40 NYS appointment fee and $20 county filing and indexing fee)

NYS DOS notifies appointee of approval of application by issuing a NYS N.P. identification card

NYS DOS forwards N.P. commission record, oath of office and $20 from $60 submitted by appointee for filing and indexing fee to local county clerk

*Effective July, 2001

by virtue of submitting the application fee. Because of the new legislation, however, the secretary of state has been authorized to charge a non-refundable examination fee of $15 for prospective notary public appointees. Then, after successfully passing the exam, another $60 fee is charged when filing the application for appointment. The requirement to file an application to be scheduled for an examination was discontinued in July 1988. All exams are conducted on a walk-in basis; no pre-registration is necessary, effective August 1988. After the notary public has qualified for office, a notary public identification card is issued, indicating the commission expiration date and registration number.

Notary Public Educational Workshops/Seminars

Prior to seeking an appointment as notary public, it is highly desirable and strongly recommended that every prospective notary public attend a notary public workshop or seminar in order to become fully aware of the office authority, duties and responsibilities. These educational programs are conducted at accredited colleges and universities throughout New York.

These classes "demystify" the office. A common misconception is that merely receiving an appointment adequately prepares a candidate to competently execute all of the official duties. It does not. The seminar provides a comprehensive view of information concerning the office. It is filled with helpful suggestions gained from actual situations experienced by notaries public working in a variety of fields. Confusing laws, concepts and procedures are clarified in plain English. Examples are provided to illuminate situations that the officer is likely to encounter, such as avoiding conflict of interest, maintaining professional ethics, charging proper fees, handling of special situations (e.g. foreign language documents), minimizing legal liability, and much more. An emphasis is placed upon realistically and practically guiding the participant through the procedures.

Examination

Examinations are administered in the cities of Albany, Binghamton, Buffalo, Elmsford, Franklin Square, Hauppauge, Newburgh,

New York City (Manhattan Borough only), Plattsburgh, Rochester, Syracuse, Utica and Watertown. Testing is performed in each city on a regular basis, typically between 9:00AM and 4:00PM, Monday through Friday. It is commonly given at a New York State or other public building. The applicant should expect to be at the site for approximately an hour and a half. Consult the department of state for a list of current test locations, dates and times. For an updated examination schedule via the internet, see: http://www.dos.state.ny.us. Check under the division of licensing services.

The need for the applicant to bring a photograph to the examination has been eliminated with the introduction of the walk-in examination procedure. The applicant will complete an examination application at the test site. The examination proctor will have each applicant place his inked thumb print on his examination application. Applicants are advised to bring some form of a generally acceptable photo identification credential to the test site. A check (business or personal) or money order drawn for $15 made payable to New York State Department of State is required at this time. No cash is accepted.

Report to the test site early. Bring several sharpened No. 2 pencils. The examination is a computer scored test using a special computer readable answer sheet; answers are chosen by darkening small ovals. Only No. 2 pencils are permitted.

The examination consists of 40 multiple-choice style questions. There are no essay questions. One hour is the maximum time limit allowed to complete the test. The examination is based upon the material as discussed in this book and may include questions relating to general knowledge and reasoning ability.

The test is administered under the supervision of the division of licensing services. These persons are not necessarily notaries public and they are not permitted to answer any questions about the content of the examination.

Since the office of notary public is synonymous with integrity and honesty, any display of dishonesty in testing will result in dismissal from the test center and jeopardize future consideration of appointment. The minimum acceptable score required for appointment is 70 percent. The maximum number of incorrect questions allowed is 12 out of 40 questions. Each question is worth two and a half points based upon a total score of 100 percent.

RESULTS NOTIFICATION

Approximately ten days to two weeks after sitting for the examination, notification will be sent from the secretary of state indicating passing or failing the test. The notification will not indicate the actual test score. Further, there is no information given regarding specific weak areas, if any.

If the acceptable score of 70 percent is not received, the candidate may write or telephone the department of state division of licensing services to request an appointment to review their test results. The request must be made within 30 days of the failure notice. Examinations are *not* permitted to be removed from direct supervision of the department of state. The candidate must review the results in one of the nine department of state offices in order to prepare for the second examination. The number of times that the test may be taken is unlimited. There is no waiting period prior to re-taking the test.

APPLICATION FOR APPOINTMENT

Previously in history, the application process was significantly more detailed than it is today. Applicants were required to provide comprehensive information including occupation, place of birth and details concerning employment dismissals. Reference letters were needed from several elected officials. Notarization of the initial application was required. Over time, these important details have been eliminated. Most recently, in 1986 the requirement for three character reference letters was dropped.

After passing the exam, in order to receive consideration for appointment, the applicant must complete and submit an official *state application for appointment* as a notary public. The form is available from New York State Department of State, Division of Licensing Services, 84 Holland Avenue, Albany, New York 12208-3490. Direct all correspondence and applications to this address. Application forms may be obtained from any department of state branch office located throughout New York. A directory of department of state office addresses and telephone numbers is located in the appendix. As a courtesy to citizens, many New York county clerks's offices provide a local source of applications for a NYS notary public commission. A directory of county clerk's offices addresses and telephone numbers is located in the appendix.

When completing the application, the applicant should be honest and straight-forward in answering the questions. Responses which are willfully incorrect will cause the rejection of an application, in addition to a criminal charge of perjury. If later revealed that there was a misstatement of a material fact on the application, the notary public may be removed from office. **Perjury** has been committed if, while under oath or by affirmation, the applicant knowingly and willfully made a materially false statement or offered materially false testimony on any matter.

The completed application and a non-refundable processing fee of $60 should be submitted to the secretary of state in Albany.

Notary's Name

The applicant should carefully consider personal name preferences before submitting the application for appointment. The name that the applicant indicates on the application for appointment is the name the commission will be issued under. Accordingly, if an applicant applies as Alfred E. Piombino, the official signature form must exactly follow the commissioned name. After appointment, it would be inappropriate for the officer to sign a document in connection with official notarial duties as A. Piombino, A. E. Piombino, Alfred Ernest Piombino, Alfred Piombino, Al Piombino or any other variation. Exclusive use of initials with a surname (last name) is prohibited.

A member of a religious order may be appointed and officiate as a notary public under the name by which he is known in the religious community.

Name Changes

When a woman notary public marries during the term for which she was appointed, she may notify the secretary of state of any change of name. She may elect to retain her maiden name or assume her new name. However, she must still perform all of her notarial functions under the name selected on her original commission for the duration of her appointment. Effective April 1989, a notary public wishing to file a change of name for his/her commission is required to pay a fee of $10. The notary public should contact the department of state for a change of name card, which must accompany the filing fee.

Effective September 30, 1999, the fee to change a name on a "license, permit, registration or other indentifying document", because of a change of marital status, was abolished under New York civil rights law. However, the New York legistature neglected to also amend New York executive law concerning the name change fee charged to holders of notary commissions. As of the publication of this edition, executive law was still conflicting with civil rights law.

Qualifying for Office

Effective January 1, 1993, the New York Legislature altered the appointment procedure. Prior to this time, rosters of successful candidates (who were commissioned) were sent from Albany to the county clerk of the county in which the candidate resided. Upon receiving the commission, the county clerk would request the candidate to qualify by filing with him the oath of office.

The county clerk would send the appointee an "*oath and signature card.*" The oath and signature card indicated the notary public's date of appointment and the expiration date of the term of office.

Although it appears illogical, New York Law now requires the applicant to be sworn in prior to commissioning by the secretary of state. Effective January 1, 1993, the department of state incorporated the oath and signature card as part of the application of appointment (and reappointment).

The notary public administering the oath of office may ask the applicant to repeat the words of the oath, or alternatively, may read the entire oath to the applicant, and thereafter inquire as to the acceptance of the oath by the applicant. The choice of protocol is the prerogative of the officiating notary public or other authorized officer. Most states require that an individual take the required oath(s) prior to being commissioned. Often the logic behind such an awkward policy as this is to minimize the amount of paperwork processing required by the government. Although increased efficiency in any government bureaucracy is admirable, it simultaneously diminishes the positive impact of being sworn into office after receiving an important official appointment. Such formal ceremony, however brief, is essential to impart the grave seriousness and honor of this and any other official appointment.

The applicant must take the constitutional oath of office orally before a notary public or other officer authorized to administer oaths, such as a judge or mayor. Upon being sworn in, the notary public will sign the oath of office and signature card. The notary public or other officer who administered the oath should endorse the oath of office at this time. The signatures and related records of the notary public commission application have now become the master references to which all future notarizations can be compared and verified, if necessary.

Effective July, 2001, the oath of office, along with the notary public commission and $20 apportioned from the application fee of $60, will be transmitted by the secretary of state to the county clerk where the notary public resides. The oath records will remain with the county clerk for the duration of the term of office.

Any person who executes any of the functions and duties of a notary public without having taken and duly filed the required oath of office is guilty of a misdemeanor.

Each notary public is responsible to take the verbal oath of office, and faithfully and honestly discharge the duties of office.

The *oath of office* is as follows:

"I do solomnly (swear) (affirm) that I will support the Constitution of the United States and the Constitution of the State of New York, and that I will faithfully discharge the duties of the office of notary public, according to the best of my ability (So help me God)."

Upon taking the oath of office, the notary public applicant will now execute the oath of office document in the presence of the notary public or other officer authorized to administer oaths.

Applicants are permitted to choose between swearing or affirming the oath of office.

The completed application for appointment with oath of office, properly executed and sworn, accompanied with a total fee of $60 should be submitted to the New York State Department of State in Albany by mail.

Effective July, 2001, the $60 application fee was established for a notary public commission. The $60 application fee breaks down into a $40 state appointment fee, and $20 county filing and indexing fee. In the event that the application for appointment is not approved, no fees paid will be refunded.

Effective July 24, 1991, New York law requires each New York State county clerk to designate at least one staff members to be available to perform notarial services at the county clerk's office. The service is available during normal business hours and is free of charge, regardless of the amount of notarial service. Each individual appointed by the county clerk to serve as the "house" notary public in the county clerk's office is exempt from all commission-related fees, including examination fee, application fee and county filing and indexing fee.

Upon the approval of an application for appointment, the newly commissioned notary public will be provided with an official notary public identification card, issued by the State of New York. This document is the official credential for the notary public, "certifying that he is a duly sworn and commissioned notary public as a constitutional officer of the State of New York." It bears the signature of the secretary of state.

The identification card will contain a multi-digit number. The registration number assigned to the notary public generally can be expected to remain unchanged throughout the notary public's service in office, provided the notary public applies for another appointment in a timely manner.

In the event that the identification card is lost or destroyed, a $10 fee is charged for a duplicate, effective April 1989.

Chapter 2 Questions

1. What are the qualifications of a notary public?
2. Discuss why a non-citizen is allowed to receive a New York notary public commission.
3. Are attorneys-at-law automatically appointed as notaries public? Explain your answer.
4. What is dual-office holding?
5. Define "moral turpitude".
6. Is a felon ever eligible to receive a notary public commission?
7. Discuss the difference between a certificate of good conduct and a certificate of relief from (civil) disabilities.
8. What other special legal procedures will allow a felon or other convict to be eligible for appointment?
9. Define "surety".
10. What is a surety bond?
11. Why are notaries sometimes required to be bonded?
12. How do surety bonds differ from malpractice, or errors and commissions insurance?
13. Why can surety bonds prove troublesome to a notary public?

Chapter 3

Maintaining A Notary Public Commission

TERM OF OFFICE

As of July, 2001 the appointment of a notary public is for a term of four years, starting on the date indicated on the notification from the secretary of state. Prior to this date, all notary public commissions expired on March 31. Commission dates were staggered to allow the state to process renewals more efficiently.

To verify the commission status of a current New York notary public, via the internet, see: http://www.dos.state.ny.us. Check under the division of licensing services.

VACANCY IN OFFICE

Circumstances in which a public officer "vacates" the office of notary public include: the officer resides in New York and moves out of the state, or a non-resident who does not keep an office or place of business in this state; resignation; removal from office; conviction of a felony or other offense (see eligibility and qualifications for detailed list); court order; failure to file the oath of office for appointment/reappointment within the required time period; and death.

If an application for appointment is filed after the expiration of the renewal period by a person who did not or was unable to reapply because of induction or enlistment in the United States armed forces, the application for reappointment may be made within a period of one year after an honorable military discharge.

Change of Residence/Address

A notary public should give *written* notice to the New York State Department of State, 84 Holland Avenue, Albany, New York 12208-3490 *and* to the county clerk of original appointment of any change in residence (or business address if nonresident), within five days of the change. Effective April 1989, a notary public must pay a fee of $10 to file a change of address with the department of state. The notary should contact the department of state for a change of address card, which must accompany the filing fee.

Resignation

In the event a notary public wishes to resign from office, a *written* resignation addressed to the secretary of state is required. If no effective date is specified in the letter, it will begin upon delivery to or filing with the secretary of state. If a date is specified, it will take place on the date specified. However, the date may not be more than 30 days after the date of its delivery or filing. If the resignation specifies an effective date that is greater than 30 days, the resignation will be 30 days from the date of its delivery or filing. A delivered or filed resignation, whether effective immediately or at a future date, may not be withdrawn, cancelled or changed, except with the approval of the secretary of state.

Once a notary public resigns, is removed from office, or his term of office expires, he may not change any mistakes on any documents previously acknowledged. Only during his term is he allowed to correct a certificate to conform with the facts of a matter.

Complaints

In the event that a notary public encounters another notary public who is performing official duties in an unscrupulous manner, he has an obligation to report the incident. Frequently, persons encountering these notaries public are unclear about the process to report the notary public. Reports should be directed to the secretary of state, not a county clerk or other official. Examples of situations which require investigating include: improper performance of duties; failure to administer oaths/affirmations to affiants or deponents; failure to take acknowledgements; failure to complete notarial certificates; asking for or receiving more than the statutory notarial fee, etc. It is vital that an incompetent or criminal notary public be exposed and, if warranted, punished in accordance with the law.

Removal

The secretary of state may suspend or remove any notary public for misconduct. No removal will be made unless the officer has been provided a copy of the charges against him and has had the opportunity of being heard.

Delegation of Authority

Previously, many states in the U.S. permitted notaries public to appoint deputies and clerks to assist the officer in performing their official duties. New York does not authorize a notary public to delegate these responsibilities and privileges to another person.

Reappointment

Effective July, 2001, the New York Legislature altered the reappointment procedure. Prior to this time, the secretary of state directly transmitted an application for reappointment to a notary public whose commissions was near expiration. The notary public would then return the application for reappointment to the department of state. Upon approval of the application, an oath and signature card would then be forwarded to the notary public which would be filed in the notary's county clerk's office.

Applicants for reappointment of a notary public commission are to submit their application, along with the incorporated oath and signature card, and the application fee of $60, to the county clerk of their residence. Upon being satisfied of the completeness of the reappointment application, the county clerk, not the secretary of state, will issue another commission to the notary public.

Effective July, 2001, the commission (issued by the county clerk) and $40 apportioned from the reapplication fee of $60, will be transmitted by the county clerk to the secretary of state. The new oath of office will remain at the county clerk's office and the remaining $20 will be retained by the county clerk for filing and indexing the oath of office.

The number of terms that a notary public may be reappointed is unlimited.

In the event that the notary public experiences a name or address change, and the change request is placed at the time of reappointment, the fees normally required for these changes are waived.

CHAPTER 3 QUESTIONS

1. What is meant by term of office?
2. Discuss how a vacancy might occur in the office of notary public.
3. Is it necessary that a notary public resign? When and how?
4. Explain the difference between an administrative action and a civil or criminal proceeding.
5. What are some circumstances that might cause a notary public to be suspended or removed from office?
6. Is a notary public commission automatically renewed?
7. Is it possible for a person to be appointed a notary public if he or she doesn't reside in the appointing jurisdiction? Explain your answer.
8. Is a notary public required to notify the commission grantor of a change of name, address, telephone number, or criminal record? Explain your answer.
9. Can a notary public delegate his authority or appoint deputies?
10. Define "para-notary". Explain what activities could be performed by a para-notary, and specifically what acts must be performed only by the notary public.

Chapter 4

Legal and Ethical Requirements

Notary's Bond

Thirty four states require the notary public to secure a bond before assuming the duties of the office. New York does not require a notary public to provide an *"official bond."*

Briefly, an official bond is purchased by a public officer to serve as a form of assurance that he will properly and faithfully perform all the duties of the office. He then submits it to the government (i.e. state). It is distinctly different from an insurance policy. Bonds serve as a public protection guarantee by providing some security to innocent citizens who are injured through the misconduct of a public officer, such as a notary public. It serves as an incentive for a notary public to "think twice" about committing an improper act.

The public officer pays a bonding company an annual premium in exchange for the company issuing a bond on his behalf. The bond serves as protection to the public by providing assurance that if the public officer does not properly or faithfully perform his duties, a citizen may sue and recover at least the amount of the bond.

Various state bond requirements range from \$500–\$10,000. In the event that a citizen obtained a judgment or court award against the public in the amount of \$10,000 for example, the citizen may receive the \$10,000 from the bond company. The bond company then would proceed to sue (if necessary) the bond holder (public officer) to recover the \$10,000 paid to the citizen. The annual premium for a \$10,000 bond at present is approximately \$100.

The notary public assumes *full* responsibility for all of his actions. Accordingly, the notary public may be held *both* criminally and civilly liable for misconduct in performing his duties. Since New York does not require a bond, a notary public would have difficulty in obtaining one from a bonding company. The difficulty is due to insurance companies not having a "market" for such bonds. Accordingly, an insurance broker may not be able to locate an underwriting insurance company to provide a bond.

The results of one government study have revealed some startling facts about the necessity of such statutory bonding requirements. The report showed that one surety company collected almost a million dollars in bond premiums during a five year period, but paid out only $750 in claims. Another company collected nearly $200,000 and dispersed about $2,000 in claims.

LEGAL LIABILITY

A subject of great concern to many notaries public revolves around the issue of legal liability in connection with performing notarial acts. As previously stated, the notary public assumes full legal responsibility for all of his actions. However, the best method of limiting his liability is a complete understanding of his duties and responsibilities.

Frankly speaking, if a notary public performs his duties correctly and carefully, he can be reasonably assured that he will not expose himself to significant legal liability. Virtually every civil suit and criminal charge involving a notarial act is the direct result of the notary public acting in a careless or negligent manner. Notary public errors and ommission insurance coverage is available. However, in the event that a notary public acted carelessly or negligently, the insurance coverage would not protect him. Before purchasing any insurance policy, a notary public should request a sample policy to review with his attorney.

As an officer authorized to take the acknowledgment or proof of execution of conveyances/instruments or certify acknowledgments or proofs, the notary public is personally liable for damages to persons injured as the result of any wrong doing on his part.

A notary public commits malfeasance if he performs an act which he has no legal right or authority to do so. All activities which are positively unlawful such as giving legal advice, drawing legal papers for another person, forgery, etc., are examples of malfeasance.

Misfeasance is committed when a notary public improperly performs a legally authorized act. Examples include issuing a false certificate, post or pre-dating an official certificate, charging a fee in excess of the lawful amount, taking an affidavit known to be false, etc.

Nonfeasance is committed when a notary public has omitted an act which he has a duty to perform. It can represent a total neglect of duty. Examples include a notary public not requiring an affiant to sign an affidavit or deposition before him, or the act of a notary public merely attaching his official signature and notary rubber stamp to a paper presented to him without performing any of his legally required duties.

Negligence is committed if a notary public fails to use the necessary standard or degree of care required in a situation. A key element in the determination of negligence is the question of whether or not another notary public, acting reasonably and prudently, would perform similarly in an identical situation. An example of negligence would be a notary's failure to identify a constituent who is not personally known to him.

American Society of Notaries

The American Society of Notaries (ASN) is a non-profit, tax-exempt, membership organization which was formed in 1965. Based in Florida, ASN is dedicated to the improvement of the office of notary public throughout the United States. It is the oldest, national, *tax-exempt* non-profit organization for notaries in the country.

The benefits of membership include the following: a subscription to *The American Notary,* a bi-monthly magazine with ASN news, notarial developments, proposed and pending laws, court decisions and duties; group insurance protection (i.e., life); low interest Mastercard/Visa; signature loan programs; low cost errors and omissions (liability) insurance for notaries public; car rental discounts; a distinguished membership certificate for framing; wallet card; and insignia.

Further information is available by contacting: American Society of Notaries, Department F, P.O. Box 7663, Tallahassee, FL 32314-7663 (800) 522-3392/(904) 671-5164. To contact the Society via the internet, see: http://www.notaries.org.

FEES

Components of the fee structure payable to notaries in New York have been in effect for over a century. These fees are governed by Public Officers Law.

Under the laws of New York, a notary public is entitled to receive the following fees in connection with performing official notarial duties:

1. administering an *oath:* $2.00 (1991);
2. administering an *affirmation:* $2.00 (1991);
3. administering an *oath* and certifying it when required: $2.00 (1991);
4. administering an *affirmation* and certifying it when required: $2.00 (1991);
5. taking and certifying the *acknowledgment* of a written instrument by one person: $2.00 (1991);
6. taking and certifying the *acknowledgment* of a written instrument for each additional person when more than one: $2.00 (1991);
7. taking and certifying the *proof of execution* of a written instrument by one person: $2.00 (1991);
8. taking and certifying the *proof of execution* of a written instrument, for each additional person when more than one: $2.00 (1991);
9. swearing each witness in the taking or certifying the acknowledgment or *proof of execution* of a written instrument: $2.00 (1991);
10. administering the *oath of office* to a member of the state legislature, military officer, inspector of election, clerk of the poll or to any other public officer or public employee: NO FEE ALLOWED;
11. *protesting* for nonpayment of any note, or for the nonacceptance or nonpayment of any bill of exchange, check or draft and giving the requisite notices and certificates of these protests (including affixing notarial seal): 75 cents (1837);
12. furnishing *notices of dishonor* on the protest of any note, bill of exchange, check or draft for each notice, not exceeding five on any bill or note: 10 cents, each (1865);
13. taking and certifying an *affidavit:* not addressed in statutes; and

14. taking and certifying a *deposition:* reasonable compensation, including reasonable and necessary expenses (i.e. actual travel costs, etc.).

While components of the present fee structure are archaic and obsolete, the majority of fees which notaries public may collect have been increased by the New York Legislature. Gov. Mario M. Cuomo approved legislation passed during the 1991–1992 session (Chapter 143 of the Laws of 1991) which elevated the major fee to two dollars. In past years, many proposals to raise the fee ranged from 75 cents to five dollars. As a comparison, the statutory fee for taking an acknowledgment in the States of California, Texas, Utah and Arkansas is $5; Florida allows a $10 fee; New York law permits $2.

It is the opinion of some individual notaries public that each public officer should be permitted to set their own fees according to what they determine would compensate for the value of the notarial services and related expenses. Clearly these individuals do not understand that they are not private practitioners, such as an attorney or certified public accountant (CPA). While notaries public in the State of New York are administered through the division of licensing services of the department of state, the office of notary public is not a licensed profession; it is a state *commission,* not a license.

One proposal to solve the fee structure problem is simply to abolish all fees for performing all official notarial acts. By doing this, the general public will be protected from uncontrolled fee variations. It is not uncommon for a person to be charged a different fee for identical notarial acts performed by different notaries public. To illustrate the point, the charge for taking an acknowledgment has been known to be from a dollar or two to over 20 dollars. If all services were to be provided at no charge, it would practically eliminate the variations now existing. Violations would be obvious and easy to detect. While notaries are legally permitted to collect a small fee, most perform their duties as a public service, not charging a fee. This does not imply that a notary public who accepts the permitted fee is acting unethically. However, many are simply embarrassed to request such a demeaning amount. From an economic perspective, forbidding the collection of such a trivial amount will not cause a significant hardship. From a professional perspective, charging this minor fee degrades the honor, significance and respect of both the duty and the office. It decreases the self-esteem of the public officer and the respect of the public. Instituting a no-fee structure would reduce public confusion and help restore public esteem of the office.

A notary public may not *charge* or *receive* a greater fee or reward than the amount allowed by law. He may not demand or receive any fee or compensation allowed to him by law, unless the service was actually performed by him. An exception is that the notary public may demand the fee in advance, before providing the service. Violation exposes the notary to punishments including removal from office, in addition to a law suit by the person, who is entitled to treble damages (three times the jury's award for actual damages).

United States law provides that a notary public who is an officer, clerk or employee of any executive department of the United States, will not charge any U.S. employee any fee for administering oaths of office which are required to be taken on appointment or promotion.

The contemporary office of notary public in New York is not structured so that the officer can establish an independent practice. A notary public in New York will typically serve the public in connection with another profession. The range of the professions include business, legal, law enforcement, medical, social service and virtually any other job position. Many students, retirees and others serve as notaries public.

Notary public commissions are not reciprocal between states, unlike license reciprocity. An example of a similar situation is when a state judge is appointed to preside in the state courts of New York, he may not preside in a court outside of New York.

Advertising

There are a number of states that prohibit certain forms of advertising by notaries public including California, Illinois, Texas and Oregon. Except through general New York consumer protection legislation, New York does not specifically address this important topic. However, certain issues must be discussed regarding advertising. It is an acceptable practice for the notary public to choose to inform the public of the available notarial services. Advertisements in various media (i.e. a telephone directory, a website on the internet, etc.) inform the public of a valuable service and promote the public image of the business firm and/or notary public. The advertising copy must not contain any wording that might mislead or misrepresent the services that are legally available. For example, to advertise as a "notary public and counsellor" is illegal. The ad copy should state simply "notary public" or "notarial services."

All advertisement wording should be entirely in English to prevent confusion among non-English speaking parties. *Notario publico, notario, notaria publico, notaria* and similarly worded or appearing phrases may cause confusion in the minds of Spanish-speaking immigrants. The position of a notary public in many Latin American countries is usually held by an attorney or similar highly trained legal professional. Some notaries public take advantage of these persons and freely demand/accept the high notary public fees typically paid by a citizen in those countries. The Immigration Reform and Control Act of 1986 caused many apprehensive immigrants to seek legal assistance in order to appropriately follow the new legal requirements. Unsuspecting immigrants asked for the advice and assistance of notaries public in connection with the completion of the intimidating Immigration and Naturalization Service (INS) documents. Numerous instances of misuse of notarial authority have been reported in connection with the new requirements for filing documents. Typically these parties are economically disadvantaged, and by dealing with a corrupt notary public, it could possibly deny the person his only opportunity to follow the requirements. State and federal law enforcement agencies are increasing prosecution of notaries who commit these acts of fraud. The authorities will prosecute abuses of public trust which violate the integrity of the office of notary public. Notaries public are advised to avoid any advertising in connection immigration and naturalization services.

During the 1987–88 session of the New York Legislature, several were bills proposed concerning notice to the public regarding notaries public advertising as notarios publicos. The proposed laws would require a non-attorney notary public who advertises the service of a notario publico, to post a bilingual notice advising citizens that the service is not by a lawyer and therefore, not authorized to give legal advice or accept fees for legal service. Failure to comply would have been a violation with a fine up to $250. These bills died in committee.

Foreign Language Documents

It is possible that a notary public could be presented with a document that is written in a foreign language. Unless the notary public is fluent in the language contained in the document, he should refer the person to the appropriate foreign consulate office. In the event that a person appearing before the notary public cannot speak English (and the notary public is not fluent in the foreign language), the notary public should decline performing an oath/affirmation, acknowledgment, or other notarial act. The person should be referred to a foreign consulate office or a notary public fluent in the foreign language.

Regarding foreign consulates, the general rule of protocol is that a consular officer will usually assist only his government's citizens residing in his jurisdiction. Accordingly, if an American citizen approaches a foreign consulate for assistance, it is unlikely that the consular officer would intervene.

Records and Journals

The secretary of state does not specifically require a notary public to maintain a journal or log book of performed official duties. While it is not mandatory, it is a highly recommended practice, especially for the notary public with a high degree of contact with the general public.

Each notarization should be documented in a permanent log book. A detailed record of each act provides essential evidence and protection. Record information including the date/time, kind/type of act, document date, kind/type of document, constituent's signature, home (residence/actual street) address, identification data and any additional relevant information, including notarial fees.

A blank, sewn-type binding log book is recommended, such as those used in accounting. Each page should be consecutively numbered. Pages should never be removed. If an error is made, draw a single line through it. Never erase or completely cross out or use any type of correction fluid, such as white, opaque correction liquid. Entries should be written in permanent, dark, black-colored ink. Keep the log book in a secure location indefinitely.

In the event that a notary public is subpoenaed to testify (subpoena ad testificandum) at a trial or hearing involving a notarial act, having basic documentation will be vital in assisting the notary public to provide accurate testimony. An accurate record could be critically important, especially if a number of years had passed since the notarial act was performed. A carefully maintained record/log book will serve as a means of protection to the notary public in the event of potential claims against him. Keeping a record would also be advantageous if the notary public was served with a subpoena to produce documents, papers or records (subpoena duces tecum) at a trial or hearing. This information could prove critical to the dispensing of justice.

Inked Hand Rubber Stamp

Thirty-two states in the U.S. require the use of an inked stamp, some in addition to the seal/embosser. New York does not specifically require an inked stamp in connection with performance and documentation of official notarial acts. However, it is customary practice to use a stamp in connection with official acts.

Executive Law section 137 requires that, beneath his signature, the notary public print, typewrite or stamp in black ink, his name, the words "Notary Public State of New York," the name of the county in which he originally qualified, and the commission expiration date. His commission registration number may be positioned on the line below "Notary Public State of New York." Although not a legal requirement, inclusion of this number is highly recommended. These items should be included on the hand rubber stamp, if the notary public chooses to use one.

Simply affixing the official signature or official signature and state commission number to an official notarial certificate is legally insufficient. The law specifically requires the notary public to use black ink for both his official signature and stamp impression. No other ink color is acceptable. Failure to conform with these laws could likely result in the document being rejected by a public recording office (e.g. county clerk).

Only the words required by law should be contained in the rubber stamp copy. For example, a number of notaries officiate with stamps that state "Residing in New York County," "Residing in and for New York County," or simply "New York County," These stamp forms should be replaced with stamps that are in legal conformity.

Whenever required, a notary public shall also include the name of any county in which his certificate of official character is filed, using the words "Certificate Filed . . . County." If he has qualified or has filed a certificate of official character in the office

JANE DOE
Notary Public – State of New York
Qualified in Excelsior County
Commission Expires 00–00–0000

JANE DOE
Notary Public – State of New York
Qualified in Excelsior County
Certificate Filed
Clinton County and Albany County
Commission Expires 00–00–0000

of the clerk, in a county or counties within the City of New York, he must also place the official number(s) (in black ink), as given to him by the clerk(s) of such county(s). If the document is to be recorded in the register's office in any county within the City of New York and the notary public has been given a number by the county register(s) (where the notary public has filed an autograph signature and certificate), these numbers should be included.

Although New York law discusses the issuance of additional numbers to notaries public by New York City county clerks, currently the practice isn't uniform with the state statute. For example, when filing a certificate of official character with the New York County clerk, the notary public is instructed to simply use the registration number issued by the state.

Further, the New York City register does not require a notary public to file a certificate of official character (in her office) as a requirement for filing a document in the register's office. Rather, the notary public should file a certificate of official character in the New York County clerk's office. (There is currently one citywide register for the City of New York.)

While the law does not specifically require an inked stamp, using one will make the actual performance of the documentation process of the official act much easier. The required notary public identification data will be legible, consistent and reproduce clearly when photo-copied or microfilmed. Using a stamp makes sure that no essential information will be left out, due to haste or carelessness. Although it is not recommended, some notaries do not put the year portion of their commission expiration on their stamps. If omitted, this could result in the rejection of the document by a county clerk or recorder, causing possible delays in finalizing an important business, legal or real estate transaction. While including the date in the copy of the stamp would mean replacing the stamp every two years, the cost of a few dollars is minor in comparison to the cost of delaying or complicating a legal or business act.

The stamp may be obtained from any stationer who produces custom rubber stamps. There is no requirement or specification for the style or size, other than the stamp word copy as discussed earlier. The type style selected should be simple and free of intricate or fancy letter design to make it easier to read and reproduce. A business-like, professional image should be the rule of selection.

Size is an important factor. Avoid selecting a type size so small that the ink from each letter runs onto one another when placed on the paper. Likewise, avoid billboard, over-sized bulky letters which many legal forms may not have the space to accommodate. A recommended type face is Gothic, Goudy or Century in nine or eight point-size type; avoid letters smaller than eight point. The average cost of this type of basic rubber stamp is approximately $10 to $12.

For those who prefer a self-inking style rubber stamp, the cost can range from $25 to $30. Portable, self-contained, self-inking stamps are available which fold into a plastic carry-case/handle.

The "traditional" notary public stamp, a metal-encased miniature rubber stamp with matching-sized inked pad, retails for about $15 from a full-service stationer. Some notaries public dislike this style, due to the "mess." The ink pad frequently stains purses, briefcases, clothing and papers. Production and delivery time ranges from two to four weeks.

Notary's Official Seal

Thirty-six states in the U.S., excluding New York, require and/or recommend notaries public use an *embossing-type seal* (producing a raised impression of letters on the paper document) in connection with their official notarial duties. However, there are laws, rules and regulations that contradict this issue. They strongly imply the notary public requires a seal for certain documents, in order to effectively perform the duties of the office to the full extent of the requirements. For example, Executive Law section 135 instructs the notary public to affix his notarial seal to a protest.

The compiled statutes of the United States instruct the notary public to attach an impression of his official seal to all oaths, affidavits, acknowledgments and proofs of execution. A document should be sealed when it is notarized and intended to be entered into the record of a United States court or according to a federal statute.

Most states legally require that a document which is to be recorded in their state (county clerk's office), meet *that* state's document preparation and filing requirements, regardless of the rules of the jurisdiction in which the document is actually executed and/or notarized. For example, if a state requires that all deeds be sealed with a raised seal and it is executed and notarized in New York (but not sealed), the county clerk or register from that state will likely reject it.

Sealing documents greatly reduces the possibility of fraud. For example, in addition to the notarial certificate, the seal should be placed onto each page of the entire document. This makes it obvious to the document recorder and/or the recipient if any pages have been replaced. The replaced pages will not have the seal impression, alerting the party to a potentially fraudulent document. Furthermore, applying the notarial seal to documents reinforces the fact that the act being performed is an official governmental function. Since the use of embossing seals is generally restricted to official actions, using the seal has a positive impact upon the constituent. It is clearly evident that the notarial service is not an act to be taken lightly. The official seal of the notary public is classified as a *public seal,* since the notary public is a public officer. By law, it is clearly distinguished from a *private seal,* which represents a private person or corporation (an "artificial" person).

New York law does not regulate the sale of notary public seals, so there are no rules or regulations controlling seal purchases. Any individual may purchase a seal through a local stationery supplier or mail-order firm, without producing the evidence of authorization to rightfully possess one.

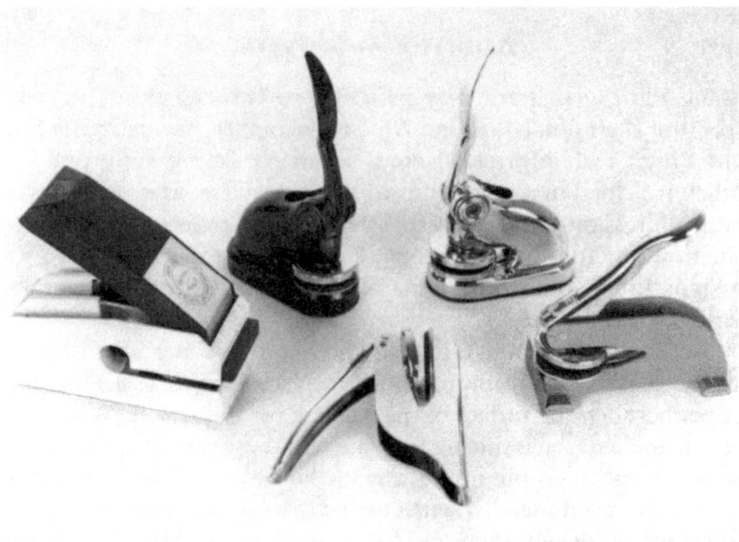

In 1986 Oklahoma passed legislation to prohibit sales of notary public seals unless the purchaser presents proof of current notary public appointment status; violations are misdemeanors. A similar bill was defeated during the same year in the California state assembly.

In 1989 the average market cost for a notary public official seal (complete with case) ranged from $23 to $35, depending on the supplier. Production and delivery time varies from three to four weeks. Because the seal does not contain information which will change (except a name change), the purchase of the seal is generally a one-time expense.

When affixing the official seal, the notary public should apply a little more force than he thinks necessary. This will ensure that the seal impression is clearly legible. If the first impression is inadequate, it is acceptable for another seal impression to be applied.

The embosser seal should be impressed in the area designated with the initials "*L.S.*," the abbreviation of the Latin words *locus sigilli* (pronounced "lowkus SEE-jill-EE") meaning "place of the seal." If the *L.S.* is not indicated, the notary public may place his seal impression on any unprinted area of the document near his official signature. The seal should not, if at all possible, be placed over any document text (except specifically over the *L.S.* notation, including signatures, dates and other important elements).

Additional Supplies

Some additional items may be useful to notaries public in performing their official duties. An "ink smudger" device applied to the raised seal impression on a document is common practice when it is filed in a public recording office. This now permits the seal impression to be easily visible allowing photographic reproduction (microfilm, photo copy, etc.). If the seal was affixed over a signature, date or other critical element, it could pose a problem at a later time.

An inexpensive and quick method of producing an instantly darkened, raised seal impression is to place a single leaf of carbon paper between the surface of the seal and the document. When the seal is applied, the resulting pressure will cause the carbon paper to make an easily visible impression of the seal. However, this practice is not recommended when utilizing a foil notarial seal.

Gummed or self-adhesive, *foil notarial seals* may be used when imprinting official seals to notarial certificates. The foil notarial

seal is positioned on a blank portion of the document, near the signature of the notary public. The notary public seal impression is placed over it, creating an impressive appearing result. Originally an actual gold leaf, the modern foil notarial seal is available

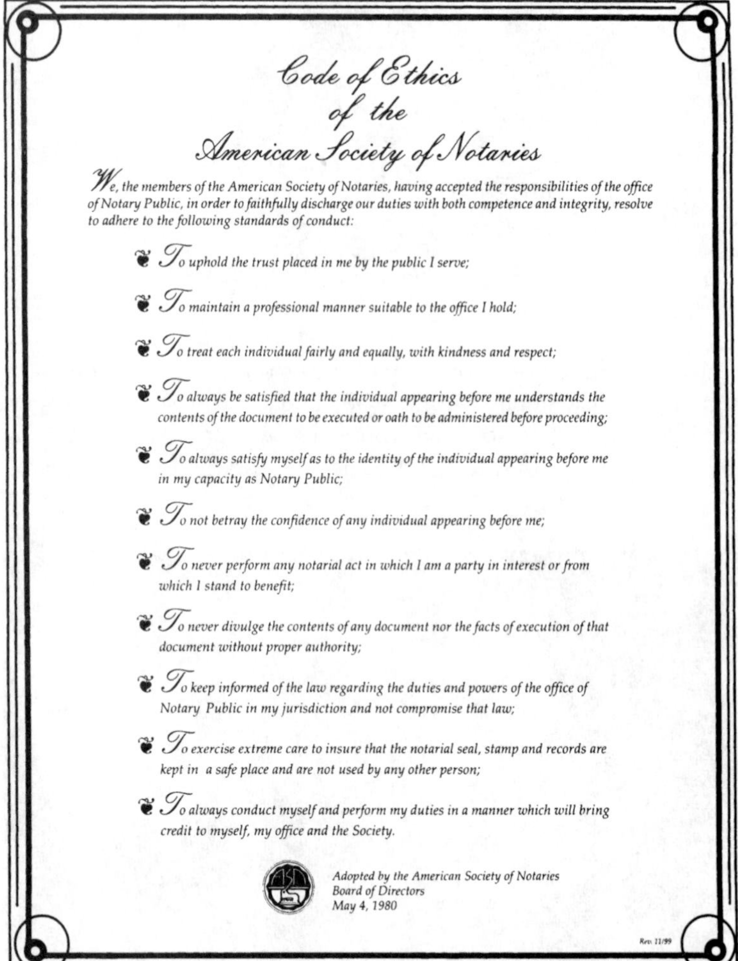

Code of Ethics of the American Society of Notaries

We, the members of the American Society of Notaries, having accepted the responsibilities of the office of Notary Public, in order to faithfully discharge our duties with both competence and integrity, resolve to adhere to the following standards of conduct:

- *To uphold the trust placed in me by the public I serve;*
- *To maintain a professional manner suitable to the office I hold;*
- *To treat each individual fairly and equally, with kindness and respect;*
- *To always be satisfied that the individual appearing before me understands the contents of the document to be executed or oath to be administered before proceeding;*
- *To always satisfy myself as to the identity of the individual appearing before me in my capacity as Notary Public;*
- *To not betray the confidence of any individual appearing before me;*
- *To never perform any notarial act in which I am a party in interest or from which I stand to benefit;*
- *To never divulge the contents of any document nor the facts of execution of that document without proper authority;*
- *To keep informed of the law regarding the duties and powers of the office of Notary Public in my jurisdiction and not compromise that law;*
- *To exercise extreme care to insure that the notarial seal, stamp and records are kept in a safe place and are not used by any other person;*
- *To always conduct myself and perform my duties in a manner which will bring credit to myself, my office and the Society.*

Adopted by the American Society of Notaries Board of Directors May 4, 1980

Rev. 11/99

through a stationer. The traditional color is gold; other colors are available. A package of 40 gummed style costs approximately $4.00; 96 self adhesive seals cost about $7.00. A two inch foil seal is recommended. The seal impression should be entirely contained within the borders of the foil seal. Various blank legal forms which the notary public may desire to have to more effectively perform his official duties include loose notarial certificates (i.e. acknowledgment certificates) and blank affidavits. A stationer which stocks blank legal forms will have these available.

CHAPTER 4 QUESTIONS

1. Discuss personal legal liability and the notary public.
2. How might a notary public minimize his or her legal liability?
3. What is "E & O" insurance and why would a notary public consider purchasing such an insurance policy?
4. Define "negligence".
5. Is an employer liable for the negligent acts of an employee/notary public for "on the job" incidents? If so, how does this affect the employee/notary public liability?
6. Explain the difference between malfeasance, misfeasance and nonfeasance.
7. Describe some examples where negligence is committed by a notary public.
8. Discuss legal liability for U.S. government employees in connection with official duties for federal business.
9. Are the fees for official services legally regulated? What fees may be charged and collected for official services? Explain your answer.
10. What are some supplemental services which a notary public might offer to clients? Is the charge for these supplemental services legally regulated?
11. Is a travel expense permitted? Does the law regulate this charge, and if so, what are the rules?
12. Is notary public service fee income subject to income taxes? Explain the Internal Revenue Service rules concerning self-employment tax and how it relates to notary public service fee income.
13. How may a notary public advertise? What are some general rules for advertisement?
14. Why are American notaries public discouraged from advertising in non-English languages?
15. What assistance will a foreign embassy provide, and who will they typically assist?
16. Explain what special precautions should be taken with a document in a language other than English.
17. Is there a prohibition against a person signing a document is a foreign language or non-English symbols or characters? Explain your answer.
18. Define "signature".
19. Is it legally permissible for a person to sign a document with a rubber stamp, instead of drawing a pen against a document? How about a fingerprint? Explain your answer.
20. Is a register required to be kept by a notary public?
21. What is a danger in not recording every notarial act in the notary public register?
22. What physical characteristics should a register possess? What are some unacceptable characteristics?

23. List the basic data to be recorded for acts performed by a notary public.
24. Name two reasons explaining the importance of client signatures in the notary public register.
25. Does an employer or the employee/notary public retain legal control and ownership of the register? Explain your answer.
26. Under what specific legal circumstances should a notary public release his or her register?
27. Explain the proper process for a notary public to issue a certified copy of a entry recorded in his register.
28. Discuss the use and value of a fingerprint taken by a notary public and recorded in a notary public register.
29. Is a notary public permitted to destroy his register after a certain period of time passes? Explain your answer.
30. What is the proper legal process for the custody of notary public register(s) and official seal(s) upon the resignation, retirement, removal or death of a notary public?
31. Is a notary public legally required to possess an official seal or rubber stamp? Explain your answer.
32. What is the physical difference between an official embossing seal and a rubber stamp?
33. Describe what information should be inscribed in an official embossing seal. Sketch a rough outline of the impression layout.
34. Name and explain at least five reasons that a notary public should possess and faithfully impress an embossed seal on every legal certificate.
35. What legally traditional treatments may be combined with the embossing seal impression to create an impressive finished appearance?
36. Is there ever a case in which the use of an embossing seal would be inappropriate?
37. Are the sales of notary public seals regulated by law? Explain your answer.
38. What does the Latin abbreviation "LS" signify? What does it mean to the notary public and what should be performed in the vicinity of this marking?
39. Explain why a notary public should never affix his embossing seal over signatures.
40. What steps should a notary public take if his official seal or other marking instruments are lost or stolen?
41. What are some of the important characteristics of a notary public trade group?
42. Since many U.S. notary associations are actually private, commercial companies (including non-profit), how can a notary public protect himself? What questions would a legitimate non-profit, tax-exempt, membership-type association freely provide to an inquirer?

Chapter 5

Organization and Management of Duties

Jurisdiction of Office

Previously, notaries public were limited to performing official duties within the geographical boundaries of the county in which they resided or qualified. Because a notary public is both a *state* and *local officer,* he has the legal authority to perform all authorized, official duties within the geographical boundaries of the *entire* State of New York, including New York City. A New York notary may act only within the confines of the territorial limits of the state, including land, sea and air space. The certificate of authentication may possibly be required where the document is to be recorded or used in evidence outside the jurisdiction of New York State, particularly involving matters of a significant, legal, business or financial nature. It is typically the responsibility of the party executing the document to determine the necessity for obtaining a certificate of authentication.

Certificate of Official Character

The notary public commission authorizes the notary public to officiate in any county of New York State. However, there are practical reasons for filing a certificate of official character with different county clerk(s). Notaries public who expect to sign documents *regularly* in counties other than that of their residence (or in which they are qualified non-New York State residents) may choose to file specimen signatures with other county clerk's offices in the state. A directory of New York county clerks is contained in the appendix. If a notary public lives in a suburban county and is employed or conducts business at a place of considerable distance, he may want to file with that county clerk. This will assist a party who wants the notarial certification/signature ***authenticated*** (or verified). Otherwise, the party would have to travel or correspond to the county clerk's office in which the notary public originally qualified. By filing a certificate of official character, it facilitates the certification or authentication process. It also reduces the constituent's expenses by eliminating the need to travel many hours or wait days if using the mail. Depending upon the nature and circumstances surrounding the document or matter, this may not be acceptable. While perhaps not a concern of some notaries public, those who are frequently involved in significant legal or business matters are certainly interested in reducing any unnecessary inconvenience and expense to those persons who receive his official services.

Any notary public may file his autograph signature and a certificate of official character in the office of any state county clerk. After filing these documents, the secretary of state or the county clerks may certify the official character and signature of the notary public.

Fee Paid $5.00

CERTIFICATE OF OFFICIAL CHARACTER OF NOTARY PUBLIC

I, [Name of County Clerk], Clerk of the Supreme and County Court of [Name of County] County do hereby certify that

[Name of Notary Public]

was appointed a Notary Public in the State of New York for the term ending [Date of Expiration], and duly qualified in my office on [Date of Filing Oath], and that I am well acquainted with the handwriting of such Notary Public or have compared the signature below with his autograph signature deposited in my office, and believe that the signature is genuine.

WITNESS MY HAND AND SEAL at [Name of County Seat] this [Date] day of [Month], [Year].

[Signature of County Clerk]
County Clerk, [Name of County] County,
[Name of County Seat], New York

[Signature of Notary Public]
[Address of Notary Public]

CERTIFICATE OF AUTHENTICATION

STATE OF NEW YORK) ss.:
COUNTY OF [Name of County])

I, [Name of County Clerk], County Clerk and Clerk of the Supreme Court of the State of New York, in and for the County of [Name of County], a Court of Record, having by law a seal DO HEREBY CERTIFY pursuant to the Executive Law of the State of New York, that

[Name of Notary Public]

whose name is subscribed to the annexed affidavit, deposition, certificate of acknowledgment or proof, was at the time of the taking the same a NOTARY PUBLIC in and for the State of New York duly commissioned, sworn and qualified to act as such throughout the State of New York: that pursuant to law, a commission or a certificate of his official character, with his autograph signature has been filed in my office; that at the time of taking such proof, acknowledgment or oath, he was duly authorized to take the same; that I am well acquainted with the handwriting of such NOTARY PUBLIC or have compared the signature on the annexed instrument with his autograph signature deposited in my office, and I believe that such signature is genuine.

IN WITNESS WHEREOF, I have hereunto set my hand and affixed my official seal this [Date] of [Month], [Year].

[SEAL OF COUNTY CLERK] [Signature of County Clerk]
County Clerk and Clerk of the Supreme Court,
[Name of County] County

If the secretary of state issues a certificate of official character, the fee is $10. All county clerks collect a fee of $5 to issue a certificate of official character/signature. An additional $10 fee is charged for filing the certificate. Therefore, the total cost for filing each certificate of official character with a county clerk or recorder is either $20 for a secretary of state issued certificate or $15 for a county clerk-issued certificate. A certificate issued by a county clerk is lawfully equivalent to a certificate issued by the secretary of state. Certificates of official character expire at the conclusion of a notary's term of office.

Authentication Or Certification of Notarial Authority

It is a generally accepted legal principle that the signed certificate of a notary public is prima-facia evidence. In other words, the signed certification by the notary is sufficient evidence to legally establish the fact that a notarial ceremony documented by the notary actually took place, unless disproved by other evidence. Therefore, if the document signed by the notary is to remain in New York state, no further certification is required.

Authentication may be required in a case where the document signed by a notary is to be entered into evidence in a court, recorded in a public recorder's or clerk's office, or utilized in some other fashion *outside* of New York state. This may occur when the document concerns a matter of significant legal or business nature. Examples include powers of attorney, agreements, bylaws, transcripts, deeds of assignment, diplomas, depositions and affidavits. It is the responsibility of the party executing the document to determine the necessity for obtaining a certificate of authentication.

Some states do not require authentication of documents signed by a notary from another state if the notary impressed his *embossing-style seal* onto the document. Documents not possessing the seal embossment will require customary authentication by the appropriate official(s) from New York state. Check with the destination officials.

County Clerk Authentication

If a document is expected to leave New York state for use in another state or nation, or if the client wishes to verify the legitimacy of a notary public, authentication is available from the appropriate county clerk and New York secretary of state. The county clerk will confirm that a commission has been issued, and an oath of office with specimen signature is on file. The county clerk will then verify that the notary was properly authorized to perform the notarial act at the time of officiating and the notary signature appears genuine. The ***certificate of authentication*** signed by the county clerk and sealed with his official seal is now attached to the document by means of a secure attachment thereby reducing the likelihood of a person tampering with the certification. Some certifications may be directly impressed onto the document by means of a rubber stamp or similar marking machine, usually with an official seal embossment. The fee for an authentication or certification of a notarial certificate and signature is $3 (each), payable to the county clerk. The fee is the responsibility of the client or document holder, not the notary public.

NEW YORK STATE AUTHENTICATION

State authentications from the New York Secretary of State are available from either Albany or New York City, and may be obtained either by mail or in-person.

State authentications may be requested from (1) New York Secretary of State, Miscellaneous Records Unit, 41 State Street, Second Floor, Albany, New York 12231. The direct telephone number is 518/474-4770; or (2) New York Secretary of State, Certification Unit, 123 William Street, Nineteenth Floor, New York, New York 10038. The direct telephone number is 212/417-5684.

Walk-in, counter service is provided at either the Albany or New York City (Manhattan) office on a while-you-wait basis, Monday through Friday, except federal and state holidays. Call ahead to verify hours of operation. Pre-payment is required by cash, business or personal check, or money order. Checks $500 and over must be certified. Checks or money orders should be made payable to the New York Department of State.

The fee for a state authentication is $10 each document, not each page. Payment of the fee is the responsibility of the client or document holder, not the notary public.

Each request should be accompanied by a cover letter making the request which contains the requester's name, mailing address, daytime telephone number, and if the document is leaving the United States, the name of the foreign nation.

For updated information via the internet from the New York Department of State on state authentications and apostilles, see: http://www.dos.state.ny.us.

A document signed by a New York notary with a county and state authentication certificate attached is permitted to be entered as evidence in any court or hearing, or be recorded in any state in the United States. There is a $10 fee to obtain an authentication certificate. Payment of the charge is the responsibility of the client or document holder, not the notary.

New York state has a *two-part authentication process.* First, the document must be presented for certification to the county clerk's office in which the notary qualified and filed his oath of office. Then, the county certified document is delivered to the secretary of state for the state authentication. The document would now be ready for inter-state use anywhere in the United States.

APOSTILLE

An ***apostille*** is a special certification issued by the New York Secretary of State. An apostille (pronounced "ah-po-steel") verifies certain document certifications and may be required if a document is to be presented or filed outside of the United States. While it may not be frequently required, an alert and conscientious notary would recommend obtaining such certification in the possible event it was necessary.

If a document is intended to be delivered to a foreign nation, there are two options for accomplishing the process called *"Legalisation for Foreign Documents"*. In the past, every document intended to be delivered to a foreign nation required a multi-step "legalisation". This process, sometimes called *"chain certification"*, is still necessary for nations not party to the *"Hague Convention on Abolishing the Requirements of Legalisation for Foreign Documents"*. However, in 1961, the United States signed this treaty called the "Hague Convention" and the authentication process has been streamlined. Kindly refer to the table of nations who have signed this treaty and will therefore accept the special apostille certification. If the destination nation is not found in the table, please contact that nation's foreign embassy or consulate to determine if that nation has since signed the treaty.

HAGUE CONVENTION ABOLISHING THE REQUIREMENT OF LEGALISATION FOR FOREIGN DOCUMENTS*

Nations Party to The Treaty

Antigua and Barbuda
Argentina
Austria
The Bahamas
Belgium
Botswana
Commonwealth of the Independent States, including:
 Belarus
 Russia
Cyprus
El Salvador

Fiji
Finland
France, including:
 Affars and the Issas
 French Guiana
 Guadeloupe
 Martinique
 New Caledonia
 Reunion
 St. Pierre and Miquelon
 Wallis and Futuna
Germany
Greece
Hungary
Israel
Italy
Japan
Lesotho
Liechtenstein
Luxembourg
Malawi
Malta
Marshall Islands
Mauritius
Mexico
Netherlands, including:
 Netherlands
 Antilles
Norway
Panama
Portugal
Seychelles
Slovinia
Spain
Suriname
Swaziland
Switzerland
Tonga
Turkey
United Kingdom of Great Britain and Northern Ireland, including:

Anguilla
Bailiwick of Guernsey
Barbados
Bermuda
British Antarctic Territory
British Guiana
British Solomon Islands Protectorate
Cayman Islands
Falkland Islands
Gibralter
Gilbert & Ellice Islands
Hong Kong
The Isle of Man Jersey
Montserrat
New Hebrides
St. Helena
St. Christopher and Nevis
Southern Rhodesia
Turks and Caicos Islands
British Virgin Islands
United States of America
Yugoslavia

*Effective January, 1997
The current text of the 1961 Hague Convention may be found in the following legal references: T.I.A.S. 10072; 32 U.S. Treaty Series (UST) 883; 527 U.N. Treaty Series (UNTS) 189, and the Martindale-Hubble International Law Digest.

The following example will illustrate the authentication process.

A client signs a power of attorney in Buffalo, New York before a New York notary (who has qualified in Erie County). The notary takes and certifies the acknowledgment of the principal signing the power of attorney. The client delivers the executed legal document to the Erie County Clerk for county clerk authentication. The oath of office and signature record of a New York notary is recorded at the county clerk's office in the county in which the notary resides. This is referred to as the county in which the notary has qualified for the office of notary. Therefore, the county clerk verifies the validity of the notary's authority on the date the acknowledgment was taken, and also verifies the signature on file with that on the document. The county clerk authenticated document is now delivered to the New York Department of State for either the state authentication or apostille certification.

If the destination nation is a Hague Treaty party, the New York Department of State will attach an apostille certificate signed by the New York Secretary of State. This step certifies that the prior certification by the county clerk was legitimate. The power of attorney is now properly "legalised" and prepared to be received at the Hague Treaty destination country with full legal recognition.

If the destination nation is not a Hague Treaty party, the New York Department of State will attach a state authentication certificate signed by the New York Secretary of State. This step certifies that the prior certification by the county clerk was legitimate. The state certified document now is delivered to the U.S. Department of State. The U.S. Department of State will attach a federal authentication certificate signed by the U.S. Secretary of State. This step certifies that the prior certification by the New York Secretary of State was legitimate. A final step may be required. A foreign consular officer at a consulate or the embassy of the foreign nation may be necessary. This step certifies that the prior certification by the U.S. Secretary of State was legitimate. The power of attorney is now properly "legalised" and prepared to be received at the non-Hague Treaty destination country with full legal recognition.

It is possible that the destination country may also require a final certification of the consul certification upon the arrival of the document in the foreign nation.

FEDERAL AUTHENTICATION

Federal authentications are necessary for documents destined for use in nations that are not parties to the Hague Treaty. Federal authentications are issued by the U.S. Secretary of State. Federal authentications are only available from the federal department of state office in Washington, D.C. and may be obtained either by mail or in-person.

Federal authentications may be requested from the U.S. Department of State, Authentication Office, 518 23rd Street, N.W., State Annex 1, Washington, D.C. 20520. The direct telephone number is 202/647-5002. The main switchboard telephone number is 202/647-4000. Information may also be obtained from the Federal Information Telephone Center at 800/688-9889 (Option #6). Call ahead to verify the office address.

Walk-in, counter service is provided at the Washington, D.C. office on a while-you-wait basis, Monday through Friday, except federal holidays. Call ahead to verify hours of operation. The limit is 15 documents per person, per day. Pre-payment is required by cash, business or personal check, money order, or MasterCard or Visa credit cards. Checks or money orders are to be made payable to the U.S. Department of State.

The fee for a federal authentication is $5 each document, not each page. Payment of the fee is the responsibility of the client or document holder, not the notary public.

For updated information via the internet from the U.S. Department of State on federal authentication, see: http://www.state.gov/www/authenticate/index.html.

SUNDAY

A notary public may administer an oath or affirmation, take an affidavit, acknowledgment, proof of execution or deposition involving a *criminal* matter on Sunday. However, a deposition in connection with a *civil* hearing or trial cannot be taken on Sunday. A notary public may perform any notarial act on any day of the week, with one exception. A deposition in connection with a civil hearing or trial cannot be taken on Sunday. However, a deposition involving a criminal matter on Sunday is allowed. A notary public may also administer an oath or affirmation, take an affidavit, take and certify an acknowledgment and proof of execution on Sunday, regarding either civil or criminal matters.

DISQUALIFICATION/CONFLICT OF INTEREST

The state statutes are unclear regarding many specific examples and circumstances when a notary public should disqualify himself from performing an official act. It is vital that the notary public maintain the highest degree of ethics and morals.

In order for the notary public to ethically perform the duties of office, it is essential that the notary public be an impartial party or "disinterested" in the act or transaction. Therefore, he may not take his own acknowledgment or administer an oath or affirmation to himself. He should neither gain nor lose as a result of the transaction.

If a notary public is a party to or directly/indirectly and (financially) interested in the transaction, he should decline to officiate. For example, a notary public who is a grantee or mortgagee in a deed or mortgage is disqualified to take the acknowledgment of the grantor or mortgagor. If he is a trustee in a deed of trust, the officer who is the grantor could not take his own acknowledgment. It would be inappropriate for a notary to acknowledge the bill of sale of personal property (i.e. a car) for his spouse.

In New York, the courts have held that an acknowledgment is null and void, when taken by a notary public who is financially or beneficially interested in and/or a party to an instrument or deed. The acknowledgment of the assignment of a mortgage before one of the assignees (who is the notary public) is invalid. An acknowledgment by one of the incorporators (who is a notary public) of another incorporator who signs a certificate is of no legal value.

Even though the state has established that these situations would disqualify a notary public, it has determined a notary public may officiate in certain circumstances. However, this does not mean that a questionable situation could not be successfully challenged in a court of law.

If the notary public is a stockholder, director, officer or employee of a corporation, he *may* take an acknowledgment or proof of execution or administer an oath or affirmation to any stockholder, director, officer, employee or agent of the corporation. The notary public may protest for non-acceptance or nonpayment, bills of exchange, drafts, checks, notes and other negotiable instruments owned or held for collection by the corporation. However, if the notary public is individually a party to or financially interested in the instrument, he may not protest the negotiable instruments owned or held for collection by the corporation. He *may not* perform an official act if he will also *sign* the document on behalf of the company. In this case, the notary public would be performing a notarial act for himself (or his own interest) which is not legally permitted.

A notary public who is an attorney at law admitted to practice in New York may administer an oath or affirmation, and take the affidavit or acknowledgment of his client in respect of any matter, claim, action or proceeding. To prevent a questionable situation and possible challenge, some lawyers will have another attorney or a legal assistant (who is a notary public) perform the act, even though the law permits the attorney to perform such acts.

New York statutes do not specifically address the topic of notarization for relatives of the notary public. If the document or act to be performed concerns matters of major significance, the notary public should decline to officiate. Examples would include (but not be limited to) contracts, deeds, mortgages, powers of attorney and incorporation or partnership papers. The notarial act could be challenged in court if there is sufficient evidence that the notary public was interested in the matter. The notarization may be declared invalid (by the court) and the act, document, or transaction voided.

IDENTIFICATION DOCUMENTS

The notary public must carefully examine the documents presented by the individual for the purpose of verifying identity. When examining the identification of the person, the notary public should be discreet and professional.

There are a variety of identification documents that are reliable and plentiful. The document should be valid and not expired. An identification document should contain a photograph, physical description, signature and be plastic laminated. Types of identification documents include passports, licenses and other identification cards.

The photograph should show the head, full face and shoulders; color is preferred over black and white, but a quality black and white photo is perfectly acceptable. The eyes of the subject should be visible in both the photo and in-person. Dark or sun glasses should be removed so that the eyes may be seen. With the popularity of tinted contact lenses, eye color authenticity and reliability is questionable.

In order to determine true identity, several key items should be carefully considered. The physical description should be *compared* from subject to identification document. A number of characteristics including eye color, hair color, race/skin color, sex and other data should be compared. The full, legible signature of the person should match the name listed on the identification documents and compared with another identification credential. Plastic lamination helps to deter modification or forgery. Examine the plastic for evidence of tampering.

The *United States Passport* is considered by many authorities to to be among the most reliable and trusted forms of identification in the United States. Issued by the U.S. Department of State, it is given to a citizen after the approval of a detailed application. In terms of appearance, the U.S. passport contains the citizen's full name, date of birth, home and foreign address (if any) and next of kin. Similar in size and style to a bank account passbook, the cover is dark blue and has gold-foil lettering stamped on the front, outside cover. The I.D. data is printed in multi-colored, fabric-type ribbon. The paper is safety, currency-type, multi-colored stock. Since 1984 newer passports have been issued with letter-quality computer printout style lettering. The entire page is plastic laminated over the data. The color photo is sealed with the seal of the U.S. Department of State, located on the first page. The citizen's signature is on the front cover (inside) page.

Armed forces (military) or *United States identification cards* are generally reliable. While sometimes not as comprehensive as the passport, they adequately satisfy the requirements for a dependable I.D. form. Due to the comprehensive "checks and balances" system for issuing these credentials, the ability to prevent forgery is increased. *State, county* and *local government I.D. cards* are dependable.

Driver's or *motor vehicle operator (MVO) licenses* issued by the state department of motor vehicles are good sources of identification. Virtually every U.S. state, including New York, issues a color photograph on the driver's license. Data listing the full name, home address, birth date, eye color and height are indicated. The holder's signature is clearly displayed. The card is sealed in plastic.

For those who do not have a driver's license, a card similar in information and appearance is available to *non-drivers* in New York and many other states. Applications are available from any county clerk. In New York State, only those without a driver's license are allowed to receive one.

A *state-issued license* with photograph may be used for identity verification purposes. Examples include professional licenses for barbers and cosmetologists, and firearm permits to possess a pistol. Locally issued identification documents such as a taxi-cab driver ("hack") license may be considered.

Some additional documents which may be presented for identity include: *Alien Identity card* (Form I-551 or the previously "green" card, now blue); *Department of Justice Immigration card; Displaced Person identification card; Medicare/Medicaid card; military discharge papers; proof of change of name; Selective Service card;* or *driver's license, learner's permit* or *non-driver I.D. card* issued by another state or country.

Be cautious in examining *foreign* identification documents, particularly passports from foreign countries, especially those which you have never heard of. *The Wall Street Journal* has reported about a U.S. company that issues passports in the former name of foreign countries which have changed names. The service is intended for those U.S. travelers going abroad who are concerned about terrorism aimed against United States citizens.

Employer-issued identification cards are commonly presented to notaries public as identification. The data contained on these cards varies widely and may be of questionable value. Some company-issued cards will contain only a name and picture sealed in plastic, while others may be comprehensive and informative. Caution is urged in using only this form of identification.

College and school identification cards may be acceptable, but are very likely to contain misinformation. This is because of the traditionally poor security surrounding their issuance. Typically issued in the library, bookstore or student activities office, a security system is usually non-existent, especially if the cards are issued by a fellow student. As an example, during a college registration, neighboring private high school students "infiltrated" the identification card process by merely walking up to the line and patiently waiting for their card. After being orally questioned for their name, date of birth, and social security number, their instant color photo was taken and they were immediately presented with their new identification card. These forms of identification are acceptable only if they are presented with another suitable form of I.D. that verifies them.

There are three significantly unreliable and generally unacceptable forms of identification: social security cards, credit cards and birth certificates.

Social security cards are not suitable because they contain only a name, social security number and signature. Unfortunately, some persons do not sign their cards. If the person was issued the card at age 13, there is usually a striking difference in signatures at age 44. Accordingly, it is not an acceptable form of identification.

Credit cards, bank teller machine cards, charge plates, check cashing courtesy cards and similar documents contain only a name, account number data and an expiration date. The cards lack necessary personal data. They do provide a space for a signature, but often the white signature strip is badly worn, grimy and illegible. Credit card crime and fraud has decreased dramatically since the "hologram" design was introduced, but these cards are still not adequate identification.

Birth certificates merely contain a name, date of birth and place of birth. Furthermore, it is reasonably easy to obtain the birth certificate of another person from a public bureau of vital records, health department or city chamberlain. Forged birth certificates are plentiful.

A good "rule of thumb" is to request at least *two* forms of identification documents, preferably a valid driver's license and another acceptable photo identification document. An indicator of possibly fraudulent documents is when all of the identification documents are sealed in new-appearing plastic lamination. Check the date of issuance to help determine authenticity.

Never officiate if the person is unable to produce acceptable forms of identification or is not personally known to you. Do not let an emotion-filled story, detailing the heart-wrenching consequences of not obtaining the notarization, prevent your thorough and positive identification of the individual.

The following are three actual instances revealing the importance of determining if the act should be declined.

1. A woman needed a social service department document acknowledged. She claimed she did not have any identification, but offered her telephone bill as the *only* proof of identity. Until she was able to produce an acceptable form of personal identification, the performance of the official notarial act was politely declined. She was referred to a notary public who knew her personally.
2. A college student missed his scheduled court appearance for an alleged traffic violation. He typed up a crudely worded and messy-appearing paragraph statement detailing his reason for not showing. The paper was presented for "notarization." The affiant (the person swearing to the facts in the affidavit) did not bring any identification whatsoever. Further, the paper did not contain many essential elements including the venue and jurat. The venue is the particular county or city where the notarial act is being performed. The jurat is the statement of the officer before whom a statement was sworn ("Sworn to before me on this 27th day of

January, 1918."). Growing impatient and agitated, the person indicated that he "never needed any I.D. before" for a notary public. After diplomatically informing the person of the requirements of law and penalties for failure to obey them, a second meeting was arranged where he could properly identify himself and we could prepare an affidavit which met the requirements of law.

3. A woman purchased an auto that had an Illinois title and tags. To transfer the legal ownership and title of an auto in Illinois, the owner must have his signature acknowledged. In this case, the seller simply signed (without the benefit of a notary public present) the title "over" to the buyer, not following the legal requirement. Unaware of this flaw, the buyer paid the seller. The seller moved out of the state the day after the sale and the buyer did not know where she had moved. The matter was further aggravated by the fact that the buyer sold her own car already. After explaining the necessary requirements to perform the acknowledgment, the woman insisted that the notarization be performed. Further questioning revealed that she attempted to have the acknowledgment performed by several other notaries public who also declined! Obviously, she was simply going to numerous notaries public until she found an officer who was willing to fulfill her need. Certainly she had a legitimate dilemma, but it was a combination of indifference on the part of the seller ("let her worry about it") and inexperience/naivete on the part of the buyer.

Identification checking guides are available to assist in positive identification of persons. These guides, available in U.S./Canada and International versions, contain full-color photographs of driver licenses, identification cards, passports and other government-issued identification documents.

Notary Public Must Officiate on Request

The penal law requires an officer (i.e. notary public) to perform the official duties when requested by a constituent. By the court order of a judge, he may be compelled to perform his duties or if he has done some act illegally, he may be ordered to correct it. This was established to prevent notaries public and other officers from abusing their powers. Refusal to perform his duty is a misdemeanor. When notaries public hear this, many become needlessly worried. An imagined scenario is a constituent making a request at three o'-clock in the morning or while at the grocery store. If unavailable at a particular time due to a legitimate previous commitment, tactfully explain this to the constituent. Make an arrangement for a meeting at a mutually convenient time or suggest a few other notaries public who may be available. The rule of being *reasonable and prudent* applies. However, if a constituent arrives at a firm at 4:45 p.m. on a Friday afternoon and the notary public is present, he must officiate regardless of the store closing at 5:00 p.m. The store cash registers may be closed-out a couple of minutes later than usual, but the public officer is obligated to officiate. Refusing to officiate based upon this reason exposes the notary public to disciplinary action including removal, jail and/or fine. A civil suit and award of damages is possible. Each notary public should put himself in the position of his constituents.

Physically Disabled Persons

If a notary public is asked to perform a notarial act by a physically disabled person unable to sign his name or make a mark, he does not have the explicit authority to assume the responsibility of signing for the individual. Even though the disabled person may be mentally competent to execute and understand a document, he is not able to have it notarized. Current New York law gives no clear legal direction for individuals in such a situation. One remedy is to have the court appoint a limited guardian for the purpose of executing a document, but this can be both costly and time consuming.

During the 1988–89 session of the New York Legislature, a proposed bill would have permited a physically handicapped person to orally direct a notary public to sign on his behalf. The proposed law would have held the notary public responsible for ascertaining the competence of the disabled individual. However, the bill died in committee. The bill was reintroduced during the 1990 Legislative session. Until such a law is passed, notaries who are approached by such persons unable to sign should advise them to consult their attorney.

CHAPTER 5 QUESTIONS

1. What is the jurisdiction of a notary public?
2. In what state is a notary public permitted to perform official services outside of his jurisdiction?
3. Under what circumstances is this notary public in this state permitted to perform these services?
4. Define an "authentication".
5. Name the three major sources of authentications.
6. Describe the authentication process, including fees.
7. What is the Hague Convention and how it relates to the authentication process?
8. Define an "apostille".
8. Are there any limitations placed upon providing official services on Sunday?
9. What is the rationale behind these limits?
10. Is there ever a situation in which a notary public should decline to provide services?
11. Describe some situations involving family members in which a notary public should decline to provide official services.
12. Explain why a corporation, bank or attorney might be legally allowed to perform official services for clients.
13. Is a notary public legally permitted to perform official services for people without identification? Explain your answer.
14. What are the four best forms of identification for positively determining personal identity of a person?
15. Compare the difference between "personally known" and "satisfactory evidence" in determining personal identity.
16. Define a "credible witness".
17. Detail the potential pitfalls in determining identity on the basis of sworn testimony of a credible witness.
18. Is an expired identification card ever acceptable for the purpose of determining personal identity? Why?
19. Explain what possible circumstances might allow the use of an expired identification to be suitable for assisting in the determination of personal identity.
20. Name at least six forms of common identification documents which are unacceptable for the purpose of determining personal identity. Explain why.
21. Explain why the use of the right thumbprint might prove helpful in the identification of a person.

22. Is it acceptable to decline service to a requester? Under what circumstances is it permissible to decline? What is the legal rationale behind this requirement?
23. What special considerations are involved in serving a physically disabled person?

Chapter 6

Basic Formalities and Concepts of Notarial Acts

NOTARIZATION

In order to legally and ethically perform his function, a notary public must possess the knowledge of a number of basic legal terms. The term "*notarization*" is not a proper, legal term. It is not found in *Black's Law Dictionary,* the reliable, court standard for accurate legal terminology. The term developed as a slang word in common usage. Use of such a term should be avoided in practice because it causes confusion and trivializes the act of a notary public. Remember, there is no one, single "notarization" or notarial act performed by a notary. There never has been such a single act. Remember, notaries do *not* simply "notarize" signatures.

As a state public officer, the notary public is authorized to perform a variety of legal acts. The two most frequently performed acts are *taking an acknowledgment* and *administering an oath.* A brief oral ceremony is required in both cases. In order for the notary public to properly perform his function, New York law requires him to recite a specific set of words to a person, who, in-turn, must reply orally in the affirmative. The notary public should *never* simply sign his name and make a stamp and seal impression without also performing the required ceremony— even if that's all a document seems to call for! Very often, an individual, or a party at a business firm or governmental agency who drafted a document simply isn't aware of the proper legal certificate language to accompany the document. As a result, documents may seem to call for only the signature and seal of a notary. However, if a notary simply signs his signature and marks his official instruments on a document, without certain additional information, the notary is subject to legal discipline by the secretary of state.

In order to correctly take an acknowledgment or administer an oath, the notary public must satisfy three components: (a) personal appearance of the requester, (b) actual performance of the legal ceremony, and (c) written documentation of such ceremony. The documentation of the ceremonial act is recorded in a certification containing "recitals" or factual statements noted in a notarial certificate which accompanies a legal instrument.

After taking an acknowledgment of the execution of a written instrument, the notary documents the act in an *acknowledgment certificate.* Likewise, upon administering an oath, the notary documents the act in a *jurat certificate,* sometimes referred to as a *verification.* Merely completing the acknowledgment certificate or jurat, without also performing the required legal ceremony, may subject the notary to suspension, removal and fine. The underlying legal or business transaction may also be rendered voidable by the negligence or misconduct of a notary for failing to perform the required act.

Legal Myths and Folklore in New York State

1. It is always necessary to sign before a notary.
   FALSE.
2. The act of a notary legalizes any document.
   FALSE.
3. The notary is "notarizing" the signature, but not the contents of the document.
   FALSE.
4. The primary reason that the notary needs the signatory present is to watch him sign the document.
   FALSE.
5. The notary doesn't need the signatory to appear before him if the notary is familiar with the identity of the signatory.
   FALSE.
6. The date that a document is executed must match the date that a notarial act for that document was performed.
   FALSE.

7. It's illegal for a notary to act on behalf of a matter for his blood or marriage relatives.
   FALSE.
8. If a person appears before a notary (who is unknown to the notary) without identification, the notary cannot proceed with any notarial act.
   FALSE.
9. A notary can limit the scope of his notarial acts to those in his employment or profession.
   FALSE.
10. A notary can refuse to perform a notarial act if he feels uncomfortable about the transaction, or doesn't feel he understands the matter presented to him.
    FALSE.
11. A notary is not legally responsible for damage to third-parties due to forgery because he failed to properly maintain adequate security for his official seal and statement of authority marking stamp.
    FALSE.
12. A notary can limit his services to only business firm customers or government agency clients.
    FALSE.
13. If an employer sponsors an employee by reimbursing the notary for all notarial related costs and expenses, the notary must surrender his official seal and marking stamp, and official register to the employer upon resignation, termination or retirement.
    FALSE.
14. A notary must proceed with a notarial act, even if he feels the capacity of the person before him is diminished, impairing the ability to understand an oath, or the "free act and deed" nature of an acknowledgment.
    FALSE.
15. A notary can refuse to administer an oath to an affiant who wishes to swear to facts in an affidavit which such notary finds morally offensive or politically distasteful.
    FALSE.

SIGNATURE

One of the most common myths about notarial acts is that a party must always sign the document in the physical presence of the notary public. This is true in some cases, but not others. Furthermore, although the standard practice in legal related matters is for a party to sign a document in black ink, it is often permissible for a signature to be made in blue ink.

It is interesting to note that the signature does *not* necessarily have to reflect the letters of which the signatory's name is composed. Whatever mark a person wishes to place onto a document to represent his signature is perfectly acceptable. If a bona-fide person presents himself to a notary, and he conforms to all of the notary requests and ceremonial acts as directed by such notary, but does not reproduce the exact replica of the signature on his presented identification, it is inappropriate for the notary to decline. The notary's duty is not to compare a person's signature on a document and his identification presented to the notary. Refusing to proceed with an act because the signature on the document and identification do not match is not acceptable, and may subject the notary to discipline by the secretary of state.

A signature may be written by hand, printed, stamped, typewritten, engraved or lithographed on an instrument. A signature is made by use of an name, including any trade or assumed name, upon an instrument, or by any word or mark. A thumb print may be impressed onto an instrument as a signature.

Standard Operating Procedure

In order for a notary to correctly perform a proper notarial act, he must fulfill a certain sequence of basic procedures. When the term notarization is utilized, it represents the official action by a notary.

Routine and habitual adherence to a standard operating procedure, step-by-step, will help to minimize legal liability and enhance credibility, especially if the notarial act is questioned.

Standard Operating Procedure for Notarial Acts

1. Personal appearance of requester is always required. Identity is made with identification credential if requester is not personally known by notary. Retain identification credential until act is completed.

2. Make entry in notarial register of the requester and notarial act. Ask requester to sign notarial register. Enter requester's thumbprint, if desired and appropriate. Match identification credential with name in document(s).
3. Examine entire document(s) for any blanks. If necessary, ask requester to complete the document. Ascertain proper ceremonies and protocols which are required by scanning document. Verify that the act venue and related notarial certificate(s) facts including date, name(s) of individual(s) and related act information is accurate. If not, notary should strike through incorrect data and make necessary hand-written corrections. Each correction should be initialed and dated by the notary.
4. Perform indicated notarial ceremony with requester.
5. Invite requester to execute the document (if not already executed). If already executed, re-execution is required only if indicated. For example, an affidavit or deposition might require execution in the presence of a notary (check the jurat for language). However, taking an acknowledgment doesn't require execution before a notary.
6. Affix official notarial signature which signifies that the notarial ceremony was legally and properly performed.
7. Apply the notarial statement of authority (by inked, mechanical stamp, or by hand or typewriter).
8. Emboss the document with a clear imprint of the notary official seal near the notarial signature (but never atop any signature).
9. Collect fee, if appropriate, and prepare receipt for requester. Enter fee, if appropriate, in notarial register.
10. Return document, identification and receipt, if applicable, to requester. Enter any remaining notes in notarial register upon the departure of requester.

Adapted from *Notary Public Handbook: Principles, Practices & Cases, National Edition* by Alfred E. Piombino. ©2000

Chapter 7

Taking Acknowledgments and Proofs of Executions

ACKNOWLEDGMENT

An ***acknowledgment*** is a formal declaration before an authorized public officer. It is made by a person executing an instrument who states that it was his free act and deed. For example, when a person completes and signs a power of attorney, the acknowledgment confirms the facts that the party actually signed the document for the purpose(s) detailed in it. Further, the person declares that he signed the document *freely and willfully,* without any undue influence (i.e. a threat of violence). The acknowledgment provides a degree of protection to the public by certifying that a document was properly executed. In order for a document to become a recordable instrument, an acknowledgment is a legal requirement. An acknowledgment of execution is required for a wide variety of documents such as contracts, bills of sale, conveyances of real property (deeds), mortgages, powers of attorney, business certificates, etc. The person must appear before the notary public. Taking an acknowledgment over the telephone is a misdemeanor. Unless the person making the acknowledgment actually and personally appeared before the notary public on the day specified, the notary public's certification is false and fraudulent.

The notary public should make sure that the document is completely executed; there should be *no* blanks. If the notary public discovers blanks, the constituent should be asked to complete the document (fill in all blanks) or draw lines through the blanks. If the constituent refuses to do this for any reason, the notary public should *decline* to officiate. While it is not the responsibility of the notary public to completely read and comprehend the document, a rapid skimming examination is reasonable and prudent. Usually the blanks are purely the result of an honest oversight on the part of the constituent. Most persons will appreciate the discovery of these flaws.

It is a duty of the notary public to make certain that the constituent is fully aware of the nature of the document, before taking the acknowledgment. It is especially critical in the instance of the young, elderly, infirmed or otherwise potentially incompetent. The outcome of the execution of a document, such as a power of attorney, requires that a person fully understand its meaning and consequences. For example, a business person may tell an elderly customer that a document is just a "legal formality" to start a home improvement job, when it is really a mortgage agreement.

If a notary public *knowingly* makes a false certification that a deed or other written instrument was acknowledged, he is guilty of forgery in the second degree. The crime is false certification with intent to defraud, a felony which is punishable by imprisonment for a term of up to seven years. Damages are recoverable for issuing a false certificate. An award of damages was upheld by the New York State Court of Appeals when a notary public had certified that a mortgagor had appeared and acknowledged a mortgage when he did not appear. In such an instance, the notary public would be held *personally* liable for the damages awarded. While a notary public is protected from criminal liability in the absence of criminal intent or guilty knowledge, a deed or other written document/instrument with a false certification is invalid because it is a forgery.

The distinction between the taking of an acknowledgment and an affidavit must be clearly understood. An acknowledgment verifies that the person before the notary public actually (and freely) signed a document for the purposes stated in it. However, *no* oath is administered. The affidavit verifies that the contents of the written statement are true. The statement is made under oath. There are some acknowledgments which are a combination of an acknowledgment and affidavit. A prudent notary public should carefully examine every document and determine the duties required.

Requirements

There are three essential components of an acknowledgment:

1. the personal appearance before the notary public;

2. positive identification; and
3. the actual acknowledgment to the notary public.

The person who is the signer of the document must personally appear before the notary public. The person executing the instrument does *not* have to sign his name in the physical presence of the notary public, unless specifically required. Therefore, the venue indicated in the acknowledgment certificate should state the exact jurisdiction where the acknowledgment is performed, not necessarily where the document was actually *signed.*

An acknowledgment must not be taken by any officer unless he personally knows or has satisfactory evidence that the person making it is the person *described in* and *who executed* the document. If the constituent is unable to produce suitable identification, decline to officiate. Recommend that he find a notary public who personally knows him.

The actual acknowledgment phase of the act must meet certain criteria. It must state that on the date specified, "Before me came (name), to me known to be the individual described in and who executed the foregoing instrument and acknowledged he/she executed the same."

The signer should not only admit the signature as his/her own, but also indicate that it was made *willingly.* The oral declaration of the signer is required.

The notary public should ask the constituent the following:

A. DOCUMENT SIGNED IN PRESENCE OF NOTARY:

"Do you acknowledge that you willfully executed (or signed) this document [state type, if known] for the purposes contained in it?"

B. DOCUMENT NOT SIGNED IN PRESENCE OF NOTARY:

"Do you acknowledge that this is your signature, and that you willfully executed (or signed) this document [state type, if known] for the purposes contained in it?"

ACKNOWLEDGMENT CERTIFICATE

Essential components on the *acknowledgment certificate* (for individuals) are:

1. venue (municipality);
2. date;

3. the fact that the person named (personally) appeared before the officer;
4. a statement that they acknowledged the execution of the instrument attached to the acknowledgment and
5. the name/title of the officer performing the official act.

The notary public should affix his inked stamp and seal beneath his signature.

Real Property Deeds, Leases and Mortgages

Certain statutory forms to be utilized by notaries public were changed by New York legislation signed into law in 1997, effective September 1, 1999. The new law amends real property law, section 309, to establish statutory forms that must be utilized by corporations for acknowledgments. In addition, the new law enacts real property law, section 309-a and 309-b which provide new forms that shall be used on conveyances and other instruments affecting real property located in New York state. These new forms are mandatory for real property deeds, long-term, recordable leases, mortgages, discharge of mortgages, property liens, powers of attorney and any other recordable instrument regarding real property situate in New York state. For matters other than those concerning New York situated real property, other similar acknowledgment forms are legally acceptable. Furthermore, the law allows some flexibility. Acknowledgments concerning real property must conform substantially, although not exactly, with the new certificate forms. Therefore, if a minor variation in an acknowledgment certificate language appears, it is inappropriate for any county clerk to reject the recording of such acknowledged instruments.

The following forms are for use by any "person", which New York law defines to include "any corporation, joint stock company, estate, general partnership (including any registered limited partnership or foreign limited liability partnership), limited liability company (including a professional service limited liability company), foreign limited liability company (including a foreign professional service limited liability company), joint venture, limited partnership, natural person, attorney-in-fact, real estate investment trust, business trust or other trust, custodian, nominee, or any other individual or entity in its own or any representative capacity."

ACKNOWLEDGMENT OF CONVEYANCE, LEASE OR MORTGAGE

STATE OF NEW YORK } SS.:
COUNTY OF. . . . .

On the (date) day of (month), in the year (year), before me, the undersigned, a notary public in and for said state, personally appeared (name), personally known to me or proved to me on the basis of satisfactory evidence to be the individual(s) whose name(s) is (are), subscribed to the within instrument and acknowledged to me that he/she/they executed the same in his/her/their capacity(ies), and that by his/her/their signature(s) on the instrument, the individual(s), or the person upon behalf of which the individual(s) acted, executed the instrument.

. . . .
Notary Public

INDIVIDUAL ACKNOWLEDGMENT: FORM A

STATE OF NEW YORK } SS.:
COUNTY OF . . . .

On the (date) day of (month), (year), before me personally came (name), to me known to be the individual described in, and who executed, the foregoing instrument, and acknowledged that he/she executed the same.

. . . .
Notary Public

Individual Acknowledgment: Form B

STATE OF NEW YORK } SS.:
COUNTY OF . . . . }

On the (date) day of (month), (year), before me personally came (name), to me personally known, and known to be one of the individuals described in, and who executed, the foregoing instrument, and duly acknowledged that he/she executed the same.

. . . .
Notary Public

Several Individual Acknowledgments

STATE OF NEW YORK } SS.:
COUNTY OF . . . . }

On the (date) of (month), (year), before me personally came (name) and (name), to me personally known, and known to me to be the individuals described in, and who executed, the foregoing instrument, and severally they duly acknowledged to me that they executed the same.

. . . .
Notary Public

Acknowledgment by Fiduciary

STATE OF NEW YORK } SS.:
COUNTY OF . . . . }

On the (date) day of (month), (year), before me personally came (name), executor under the last will and testament of (name), to me known, and known to me to be the individual described in, and who executed, the foregoing instrument, and he duly acknowledged to me that he executed the same as such executor.

. . . .
Notary Public

PARTNERSHIP ACKNOWLEDGMENT

STATE OF NEW YORK } SS.:
COUNTY OF . . . . }

On the (date) day of (month), (year), before me personally came (name), to me personally known, and known to me to be a member of the firm of (name & name), and known to me to be the individual described in, and who executed, the foregoing instrument in the firm name of (name & name), and duly acknowledged to me that he/she executed the same for and in behalf of the firm.

. . . .
Notary Public

ACKNOWLEDGMENT BY ATTORNEY-IN-FACT

STATE OF NEW YORK } SS.:
COUNTY OF . . . . }

On this (date) day of (month), (year), before me personally came (name), to me known to be the individual described in, and who executed, the foregoing instrument, and to me known to be the attorney-in-fact of (name), the individual described in, and who by his attorney-in-fact executed the same, and acknowledged that he executed the instrument as the act and deed of said (name) by virtue of a power of attorney dated (month/day), (year), and recorded in the office of the (title) of the County of (name) on (month/day), (year), in liber (number) of powers of attorney, at page (number).

. . . .
Notary Public

Acknowledgment by Corporate Attorney-in-Fact

STATE OF NEW YORK } SS.:
COUNTY OF . . . . }

On this (date) day of (month), (year), before me personally came (name), to me known and known to me to be president of the (name) Corp., which corporation is known to me to be the attorney-in-fact of (name), the individual described in the foregoing instrument and who by the attorney-in-fact executed the foregoing instrument, and (name) being duly sworn, did depose and say that he resides at (number) (name) street, in the Borough of (name), City of (name); that he is the president of (name) Corp., the corporation described in, and which executed the foregoing instrument; that he knew the seal of the corporation; that the seal affixed to the instrument was such corporate seal; that it was so affixed by order of the board of directors of the corporation, and that he signed his name thereto by like order, and that the seal was affixed and the instrument was executed by the corporation as the act and deed of the (name) under and by virtue of a power of attorney dated (month/day), (year), and recorded on (month/day), (year), in the office of (name) of the County of (name), in liber (number) of powers of attorney, at page (number).

. . . .
Notary Public

Acknowledgment Before a Mayor

STATE OF NEW YORK } SS.:
COUNTY OF . . . . }

On this (date) day of (month), (year), before me, the Mayor of the City of (name), came at the City (Hall), to me known to be the individual described in and who executed the foregoing instrument, and duly acknowledged that he executed the same.

IN WITNESS WHEREOF, I have hereunto set my hand and affixed the seal of the city, the day and year first above written.

. . . .
Notary Public

Acknowledgment by Husband and Wife

STATE OF NEW YORK } SS.:
COUNTY OF . . . .

On the (date) day of (month), (year), before me personally came (name) and (name), a husband and wife, to me personally known, and known to me to be the individuals described in, and who executed, the foregoing instrument, and severally they acknowledged to me that they executed the same.

The acknowledgment of an instrument on behalf of a corporation must be made by a corporate officer. In the case of a dissolved corporation, an officer or director authorized by the corporation board of directors may execute the document.

Corporate Acknowledgment

STATE OF NEW YORK } SS.:
COUNTY OF . . . .

On the (date) day of (month), in the year (year), before me personally came (name), to me known, who, being by me duly sworn, did depose and say that he/she/they reside(s) in (city) (if the place of residence is in a city, include the street and street number, if any, thereof); that he/she/they is (are) the (president or other officer or director or attorney in fact duly appointed) of the (name of corporation), the corporation described in and which executed the above instrument; that he/she/they know(s) the seal of said corporation; that the seal affixed to said instrument is such corporate seal; that it was so affixed by authority of the board of directors of said corporation, and that he/she/they signed his/her/their name(s) thereto by like authority.

. . . .
Notary Public

Corporate Acknowledgment

STATE OF NEW YORK } SS.:
COUNTY OF . . . . }

On the (date) day of (month), in the year (year), before me personally came (name), to me known, who, being by me duly sworn, did depose and say that he/she/they reside(s) in (city) (if the place of residence is in a city, include the street and street number, if any, thereof); that he/she/they is (are) the (president or other officer or director or attorney in fact duly appointed) of the (name of corporation), the corporation described in and which executed the above instrument; and that he/she/they signed his/her/their name(s) thereto by authority of the board of directors of said corporation.

. . . .
Notary Public

The notary public should carefully review the language of the acknowledgment certificate to ensure that all legal requirements are being fulfilled. For example, corporation acknowledgment certificates state that the person executing the instrument on behalf of the corporation, swear to the notary public that he did so with the express authority of the board of directors. However, a state grant contract, for example, might not only require this standard language, but stipulate that the original resolution authorizing the execution of the instrument be attached. It is the responsibility of the notary public to assure that all of the requirements outlined in the certificate are satisfied, *before* affixing his official signature and seal.

Sometimes the state laws are a little "behind the times." A New York statute has declared that the acknowledgment or proof of execution of any document/instrument, including conveyances (deeds) of real property, "may be made by a married woman the same as if unmarried." There was a period in recent history when a married woman required the approval and signature of her husband to own or transfer real property.

An acknowledgment may be taken on Sunday.

An affidavit *cannot* be a substitute for an acknowledgment. The jurat to an affidavit does not contain the information required in a certificate of acknowledgment.

If the document signer is present before the notary public, an acknowledgment is the appropriate notarial act. If a person saw another party sign the document, and he knew them as described and that party executed the document, a proof of execution is required.

Proof of Execution

A ***proof of execution*** is the formal declaration made by a subscribing witness to the execution of a document. When the execution of a document is proved by a subscribing witness, he must: state his own place of residence; if his residence is in a city, the street and street number (if any), and that he knew the person described in and who signed the document. The proof must not be taken unless the notary public is personally acquainted with the witness or has satisfactory evidence that he is the same person who was a subscribing witness to the document.

Requirements

The information required for the certificate of proof are:

1. venue (municipality);
2. date;
3. the fact that the witness making the proof personally appeared before the notary public;
4. the statement that the witness took an oath or affirmation that he saw the document to which his name was signed as witness;
5. that he signed his name as a witness at that time;
6. the residence of the proving witness;

7. the fact that the witness knew the person described in and who executed the instrument; and
8. the fact that he was an uninterested and competent subscribing witness to the instrument.

Certificate of Proof of Execution

Effective September 1, 1999, the following is the form of the certificate of proof of execution by a subscribing witness known to the notary public:

STATE OF NEW YORK } SS.:
COUNTY OF . . . . }

On the (date) day of (month), in the year (year), before me, the undersigned, a notary public in and for said state, personally appeared (name), the subscribing witness to the foregoing instrument, with whom I am personally acquainted, who, being by me duly sworn, did depose and say that he/she/they reside(s) in (city) (if the place of residence is in a city, include the street and street number, if any, thereof); that he/she/they knows (name) to be the individual described in and who executed the foregoing instrument; said subscribing witness was present and saw said (name) execute the same; and that said witness at the same time subscribed his/her their name(s) as a witness thereto.

. . . .
Notary Public

If there are any mistakes made in a certificate of acknowledgment, a notary public can correct them only during his term of office. If his term has expired, he is ineligible to take this action. It will be necessary to then bring the document to a currently commissioned notary public to perform another acknowledgment and complete a new certificate of acknowledgment.

An officer authorized to take the acknowledgment or proof of execution of conveyances/instruments or certify acknowledgments or proofs (i.e. notary public) is personally liable for damages to persons injured as the result of any wrongdoing on the part of the officer.

X 201 — Certificate of Conducting Business under an Assumed Name For Individual. 11-98

BlumbergExcelsior, Inc. PUBLISHER NYC 10013

Business Certificate

I HEREBY CERTIFY *that I am conducting or transacting business under the name or designation of*

at

City or Town of *County of* *State of New York.*

*My full name is**
and I reside at

I FURTHER CERTIFY *that I am the successor in interest to*

the person or persons heretofore using such name or names to carry on or conduct or transact business.

IN WITNESS WHEREOF, *I have signed this certificate on*

* Print or type name.
* If under 21 years of age, state "I am .... years of age".

ACKNOWLEDGMENT IN NEW YORK STATE (RPL 309-a)

State of New York
County of } ss.:

On before me, the undersigned, personally appeared

personally known to me or proved to me on the basis of satisfactory evidence to be the individual(s) whose name(s) is (are) subscribed to the within instrument and acknowledged to me that he/she/they executed the same in his/her/their capacity(ies), and that by his/her/their signature(s) on the instrument, the individual(s), or the person upon behalf of which the individual(s) acted, executed the instrument.

(signature and office of individual taking acknowledgment)

ACKNOWLEDGMENT OUTSIDE NEW YORK STATE (RPL 309-b)

State of
County of } ss.:

On before me, the undersigned, personally appeared

personally known to me or proved to me on the basis of satisfactory evidence to be the individual(s) whose name(s) is (are) subscribed to the within instrument and acknowledged to me that he/she/they executed the same in his/her/their capacity(ies), and that by his/her/their signature(s) on the instrument, the individual(s), or the person upon behalf of which the individual(s) acted, executed the instrument, and that such individual made such appearance before the undersigned in

(insert city or political subdivision and state or county or other place acknowledgment taken)

(signature and office of individual taking acknowledgment)

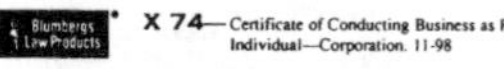
X 74—Certificate of Conducting Business as Partners
Individual—Corporation. 11-98

BlumbergExcelsior, Inc.
PUBLISHER NYC 10013

Business Certificate for Partners

The undersigned do hereby certify that they are conducting or transacting business as members of a partnership under the name or designation of

at

in the County of , State of New York, and do further certify that the full names of all the persons conducting or transacting such partnership including the full names of all the partners with the residence address of each such person, and the age of any who may be infants, are as follows:

NAME Specify which are infants and state ages.	*RESIDENCE*
....	....
....	....
....	....
....	....
....	....
....	....

WE DO FURTHER CERTIFY that we are the successors in interest to

the person or persons heretofore using such name or names to carry on or conduct or transact business.

In Witness Whereof, *We have this day of made and signed this certificate.*

....

....

....

....

....

State of New York, County of ss.: ACKNOWLEDGMENT RPL309-a (Do not use outside New York State)

On before me, the undersigned, personally appeared

personally known to me or proved to me on the basis of satisfactory evidence to be the individual(s) whose name(s) is (are) subscribed to the within instrument and acknowledged to me that he/she/they executed the same in his/her/their capacity(ies), and that by his/her/their signature(s) on the instrument, the individual(s), or the person upon behalf of which the individual(s) acted, executed the instrument.

(signature and office of individual taking acknowledgment)

ACKNOWLEDGMENT IN NEW YORK STATE (RPL 309-a)

State of New York
County of } ss.:

On before me, the undersigned, personally appeared

personally known to me or proved to me on the basis of satisfactory evidence to be the individual(s) whose name(s) is (are) subscribed to the within instrument and acknowledged to me that he/she/they executed the same in his/her/their capacity(ies), and that by his/her/their signature(s) on the instrument, the individual(s), or the person upon behalf of which the individual(s) acted, executed the instrument.

(signature and office of individual taking acknowledgment)

ACKNOWLEDGMENT OUTSIDE NEW YORK STATE (RPL 309-b)

State of
County of } ss.:

On before me, the undersigned, personally appeared

personally known to me or proved to me on the basis of satisfactory evidence to be the individual(s) whose name(s) is (are) subscribed to the within instrument and acknowledged to me that he/she/they executed the same in his/her/their capacity(ies), and that by his/her/their signature(s) on the instrument, the individual(s), or the person upon behalf of which the individual(s) acted, executed the instrument, and that such individual made such appearance before the undersigned in

(insert city or political subdivision and state or county or other place acknowledgment taken)

(signature and office of individual taking acknowledgment)

INDEX No.

Certificate of Partners

CONDUCTING BUSINESS UNDER THE NAME OF

CHAPTER 7 QUESTIONS

1. What is an "acknowledgment"?
2. Does the notary public have to make a certain inquiry of the acknowledger? Explain your answer.
3. What three words describe the chief function of an acknowledgment?
4. In what general group of documents are acknowledgments typically utilized?
5. Is personal appearance a mandatory step? Explain why.
6. Is it ever possible to take an acknowledgment over the telephone? Explain your answer.
7. Should a notary public serve as a subscribing witness in connection with a document? Explain your answer.
8. Explain the distinction between taking an acknowledgment and an affidavit.
9. What is a "venue"?
10. What is the recommended method of manually correcting an incorrect venue? Name three inappropriate methods of making a correction.
11. Explain the potential risk to a legal transaction in the event that the venue is incorrect.
12. Explain the risk and potential outcome to a secured mortgage transaction if the venue isn't accurate. What are the steps that a challenger would take to invalidate the recording?
13. A notary public is presented with a power of attorney (POA) by the principal. The principal has already signed the POA document, but not in the presence of the notary. Further, the document is dated six months earlier. What steps should the notary public take in this situation? Do the dates need to match? Explain your answer.
14. What two key elements must be contained in the standard acknowledgment taken by the notary public?
15. What is the verbal "script" of the legal ceremony for an acknowledgment to be taken for a: (a) document signed in the presence of the notary public; and (b) document not signed in the presence of the notary public?
16. Name the eight essential components of the standard acknowledgment.
17. Name at least six types or styles of acknowledgment certificates.
18. A person presents himself to a notary public with a document to be signed on behalf of another person. What is this person legally termed and what should the person present to the notary to substantiate his claim of status?
19. Explain what special steps to reduce fraud should be taken by a notary public when presented with a power of attorney.
20. In a corporation acknowledgment, who may legally make an acknowledgment on behalf of a corporation?
21. What special situation must exist for a person other than a corporation officer to execute a document on behalf of the corporation? What document should be presented to the notary public for examination?

22. In some jurisdictions, in addition to the customary acknowledgment for corporations, what additional ceremony might be incorporated? Explain why this extra legal ceremony actually assists the notary public.
23. In a corporation acknowledgment, is it necessary to determine actual corporation authority? Is it reasonable to demand production of a corporation identification card? How about a partnership or other entity? Explain your answer.
24. Describe the special notarial powers granted under law to U.S. military and consulate personnel. Who may take such acknowledgments? How would the acknowledgment certificate differ from a civilian-type certificate? Where may the acknowledgment be taken?
25. What special legal act is appropriate if the acknowledger is unable to appear before a notary public?
26. Under what unusual circumstances would this special procedure be employed?
27. List the eight primary components of a proof of execution and accompanying certificate of proof.

Chapter 8

Sworn Proceedings: Administering Oaths and Affirmations

Oath

An ***oath*** is an outward, oral pledge given by a person taking it that his promise is made under an immediate sense of his responsibility to God. It is a solemn invocation or call for the punishment of God upon the oath taker (affiant, deponent or witness), if he does not declare the whole truth. The casual and careless administration of oaths is unacceptable. An oath must be administered in the form required by law. The person taking the oath *must* declare acceptance of the oath by saying the words "I do" or "yes" after the notary public has read the statement out loud. To further impress upon the person the seriousness of taking the oath the notary public might incorporate two subtle, but powerful, symbolic gestures. First, raise your right hand and ask the person to raise his right hand when taking the oath. Second, ask the person to place his left hand on a Bible or other religious book compatible with the religious beliefs of the person. The courts expect that the solemn oath ceremony will be executed seriously and professionally, simulating the courthouse experience.

Affirmation

An ***affirmation*** is similar to an oath in that they are both equally binding under the law. The difference is that an affirmation is a solemn and formal declaration, made under the penalty of perjury, by a person who refuses to take an oath. It is based upon the person's ethical or religious beliefs. For example, there are some religions which do not allow their followers to swear to God (or anything).

Therefore: the affirmation does not contain any words which requires "swearing"; the person "declares and affirms."

The state source of the official legal forms of oaths/affirmations is the New York Civil Practice Law and Rules.

FORMS OF OATHS

The following are the forms of oaths for an affidavit and deposition:

(AFFIDAVIT) "You do solemnly swear that the contents of this affidavit are known to you and that the (said) facts are true to the best of your knowledge and belief?"

(DEPOSITION) "You do solemnly swear that the evidence you shall give, relating to the matter in difference between __________, plaintiff, and __________, defendant, shall be the truth, the whole truth and nothing but the truth?"

The simplest form in which an oath may be lawfully administered (for affidavits) is: You do solemnly swear that the contents of this affidavit subscribed by you are correct and true?"

OATH (AFFIRMATION)

"Do you solemnly swear (or declare and affirm) that the contents of this document are known to you, and that the information is true? So help you God? (or under the penalty of perjury?)"

Courtesy of Alfred E. Piombino © 1996
Reorder USA Toll-Free 1-800-405-1070
Distributor of Piombino's Notary Public Handbooks, Notary Public Register & Fingerprinting Supplies

FORMS OF AFFIRMATIONS

The following are the forms of affirmation for an affidavit and deposition:

(AFFIDAVIT)	"You do solemnly, sincerely and truly, declare and affirm that the contents of this affidavit are known to you and that the said facts are true to the best of your knowledge and belief?"
(DEPOSITION)	"You do solemnly, sincerely and truly, declare and affirm that the evidence you shall give relating to this matter in difference between __________, plaintiff, and __________, defendant, shall be the truth, the whole truth and nothing but the truth?"

REQUIREMENTS

For an oath or affirmation to be valid, it is required that the person:

1. swearing or affirming personally be in the presence of the notary public (not over the telephone);
2. unequivocally (clearly) swears or affirms that what is stated is true;
3. swears or affirms as of that time; and
4. conscientiously takes upon himself the obligation of an oath.

The criteria for determining who may take an oath are intelligence, competency and morals. The notary public should have a reasonable belief that the constituent is capable of understanding the seriousness of the act. For example, if a child has the ability to understand what an oath is and the consequences of not being truthful, then it may be concluded that he/she is "capable."

A corporation or a partnership *cannot* take an oath. An oath can only be taken by a "natural" person. A business firm such as a corporation is an artificial person. An individual representing the organization must take the oath. His relationship to the business or organization should be stated in the document.

Perjury has been committed if upon testimony on a material matter, under oath or affirmation, the person has stated the testimony to be true, yet knowingly and willfully making the statement or testimony false.

A notary public before whom a will and testament is acknowledged and sworn to, or self-proved (discussed in chapter 11), cannot also serve as a witness to the will, because he is without authority to administer an oath to himself. Under no conditions is a notary public authorized to act as his own notary public.

Key factors in successful perjury prosecutions include the following: evidence that the alleged perjurer knew his statements were false when made; false swearing made in an instruments which was specifically required or authorized by law; and that the false statements were material to the relevant issue or matter involved in the case.

There are major classifications of documents requiring the administration of an oath or affirmation. Affidavits and depositions, discussed in detail in the next two chapters, are formal classes of documents requiring swearing or affirming which conform to a prescribed pattern of construction. However, an infinite number of documents require a relatively simple procedure called verification. Verification is the confirmation of the truth of facts in a document, attested by swearing or affirming. Virtually every paper submitted to a court needs verification. Countless numbers of documents in court, commerce and governmental administration require verification. The terms "verified", "sworn" and "affirmed" are sometimes referred to interchangeably.

The jurat is the clause on the bottom of a document which is evidence that an oath or affirmation was administered. It is the written evidence indicated on a document that oath or affirmation ceremony has occurred. The most common forms of jurats are "Subscribed and sworn to before me on (date)" or "Sworn to before me on (date)".

Some statutes specifically prescribe that the jurat conform "substantially" to the following form:

Sworn to and subscribed†
before me this . . . day of . . ., 19 . . .
Personally Known . . . OR Produced Identification† . . .
Type of Identification Produced ________________

†Not required in every state

However, numerous jurats on hundreds of legal, business and government forms (and the rest of the nation) are not fashioned in this new form. For example, an affidavit prepared in New York (and according to New York Law), might not require any further information than the basic "Sworn to before me on (date)" jurat form. Even many government forms in circulation are in need of the updated legal information. However, it is perfectly acceptable for a notary public to make the addition of the new language for the jurat, the notary public is responsible to ammend the document to properly conform to the law. If required by statute, the notary public can be held responsible for not making the appropriate changes in the jurat form.

Although it is not specifically mandated by law, the venue of the notarial act should be placed immediately above the jurat on the document. The venue is the jurisdiction (state, county and sometimes municipality) in which the notarial act transpired:

STATE OF NEW YORK . . . . .] ss.:
COUNTY OF . . . . .]

Competency

The issue of *competency* is an important factor to consider. Take the instance of a patient who is taking medication or "medicated." It is both reasonable and prudent for the notary public to courteously (and tactfully) determine the patient's ability to understand the situation. Through a short conversation, the notary public may assess a person's ability to make a rational, informed decision. Objective questions to ask the person include:

1. his name and home address;
2. his whereabouts (i.e. facility name) and the circumstances surrounding his admittance (i.e. surgery, accident, etc.); and
3. the nature of the act to be performed (i.e. the seriousness of making sworn testimony).

If the patient is having continued difficulty in producing reasonable responses, decline to officiate.

Oaths of Office

There are two *different* types of oaths. The first is an oath or affirmation that is generally associated with an *affidavit* or deposition. It requires a written certificate to be completed by the officer administering it. The second type of oath is connected with the *oath of a public officer.* This oath typically involves written documentation of the oath being administered. The oath of office that the notary public is required to take is the same form required by (state law) for all other public officers.

Notaries public may legally administer either form of oath. However, not all public officers who are empowered to administer the oath or affirmation are equally authorized to administer an oath of office to a public officer.

Some examples of public officers requiring an oath of office include: members of a municipal urban renewal agency, town or city planning board, town or city zoning board of appeals, or county fire safety advisory board; town or city public library trustees; fire policemen; members of an industrial development agency or community college board of trustees; village treasurers; town superintendents of public works; village police justices; mayors; town supervisors; registrars of vital statistics; board of health members; town assessors ; and highway superintendents.

The deciding factor which determines whether a specific public servant requires an oath of office to be administered is based on law. Not all public employees are classified legally as public officers.

An oath of office may be administered to any state or local officer who is a member of the U.S. armed forces by a commissioned officer (in active service). In addition to any other legal requirements, the certificate of this officer administering the oath of office will state (a) the rank of the officer administering the oath, and (b) that the person taking the oath was at the time, enlisted, inducted, ordered, or commissioned in or serving with, attached to or accompanying the U.S. armed forces. Further, the fact that the officer administering the oath was (at the time) duly commissioned and in active armed force service, must be certified by the U.S. Secretary of the Army, Navy or Air force (or his designee). The place where the oath of office was administered is not required.

Chapter 8 Questions

1. Define an "oath".
2. What is the standard oath ceremony script for an affidavit? For a deposition?

3. Describe the supplemental features which should be incorporated into any oath ceremony to increase awareness of this important act.
4. Define an "affirmation"?
5. List the four legal requirements of an oath and/or affirmation.
6. What steps should be taken by a notary public to determine competency of a person?
7. Define "perjury".
8. What are the key factors in a successful perjury prosecution?
9. Define "jurat".
10. Describe three forms of jurat certificates.
11. If an affirmation is administered instead of an oath, is a special jurat certificate required?
12. What are some terms interchanged with sworn?
13. Is it always necessary to have an oath taker sign in the presence of a notary public? Explain your answer.
14. Describe the special notarial powers granted under law to U.S. military and consulate personnel. Who may administer oaths? How would the jurat certificate differ from a civilian-type certificate? Where may the oaths be administered?
15. Describe the two types of oaths.
16. What President of the United States was sworn into office by a notary public? Who was the notary public and what was his connection to the President?
17. Name at least six public office holders who, if appropriate, may be sworn into office by a notary public.
18. Upon completing the verbal oath of office ceremony, what documentation must be completed by the presiding notary public?
19. Describe some supplemental features which could be incorporated into a "swearing-in" ceremony to increase enjoyment and pride at this memorable event?

Chapter 9

Sworn Proceedings: Taking and Certifying Affidavits

Affidavit

An ***affidavit*** is a written or printed statement or declaration of facts, made voluntarily and confirmed by the oath or affirmation of the party making it. The party is *sworn* before a notary public or other authorized officer. The affidavit must be made voluntarily by one party or ***ex-parte***. The party making the statement is the ***affiant***. The range of circumstances in which an individual would use an affidavit is limitless. Examples are documentation of employment, verification of facts, documentation of a promise to perform a service, certification of eligibility of a benefit, etc.

The willful making of a false affidavit is ***perjury***. A notary public will be removed from office for preparing or taking the oath of an affiant making a statement that the notary public knew to be false.

Authentication of the notarial certificate for an affidavit is identical to the procedure for an oath.

Components

The general parts of the affidavit are:

1. caption;
2. venue;
3. body;
4. affiant's signature; and
5. jurat.

The ***caption*** is commonly referred to as the title and designates

Z 116—Blank Affidavit

JULIUS BLUMBERG, INC., LAW BLANK PUBLISHERS
80 EXCHANGE PL. AT BROADWAY, N. Y. C. 10004

State of
County of .... } *ss.*

....*being duly sworn, says that*

....

Sworn to before me, this..................................*day*
of...................................*19*

the title of the case or proceeding (if submitted in the course of litigation). If unknown or not applicable, omit.

Venue refers to the geographical place where the affidavit was taken, consisting of the state, county and city/town/village—the municipality is optional, unless specifically required by law. An affidavit containing no venue or a venue which does not designate the place where it was taken is insufficient.

Immediately following the venue, the abbreviation "SS" is printed. It designates an abbreviation for the Latin word *scilicet* (pronounced "sila set") which means "namely" or "in particular." The omission of the letters "SS" from the venue of an affidavit is immaterial.

The ***body*** consists of the collection of sworn statements of the affiant. It is recommended that the body be introduced with one of the following statements:

1. "(name of affiant) being duly sworn (or affirmed) deposes and says:"; OR
2. "(name of affiant), of (municipality), County of . . . , and State of . . . , being duly sworn, deposes and says"; OR

P 117—Blank Affidavit.

JULIUS BLUMBERG, INC., PUBLISHER, NYC 10013

Affidavit

State of .... } ss.
County of ....

....being duly sworn, says that

....

....

Sworn to before me, this .... day
of .... 19 ....

....

3. "(name of affiant), personally appears before me, (name), notary public, in and for the County of . . . , State of New York, residing at (municipality), and now on the (date) day of (month), in the year (0000), at (time-am/pm) of said day, in my (home/office), (street address), in said (municipality), County of . . . , and State of New York, being by me duly sworn on his oath, deposes and says that he/she is a resident of the (municipality), County of . . . and State of New York; that:".

A failure to insert the deponent's name in the beginning of the affidavit is not "fatal" to the validity of the affidavit, but it is essential that the name of the affiant be included in the body. If the person signing the affidavit is not the same person named as having been sworn, the affidavit is void. The affidavit must be dated. The statements made in the body should be clear and factual. No erasures should be made. Opaque-type correction fluid is unacceptable. Have the affiant draw a single line through any error and instruct the affiant to initial the correction.

It is *not* the duty of the notary public to examine or investigate the statements of the affiant. However, it must be emphasized that a notary should not notarize any affidavit if he knows it contains false statements. It is the duty of the affiant to truthfully detail the facts, under the penalty of perjury. Reading the affidavit back to the affiant, for example, is a method of making certain that the person is aware of the statements given.

The ***affiant's signature*** should be placed at the conclusion of the body. The affiant should sign the full name exactly as written at the beginning of the body. Social or professional titles, including Mr., Mrs., Ms., Dr., Prof., are not appropriate. A suffix is appropriate (i.e. M.D.), however.

The ***jurat*** consists of those words which are placed directly after the signature in the affidavit. It states that the facts stated were sworn to or affirmed before the notary public, together with his official signature. The failure of an affidavit to contain a jurat or the failure of the officer to sign the jurat causes the affidavit to become invalid. Further, the failure of the officer signing the jurat to add a statement of his office or of the territory to which he holds office does not invalidate the affidavit; it is presumed that he is an authorized officer (i.e. Mayor of City of New York). The following jurat form is to be placed immediately after the signature of the affiant:

"Subscribed and sworn to (or affirmed) before me this (date) day of (month), in the year (0000)."

. . . .
Notary Public

L.S.
(EMBOSSING SEAL) (INKED NOTARY STAMP)

The notary public should sign his name in permanent, *black* ink. Beneath the official signature, the notary public should make an impression of the (black) inked notary public stamp. If not available, the following information should be noted:

1. full name of notary public
2. notary public State of New York

AFFIDAVIT

STATE OF NEW YORK)
) ss.:
COUNTY OF ....)

.... personally appears before me, the undersigned officer duly authorized by the laws of the State of New York to administer oaths and take affidavits, and now on this .... day of .... , in the year 200.. , at ...... am/pm of said day, being by me first duly sworn on his/her oath, deposes and says:

....
....
....
....
....
....
....
....
....
....
....
....
....
....

....
Signature of Affiant
....
Printed Name of Affiant

Sworn to and subscribed before me on this .... day of ...., 200.. .

(NOTARY OFFICIAL EMBOSSING SEAL IMPRESSION BELOW

....
Signature of Notary Public

[STATEMENT OF AUTHORITY BELOW]

Corporation
Affidavit

```
STATE OF NEW YORK       )
                        ) ss.:
COUNTY OF .......... )

............................. personally appears before me,
the undersigned officer duly authorized by the laws of the State
of New York to administer oaths and take affidavits, and now on
this ............. day of .............. , in the year A.D.
200.. , at ...... am/pm  of said day, being by me first duly
sworn on his/her  oath, deposes and says that  he/she  is the
(President or other officer) of ..............................
.................................... and that  he/she  makes
this affidavit for and on behalf of said corporation and that:
...............................................................
...............................................................
...............................................................
...............................................................
...............................................................
...............................................................
...............................................................
...............................................................
...............................................................
...............................................................
...............................................................
...............................................................
...............................................................
...............................................................

                     ..........................................
                     Signature of Affiant
                     ..........................................
                     Printed Name of Affiant


Sworn to and subscribed before me
on this ....... day of ........, 200..  .


.........................................     (NOTARY OFFICIAL
Signature of Notary Public                     EMBOSSING SEAL
                                              IMPRESSION BELOW)
[STATEMENT OF AUTHORITY BELOW]
```

3. qualified in . . . county
4. commission expires (00-00-0000)

The embosser seal should be impressed in the area designated with the initials "*L.S.*", the abbreviation of the Latin words *locus sigilli* (pronounced "lowkus SEE-jill-EE"), meaning "place of the seal." If the *L.S.* is not indicated, the notary public may put his impression on any unprinted area of the document, preferably near the jurat. Avoid putting the seal over any document text, except specifically over the *L.S.* notation.

Affidavit of Service by Publication [Form--SCPA 314]

SURROGATE'S COURT: COUNTY OF _______

[Add title of proceeding]

AFFIDAVIT OF SERVICE

File No. _______

STATE OF NEW YORK) ss.:

COUNTY OF _______)

_______, being duly sworn, deposes and says:
1. I am over eighteen years of age.
2. I am the printer [or publisher or foreman or principal clerk] of [name of newspaper], a newspaper in the English [or other] language published iin the City of _______, County of _______, State of New York.
3. The citation to _______, the respondent, copies of which are annexed hereto, were published in the aforesaid newspaper once in each of four successive weeks.
4. The first publication was made on the _______ day of _______, ___.
5. The second publication was made on the _______ day of _______, ___.
6. The third publication was made on the _______ day of _______, ___.
7. The fourth publication was made on the _______ day of _______, ___.

[Signature]

[Type Name]

[Signature]

[Type Name]

Attorney for ______________________________

P.O. Address

Tel. No.

Sworn and subscribed before me
on [Date].

[Signature]

[Type Name]
Notary Public State of New York
Qualified in [County Name]
Commission Expires [Date]

AFFIDAVIT/APPLICATION FOR CERTIFICATE OF RESIDENCE

An affidavit which is commonly presented to notaries public in New York is the "affidavit (or affirmation) and application for certificate of residence". This affidavit is utilized in connection with attendance at a community college in New York. Although students attending a community college present this form to notaries, many people do not understand that it is an affidavit and

AFFIDAVIT (OR AFFIRMATION) AND APPLICATION
FOR CERTIFICATE OF RESIDENCE

PURSUANT TO SECTION 6305 OF THE EDUCATION LAW,
IN CONNECTION WITH ATTENDANCE AT A COMMUNITY COLLEGE*

STATE OF NEW YORK)
)
COUNTY OF)

..........................does hereby swear (or affirm) that he/she resides at........................in the (City) (Village) (Town) of........County of......State of New York; that he now is, and has for a period of at least one year immediately prior to the date of this affidavit (or affirmation) and application been a resident of the State of New York; that he now is, and has for a period of at least six months immediately prior to the date of this affidavit (or affirmation) and application been, a resident of the County of ....and that he has lived at the following places during the year immediately prior to the date of this affidavit (or affirmation) and application:

Addresses	Dates
....	....
....	....
....	....

Applicant further states that he plans to enroll in......................... (College or Institute) and that his affidavit (or affirmation) and application is made for the purpose of securing from the Chief Fiscal Officer of the County of ....a certificate that applicant has met the residence requirements of Article 126 of the Education Law.

....
Signature of Applicant

....
Social Security Number

Sworn to (or affirmed) before me this
....day of...................19.....
....
Notary Public or Commissioner of Deeds

THIS SPACE FOR USE OF CHIEF FISCAL OFFICER OF COUNTY

Certificate Issued () Certificate Not Issued()
Date........By........................

*Education Law, Section 6305, provides: "The Chief fiscal officer of each county, as defined in section 2.00 of the local finance law, shall, upon application and submission to him of satisfactory evidence, issue to any person desiring to enroll in a community college as a non-resident student, a certificate of residence showing that said person is a resident of said county...Such person shall, upon his registration for each college year, file with the college such a certificate of residence issued not earlier than two months prior thereto, and such certificate of residence shall be valid for a period of one year from the date of issuance." Education Law Section 6301, paragraph 4, defines: "Resident - A person who has resided in the state for a period of at least one year and in the county, city, town, intermediate school district or school district, as the case may be, for a period of at least six months, both immediately preceding the date of such person's registration in a community college or, for the purposes of section sixty three hundred five of this chapter, his application for a certificate of residence."

8/23/56 Rev.
SUNY-B-80

Blumbergs Law Products C 73—Judicial Subpoena; with Witness' Stipulation to remain subject to call. Blank Court. 12-88

Plaintiff

against

Defendant

Index No.
Calendar No.
JUDICIAL SUBPOENA

The People of the State of New York

TO

GREETING:

WE COMMAND YOU, *That all business and excuses being laid aside, you and each of you appear and attend before*

on the day of 19 at o'clock, in the noon, and at any recessed or adjourned date to give testimony in this action on the part of the

Failure to comply with this subpoena is punishable as a contempt of Court and shall make you liable to the person on whose behalf this subpoena was issued for a penalty not to exceed fifty dollars and all damages sustained by reason of your failure to comply.

WITNESS, *Honorable one of the of said Court, at the day of 19*

Attorney(s) for

Office and Post Office Address

what that means. For example, many college administrators believe that the notary is actually verifying the information contained in the affidavit and application. However, this affidavit is like all others; the only responsibility the notary public has is to properly complete the affidavit and actually swear the affiant. It is illogical to think that the notary public is making a "check" of the information. The notary public has no legal or moral duty to do so. It is the affiant, the student, who swears that "the contents of the affidavit are known to him and that the said facts are true to the best of his knowledge and belief".

After the student has the affidavit sworn and subscribed, he presents it to his county chief fiscal officer (county treasurer or commissioner of finance). After confirming the facts in the affidavit regarding the address, he issues a separate certification of residence.

AFFIDAVIT OF SERVICE

State of New York, County of ss:

The undersigned, being duly sworn, deposes and says; that deponent is not a party to the action, is over 18 years of age and resides at

That on 19 at

deponent served the within subpoena on witness

INDIVIDUAL 1. ☐ by delivering a true copy to said witness personally; deponent knew the person so served to be the person described as said witness therein.

CORPORATION 2. ☐ a corporation. by delivering thereat a true copy to

personally, deponent knew said corporation so served to be the corporation described in said subpoena as said corporate witness and knew said individual to be

thereof.

SUITABLE AGE PERSON 3. ☐ by delivering thereat a true copy to

a person of suitable age and discretion. Said premises is witness'—actual place of business—dwelling place—usual place of abode—within the state.

AFFIXING TO DOOR, ETC. 4. ☐ by affixing a true copy to the door of said premises, which is witness'—actual place of business—dwelling place—usual place of abode—within the state. Deponent was unable, with due diligence, to find witness or a person of suitable age and discretion thereat, having called there

MAILING TO RESIDENCE USE WITH 3 OR 4 5A. ☐ Within 20 days of such delivery or affixing, deponent enclosed a copy of same in a postpaid envelope properly addressed to witness at witness' last known residence, at

and deposited said envelope in an official depository under the exclusive care and custody of the U.S. Postal Service within New York State.

MAILING TO BUSINESS USE WITH 3 OR 4 5B. ☐ Within 20 days of such delivery or affixing, deponent enclosed a copy of same in a first class postpaid envelope properly addressed to witness at witness' actual place of business, at

in an official depository under the exclusive care and custody of the U.S. Postal Service within New York State. The envelope bore the legend "Personal and Confidential" and did not indicate on the outside thereof, by return address or otherwise, that the communication was from an attorney or concerned an action against the witness.

Index No.

Plaintiff

against

Defendant

Judicial Subpoena

Attorney(s) for

Office and Post Office Address

It is stipulated that the undersigned witness is excused from attending at the time herein provided or at any adjourned date but agrees to remain subject to, and attend upon, the call of the undersigned attorney.

Dated:

.... Witness

.... Attorney

DESCRIPTION USE WITH 1, 2, or 3 ☐

	☐ Black Hair	☐ 51-65 Yrs.
	☐ Brown Hair	☐ Over 65 Yrs.
	☐ Blonde Hair	
	☐ Gray Hair	☐ Under 5'
	☐ Red Hair	☐ 5'0"-5'3"
	☐ White Hair	☐ 5'4"-5'8"
☐ Male	☐ Balding	☐ 5'9"-6'0"
☐ Female	☐ Mustache	☐ Over 6'
☐ White Skin	☐ Beard	☐ Under 100 Lbs.
☐ Black Skin	☐ Glasses	☐ 100-130 Lbs.
☐ Yellow Skin	☐ 14-20 Yrs.	☐ 131-160 Lbs.
☐ Brown Skin	☐ 21-35 Yrs.	☐ 161-200 Lbs.
☐ Red Skin	☐ 36-50 Yrs.	☐ Over 200 Lbs.

Other identifying features:

At the time of said service, deponent paid (tendered) in advance $ the authorized traveling expenses and one day's witness fee.

....
Print name beneath signature

Sworn to before me on

B 69—Subpoena duces tecum, blank court, with witness' stipulation to remain subject to attorney's call. 10-97

COURT

COUNTY OF

Index No.

Calendar No.

Plaintiff

against

JUDICIAL SUBPOENA DUCES TECUM

Defendant

The People of the State of New York

TO

GREETING:

WE COMMAND YOU, *That all business and excuses being laid aside, you and each of you appear and attend before*
at
on the day of at o'clock, in the noon,
and at any recessed or adjourned date to give testimony in this action on the part of the

and that you bring with you, and produce at the time and place aforesaid, a certain

now in your custody, and all other deeds, evidences and writings, which you have in your custody or power, concerning the premises.

Failure to comply with this subpoena is punishable as a contempt of Court and shall make you liable to the person on whose behalf this subpoena was issued for a penalty not to exceed fifty dollars and all damages sustained by reason of your failure to comply.

WITNESS, *Honorable one of the*
of said Court, at the day of 19

....

Attorney(s) for

Office and Post Office Address

AFFIDAVIT OF SERVICE

STATE OF NEW YORK, COUNTY OF SS: The undersigned, being duly sworn, deposes and says; deponent is not a party herein, is over 18 years of age and resides at

That on at M., at

deponent served the within subpoena on witness therein named,

INDIVIDUAL 1. ☐ by delivering a true copy to said witness personally; deponent knew the person so served to be the witness described in said subpoena.

CORPORATION 2. ☐ a corporation, by delivering thereat a true copy to personally, deponent knew said corporation so served to be the corporate witness and knew said individual to be thereof.

SUITABLE AGE PERSON 3. ☐ by delivering thereat a true copy to a person of suitable age and discretion. Said premises is witness'—actual place of business—dwelling place—usual place of abode—within the state.

AFFIXING TO DOOR, ETC. 4. ☐ by affixing a true copy to the door of said premises, which is witness'—actual place of business—dwelling place—usual place of abode—within the state. Deponent was unable, with due diligence to find witness or a person of suitable age and discretion thereat, having called there

MAILING TO RESIDENCE USE WITH 3 OR 4 5A. ☐ Within 20 days of such delivery or affixing, deponent enclosed a copy of same in a postpaid envelope properly addressed to witness at witness' last known residence, at and deposited said envelope in an official depository under the exclusive care and custody of the U.S. Postal Service within New York State.

MAILING TO BUSINESS USE WITH 3 OR 4 5B. ☐ Within 20 days of such delivery or affixing, deponent enclosed a copy of same in a first class postpaid envelope properly addressed to witness at witness' actual place of business, at in an official depository under the exclusive care and custody of the U.S. Postal Service within New York State. The envelope bore the legend "Personal and Confidential" and did not indicate on the outside thereof, by return address or otherwise, that the communication was from an attorney or concerned an action against the witness.

DESCRIPTION USE WITH 1, 2, OR 3 ☐

☐ Male	☐ White Skin	☐ Black Hair	☐ White Hair	☐ 14-20 Yrs.	☐ Under 5'	☐ Under 100 Lbs.
☐ Female	☐ Black Skin	☐ Brown Hair	☐ Balding	☐ 21-35 Yrs.	☐ 5'0"-5'3"	☐ 100-130 Lbs.
	☐ Yellow Skin	☐ Blonde Hair	☐ Mustache	☐ 36-50 Yrs.	☐ 5'4"-5'8"	☐ 131-160 Lbs.
	☐ Brown Skin	☐ Gray Hair	☐ Beard	☐ 51-65 Yrs.	☐ 5'9"-6'0"	☐ 161-200 Lbs.
	☐ Red Skin	☐ Red Hair	☐ Glasses	☐ Over 65 Yrs.	☐ Over 6'	☐ Over 200 Lbs.

Other identifying features:

At the time of said service, deponent paid (tendered) in advance $ the authorized traveling expenses and one day's witness fee.

Sworn to before me on PRINT NAME BENEATH SIGNATURE ....

License No. ....

Index No.

COUNTY OF COURT

Plaintiff

against

Defendant

Judicial Subpoena
DUCES TECUM

Attorney(s) for

Office; Post Office Address; Telephone No.

It is stipulated that the undersigned witness is excused from attending at the time herein provided or at any adjourned date but agrees to remain subject to, and attend upon, the call of the undersigned attorney.

Dated:

.... *Witness*

.... *Attorney(s) for*

It is vital that the notary public be familiar with this special affidavit and follow all of the usual and customary procedures.

CHAPTER 9 QUESTIONS

1. Define an "affidavit" and "affiant".
2. What is the standard oath ceremony script for use at an affidavit?
3. Define the term "ex-parte" regarding affidavits.
4. Why are affidavits useful to the legal process, as well as many common business and consumer purposes?
5. Name some examples of affidavits and how these documents are specifically useful to the legal and commercial systems.
6. List the five components of an affidavit.
7. Define the term "venue" and explain its significance in a legal document, including affidavits.
8. Define the Latin abbreviation *"ss."* and why it is often incorporated in legal documents?
9. Why is it significant to have the affiant sign the document in the presence of the notary public? Is it always legally required? Explain your answer.
10. Define the term "jurat". Why is the inclusion of a jurat necessary on a sworn document? What is the result of the omission of the jurat? Explain your answer?
11. Explain the difference between an oath and a jurat.
12. What does the Latin abbreviation *"L.S."* signify? What does it mean to the notary public and what should be performed in the vicinity of this marking?
13. Explain the legal significance of an affidavit which has not been sworn to before a notary public with a proper, verbal oath. Explain your answer.
14. What is a notarial protest? Are there different forms of notarial protests? Describe them.

Chapter 10

Sworn Proceedings: Taking and Certifying Depositions

Deposition

A ***deposition*** is the written testimony of a witness taken out of court or other hearing proceeding, under oath or affirmation, before a notary public or other legally authorized person. It is intended to be used at the trial or hearing of a civil action or criminal prosecution. The basis for the examination is a collection of questions determined and provided by either an attorney or judge.

The ***deponent*** is the party who gives testimony under oath which is transcribed to a written statement.

A deposition differs from an affidavit in that a deposition is an involuntary procedure by a witness in a *civil* or *criminal* matter. An affidavit is generally a *voluntary* act of making a sworn statement not intended for use in a court or hearing proceeding. If a witness in a legal proceeding is unable to attend the hearing or trial to give sworn testimony, it is legally acceptable for the testimony to be put into writing. The written testimony or deposition must be signed by the witness and sworn to in the presence of the notary public.

The testifying witness is subject to cross-examination by the opposing party.

Procedures

A deposition cannot be taken on Sunday in a *civil* hearing or trial. However, a deposition may be taken on Sunday in reference to a *criminal* hearing or trial matter.

The supervising officer will put the witness under oath. The testimony will be transcribed by the officer or someone acting under his direction.

The officer will note all objections made regarding:

1. the qualifications of the officer taking the deposition;
2. the person recording it;
3. the manner of taking it;
4. the testimony presented;
5. the conduct of any person and;
6. other objections to the proceedings. It will proceed subject to the right of a person to apply for a protective court order.

The deposition will be taken continuously and without interruption, unless the court otherwise orders or the witness and parties present otherwise agree. Instead of participating in an oral examination, any party given notice of taking a deposition may provide questions to the officer, who will then ask them to the witness and record the answers.

Examination and cross-examination of deponents will continue as permitted in the trial of actions in open court. When the deposition of a party is taken at the request of another party, the deponent may be cross-examined by his own attorney. Cross-examination need not be limited to the subject matter of the examination in chief.

If the witness to be examined does not understand the English language, the examining party must at his own expense provide a translation of all questions and answers. When the court settles matters, it may settle them in the foreign language and in English.

The deposition will be given to the witness for examination and read to or by him. Any changes he wants are entitled to be entered at the end of the deposition with a statement of reasons given by the witness for making them. The deposition is signed by the witness before any officer authorized to administer an oath (e.g. notary public). If the witness fails to sign the deposition, the officer should sign it and state on the record the fact of the witness' failure or refusal to sign, together with any reason given. The deposition may then be used as legally proper (as though signed). The officer who takes a deposition will certify on it that the witness was duly sworn by him and that it is a true record of the testimony given by the witness. All appearances by the parties and attorneys will be listed by the officer. If the deposition was taken on written questions, the officer will attach the copy of the notice and written questions received. The deposition will then be securely sealed in an envelope, marked with the title and index number of the action (if assigned) and "Deposition of (name of witness)" and promptly filed or sent by registered or certified mail to the clerk of the court where the case is to be tried.

The deposition will always be open to inspection by the parties and they may choose to make copies of the document. If a copy of the deposition is given to each party or if the parties agree to waive filing, the officer need not file the original, but may deliver it to the party taking the deposition.

Documentary evidence exhibited before the officer or exhibits marked for identification during the examination of the witness will be attached to and returned with the deposition. However, if requested by the party producing documentary evidence or an exhibit, the officer will mark it for identification as an exhibit in the case, give each party an opportunity to copy or inspect it, and return it to the party offering it. It may then be used in the same manner as if added to and returned with the deposition.

Unless the court orders otherwise, the party taking (requesting) the deposition will bear the expenses of it. The costs incurred with the deposition are not the responsibility of the officer.

Errors of the officer or stenographer or other person transcribing the deposition are waived unless a "motion to quash" the deposition (or some part of it) is made within a reasonable time after the defect is, or with careful attention might have been, determined. If the notary public is an interested party to the legal proceeding or its outcome, it is inappropriate and improper for him to take the deposition. If the notary public were related to the deponent by blood or marriage, connected in any way by employment or business, including an attorney or employee of an attorney, or in any way interested in the outcome of the litigation, he should not participate in the administration of the deposition in any way.

The topic of depositions is complex. The preceding discussion was provided strictly as a brief overview of the process. There are volumes of rules and procedures which specify the manner in which a deposition will be conducted. Commonly, trained individuals who are certified shorthand reporters will be employed to take or record the proceedings. The reporters may be notaries public. In some instances, a deposition may be taken and prepared by a shorthand reporter and brought to a notary public (by the deponent) for administration of an oath or affirmation. However, every notary public should be familiar with the topic of depositions and the general process of taking/certifying these legal documents.

GENL-4 (REV. 4/87)

SUPPORTING DEPOSITION (CPL §100.20) New York State Police

STATE OF NEW YORK

______________ COURT

COUNTY OF ______________

______________ of ______________

THE PEOPLE OF THE STATE OF NEW YORK)
)
– vs.)
)
______________)
)
______________)
(Defendant(s))

SUPPORTING DEPOSITION

STATE OF NEW YORK)
COUNTY OF ______________) ss.
)
______________ of ______________)

On [DATE] at [TIME STARTED : ☐a.m. ☐p.m.] I, [FULL NAME]

[DATE OF BIRTH] [NO. & STREET] [C/T/V] [STATE]

state the following:

NOTICE
(Penal Law §210.45)

In a written instrument, any person who knowingly makes a false statement which such person does not believe to be true has committed a crime under the laws of the state of New York punishable as a Class A Misdemeanor.

Affirmed under penalty of perjury

this ______ day of ______________, 19 ____.

– OR –

*Subscribed and Sworn to before me

this ______ day of ______________, 19 ____.

____
(SIGNATURE OF DEPONENT)

____
(WITNESS)

______________ [TIME ENDED ☐a.m. ☐p.m.]
(NAME OF PERSON TAKING DEPOSITION)

*This form need be sworn to only when specifically required by the court.

JACK SMITH,

called as a witness on behalf of the defendant, having been first duly sworn, testified on his oath as follows:

EXAMINATION

BY MR. RICO:

Q Would you please state your full name, and every name you have used in the past, and the dates you have used each name?

A My name is Jack Smith and I haven't assumed any other names in the past.

Q State the date and place of your birth.

A I was born October 9, 1962 in Frost Mills, New York.

Q At the time of the incident, did you have a driver's license? If so, state the issuing entity, license number and type, date of issuance and any restrictions.

A I was licensed to drive by New York, license number 12345678, issued on October 9, 1995, with no restrictions.

Q State your present residence address.

A Lake Shore Drive, Plattsburgh, New York.

Q State your residence addresses for the last five years and the dates you lived at each address.

A I have had no other residences during the last five years.

Q State the name and address of your present employer, or place of self-employment.

A I am a member of the New York State Police,

```
STATE OF NEW YORK      )
                       ) ss.:
COUNTY OF CLINTON      )
```

I, Jack Smith, hereby certify that I have read the foregoing transcripts of my deposition taken June 16, 1995, at approximately 9:00 a.m. at Plattsburgh, New York pursuant to the applicable New York Civil Practice Law and Rules, and that the foregoing 41 pages of transcript are in conformity with my testimony given at that time (with the exception of any corrections made by me, in ink, and initialed by me).

s/

____
JACK SMITH

Subscribed and sworn to before me on this twenty-first day of June, in the year of our Lord, nineteen hundred and ninety five.

s/

____
Jane Doe
Notary Public State of New York
Qualified in St. Lawrence County
Commission Expires

CHAPTER 10 QUESTIONS

1. Define a "deposition" and a "deponent".
2. What is the standard oath ceremony script for use at a deposition?
3. What is meant by an "EBT"? How are they utilized in a legal case?
4. What is "hearsay"?
5. Explain how a deposition differs from an affidavit.
6. Can a person refuse to make a deposition? Describe the legal remedy for a situation in which a person refuses to appear to make a deposition.
7. Compare a "de bene esse deposition" and "discovery deposition".
8. Define "interrogatories".
9. Explain the legal significance of a deposition which has not been sworn to before a notary public with a proper, verbal oath.
10. Are there any restrictions on taking depositions on Sunday? Explain your answer.
11. Discuss the subject of the telephone and taking a deposition.
12. What unique feature of document construction makes a deposition easy to recognize?
13. Is it ever possible to take an oath for a deposition over the telephone? Explain your answer.
14. Can a person take an oath by proxy for a deposition?
15. How does a videotaped deposition compare to a conventional deposition?

16. What are some of the advantages and disadvantages of a videotaped deposition?
17. A written transcription is taken in conjunction with a videotaped deposition. Explain why this is important.

Chapter 11

Handling Special Situations

MARRIAGES

Notaries in four states may perform legal, civil marriage ceremonies: Maine, South Carolina, Florida and West Feliciana Parish, Louisiana. A bill authorizing Kentucky notaries to perform civil marriage ceremonies was defeated in 1986.

WILLS AND TESTAMENTS

The subject of the last will and testament or testamentum is of great concern and confusion for many notaries public and the general public. A notary public should not become officially involved in the creation of a will. A notary public is cautioned not to take an acknowledgment of the execution of a will. This acknowledgment cannot be considered legally comparable to a testimonial clause concluding a will where the witnesses place their signatures below the signature of the testator.

A testator is a man who makes a will and a testatrix is a woman who makes a will. The witnesses who observe the testator or testatrix execute the will are sometimes referred to as subscribing witnesses or testes.

A New York judicial decision has concluded that the execution of wills under the supervision of a notary public acting in effect as a lawyer, "cannot be too strongly condemned, not only for the reason that it means an invasion of the legal profession, but for the fact that testators thereby run the risk of frustrating their own solemnly declared intentions and rendering worthless maturely considered plans for the disposition of estates whose creation may have been the fruits of lives of industry and self-denial."

In other words, the court does not want a non-attorney notary public drafting the will of a client who might feel that the notary is as qualified as a lawyer to assist in handling the will preparation. While it may be lawful for a client to draw his own will, involvement of a notary public in drafting the will is illegal and discouraged. For example, a well-meaning client might create his own will at his dining room table and seek to execute the will in the presence of a notary public to "legalize" it. Not only would the notary public potentially be misrepresenting himself by intervening, but he might give the person a sense of false confidence regarding his estate plans.

If the notary public has definite knowledge that the client received the counsel of an attorney who prepared the will, it is appropriate for the notary public to act as a citizen and serve as a lay witness. In such cases, it is essential that the notary public clearly indicate (to the testator and all others present) that his act of being a witness is as a lay citizen and not in connection with any official duty. Therefore, the notary public should not affix his official instruments or any language which designates his official position on the will. Even innocent and well-intentioned acts, in fact, could cause the otherwise lawful will to become invalid. A notary public before whom a will is acknowledged and sworn to, or self-proved, cannot also serve as a witness to the will, because he is without authority to administer an oath to himself.

In the event a notary public is presented with a will which apparently has been prepared by an attorney (who provides an affidavit of execution or subscribing witness affidavit at the conclusion of the will), the notary public may proceed to place the testator and subscribing witnesses under oath.

The notary public is cautioned to carefully examine the will. Suggested evidence of an attorney-prepared will would include a document prepared on legal paper stock with the law firm or lawyer's name, address and telephone number printed in the margin (or top of) each page. In the event that a notary public is presented with a will prepared on a formal, law blank form, the lawyer's name and related data should be typed, printed or stamped clearly on the document. If the will is not prepared by attorney, but appears complete with necessary affidavit, the notary public may proceed to swear the parties.

Caution and professional questioning should be the rule when a notary public is presented with a will. It is a reasonable rule of

Blumberg's Law Products T 175—Affidavit of Subscribing Witnesses To Will Made at Testator's Request: SCPA 1406, 1-81

JULIUS BLUMBERG, INC. PUBLISHER NYC 10013

Affidavit of Subscribing Witnesses

STATE OF NEW YORK } ss:
COUNTY OF

On 19 personally appeared before me, a Notary Public in and for the County of State of New York,

*who being severally sworn state under oath that they witnessed the execution of the **Will** of the within named Testator(trix), on 19 ; the Testator(trix), in their presence, subscribed the **Will** at the end and at the time of making the subscription declared the instrument to be the Testator(trix)'s Last Will and Testament; at the request of the Testator(trix) and in the Testator(trix)'s sight and presence and in the sight and presence of each other, they witnessed the execution of the **Will** by the Testator(trix) by subscribing their names as witnesses to it; and the Testator(trix) at the time of the execution of the **Will**, was over the age of 18 years and appeared to them of sound mind and memory and was in all respects competent to make a will and was not under any restraint.*

The subscribing witnesses further state that this affidavit was executed at the request of

*at the time of the execution of this affidavit the original **Will**, above described, was exhibited to them and they identified it as such **Will** by their signatures appearing on it as subscribing witnesses.*

*The subscribing witnesses further state that the **Will** was executed under the supervision of attorney(s) for the Testator(trix), at*

Severally subscribed and sworn to before me on
, 19

....
Notary Public

Signature ....
Print Name ....
Address ....

Signature ....
Print Name ....
Address ....

Signature ....
Print Name ....
Address ....

practice to suggest that the party consult an attorney, if it appears that the will is incomplete. If necessary, the notary public might contact the attorney who prepared the will to request further information or instruction.

While the law does not require that a will be brought before a notary public to be legally sufficient, the probate process can be greatly simplified by having the testator and witnesses "self-prove" the will before a notary.

Probate is the legal process of determining whether or not a deceased individual left a valid will, and the court's monitoring to assure that the estate is disposed of in accordance with the wishes of the deceased as outlined in the will. A will is filed for probate by having a petition for probate filed with the proper court. After the will has been admitted to probate, the court will supervise the administration of the estate.

In self-proving a will, the testator and witnesses will swear to and sign an affidavit before a notary public declaring that the document is truly the testator's will and that it was lawfully executed. The affidavit is proof that the testator had testamentary capacity, and is attached to the will, but is not a part of the actual will document.

The principal reason to "self-prove" a will is to minimize the likelihood that the witnesses to the will be required to appear in court after death of the testator.. In the event that the witnesses are unable to appear in court, this affidavit can be quite valuable.

Although it is legally permissible for the witnesses to swear to and execute such an affidavit after the testator dies, it is strongly advisable to accomplish this important act at the time the testator actually signs his will. In the event that either or both of the witnesses predecease the testator, or simply cannot be located, the probate process could become unnecessarily complicated without such an affidavit.

In the instance where a person appears before a notary public and requests that his will be "notarized", he probably is not aware of the correct terminology of the notarial act to be performed. If a client makes such a vague request, the notary public should politely request to examine the documents to better ascertain exactly what service the client requires from the notary public.

When handling an affidavit of execution or subscribing witness affidavit, the notary public should treat the affidavit in the same manner as any other affidavit. Caution should be exercised, however, to assure exact and full compliance with the legal ceremony requirements and language contained in the affidavit of execution. It is especially important to review the language of the affidavit with the testator and witnesses. Furthermore, it should be assured that the testator "signs, swears and acknowledges" and each witness "sign and swear and acknowledge" in the personal presence of the notary public. If all concerned parties cannot appear before the notary public at the same time, he should suggest that the execution of the affidavit be postponed until such time as all parties are able to report to a single notary public. Failure to comply with these requirements explicitly could prove fatal in the process to probate the will.

Although the notary public should never affix any signature, stamp or embossing official seal to the actual will and testament, it is acceptable and frequently necessary to affix these instruments to the affidavit of execution. If the affidavit of execution is physically printed on the reverse of a commercially printed blank form, it is permissible for the notary public to proceed to affix his official instruments to the affidavit, even though the instruments will appear to be affixed to the will document.

If required, the completed and sworn affidavit of execution should now be securely stapled to the will and testament.

In the case where the testator and subscribing witnesses have executed the will, but failed to subscribe and swear an affidavit of execution prior to the death of the testator, it will be necessary to have the subscribing witnesses personally appear before the particular court handling the probate matter.

If it is not convenient for the witnesses to appear in court for satisfactory reason (e.g. witness resides in another state), the attorney for the estate may petition the court to appoint a commissioner. A commissioner is an individual appointed as a temporary official to act on behalf of the probate court. Commonly a notary public and/or an attorney in the locale of the subscribing witness, this officer will summon the subscribing witness to testify before such officer and subscribe and swear to the facts surrounding the execution of the will. This procedure is sometimes referred to as a proof of execution. Although uncommon, but nonetheless authorized when appropriate, the court-appointed commissioner can issue a warrant which directs the local sheriff to place a recalcitrant witness in custody until the witness agrees to testify in response to the order of the probate court.

Personal Representative

The personal representative is the individual designated by the court to act for the estate. If the testator names his personal representative in the will, the person is called an executor if he is male, and an executrix if she is female. In the event that no individual was specifically named, but a valid will exists, the representative is known as the administrator with will annexed. If no valid will exists, the representative is referred to as the administrator. A female administrator is known as an administratrix.

After a brief period of time subsequent to death, the attorney handling the estate files the will and related papers with the proper probate court, and requests or petitions the court to issue a document called letters testamentary. This court order or decree provides the executor with written evidence of the authority that he has been granted to handle estate matters. In the event the court appoints an administrator, the document is referred to as letters of administration.

If a person appears before a notary public wishing to execute documents on behalf of a deceased person, he should be requested to produce the letters testamentary or letters of administration.

Living Wills/Health Care Directives and Proxies

One of the newest legal documents to be brought before the notary public is the living will and health care directive or health care proxy. Because of the proliferation and variety of these instruments, a notary public can be placed in a dilemma when confronted with the request to "officiate" in these matters.

The living will, a signed, dated and witnessed document, allows a person to make his or her wishes about life-sustaining treatment known, so that they can guide the family and physician in case of incapacitation or inability to communicate.

Most United States' courts have recognized that people have "a constitutional or common law right to have treatment withheld or withdrawn." Further, the courts have decreed that "a living will can be the best evidence of a patient's intentions." Regarding the issue of health care proxies, the courts permit the appointment of an agent or surrogate to make such related decisions, and have approved decision making by family members (or other appropriate representatives if there is no family available), based on a general knowledge of the patient's feelings.

The United States Supreme Court has held that family members who assert a "right to die" may be barred from ending the lives of permanently comatose relatives who have not made their wishes known conclusively.

Ruling in its first such case, the court gave states broad power to keep such patients on life support systems. A majority of the court did suggest that there may be a constitutional right to refuse medical treatment that can be exercised by competent persons, encouraging living will supporters.

Often within the living will is an optional durable power of attorney provision, which allows a person to name another person who will possess the power to make medical treatment decisions for the injured or ill person.

An ordinary power of attorney authorizes another person (an attorney-in-fact) to make decisions for the principal. This form of power of attorney, however, lapses if the principal becomes incompetent. A durable power of attorney remains effective (or, in some states, takes effect) if the principal becomes incompetent.

A method of designating an individual to make medical decisions on behalf of another is to appoint a health care proxy or designate a health care surrogate within the living will, or attached to it. A proxy's or surrogate's decision-making power under a living will statute is usually limited to a terminal condition.

A health care agent and a medical attorney-in-fact may have interchangeable roles. Appointed under a durable power of attorney, they can usually make a series of decisions for the principal, whether or not the condition is terminal. An advanced Alzheimer's patient, for example, may be quite incapable of making decisions, but may not be terminally ill. Similarly, accident victims who may be temporarily incapacitated but will eventually recover, must have medical decisions made during the period of their incapacity.

Under most circumstances, living wills, health care proxies and designation of health care surrogates do not require notary service. Instead, the typical requirement is for two or three uninterested witnesses to sign. In some instances, however, the form may prescribe either an individual acknowledgment or a form of a jurat.

Some states do not mandate a specific form for either a designation of health care surrogate or a living will. Rather, the law provides suggested forms which are provided in this chapter. Further, it is highly recommended that the principal executing his living will and designation of health care surrogate appear before a notary and have his acknowledgment taken. Even though most state laws do not legally compel parties to have the acknowledgments taken for these matters, it is strongly recommended for the following reasons.

First, use of the acknowledgment is excellent independent proof that the principal appeared before a notary public, was identified, and admitted that the execution of the document(s) were his free act and deed for the purposes contained within the document(s). Second, with respect to the use of conventional witnesses, it is not unusual for such witnesses to be impossible to locate, or pre-decease the principal. Even if the notary public is impossible to locate, or dies before the principal, the certificate of acknowledgment is considered prima facie evidence of the act that the notary recited in the written acknowledgment certificate. In the absence of fraud or duress, the certificate of a notary public is conclusive as to the facts stated.

When presented with a living will, the notary public should scan the instrument to ascertain exactly which procedure is required.

Attested or Notary-Certified Copies

Notaries public may be requested to "certify" copies of documents. The authority permits the notary public to supervise the making of a photocopy of an original document, and then attest to the trueness of such copy.

Notaries public, however, are not authorized to issue attested copies of official or public records, unless the copy cannot be provided by another public official.

Most state laws define a certified copy as a copy of a public record signed and certified as a true copy by the public official having custody of the original. Examples would be: the clerk or register of deeds issuing a certified copy of a deed or mortgage which is recorded and filed in his office; the department of motor vehicles (DMV) issuing a certified copy of an accident report filed with their department; or the health department issuing a certified copy of a birth certificate.

Under no circumstances should a notary public issue an attested copy of any school diploma, college or university degree or

Fax completed request to the participating agency where the birth occurred.

VITAL RECORD REQUEST

Credit Card ________________ Expires ________

Certificate Holder's Name ________________
(first) (middle) (last)

Father's Name ________________
(first) (middle) (last) Must include place of birth for Canadian orders only.

Mother's Maiden Name ________________
(first) (middle) (last) Must include place of birth for Canadian orders only.

Birth Date ________ County/City ________

Hospital ________ Sex ❑ Male ❑ Female

Relationship ❑ Self ❑ Mother ❑ Father ❑ Other ________

Reason ________________

Ship Method ❑ Overnight Courier ❑ Regular Mail
(Some states only offer Overnight Delivery for this service. Check with your individual state.)

Ship To Name ________________

Address ________________

City ________ State ________ Zip ________

(photo ID)

Required in Arizona, Idaho, New York, Virginia, Wyoming, San Antonio, TX., Lake/Waukegan, IL., and Indiana (including all Indiana counties).

Day Phone ________

Signature Date

VitalChek® Network Inc. - For further information call toll free 1-800-255-2414.

VCN 7/18/97

certificate, school transcript or grade report, or similar document issued by an educational institution. Notaries public are often requested to assist students with these matters. Requesters should be referred to the registrar of the educational institution. If the institution is now closed, educational records of closed institutions (public or private) are turned over to the state education department, and the requester should contact those authorities.

Affidavit and Request For
a Notary Attested/Certified Copy

```
STATE OF NEW YORK    )
                     ) ss.:
COUNTY OF .......... )

I, ..............................................................
residing at ....................................................,
hereby appear before the undersigned Notary Public and now on
this .............. day of .............. , in the year A.D.
200.. , at ........ am/pm  of said day, being first duly sworn
on my oath, depose and say:

1.  I am the lawful custodian of the following document,
    hereby described:
    .........................................................
    .........................................................
    ........................................................;

2.  The document is an original and consists of ............
    pages, including cover pages/s, if any;

3.  A certified copy of the purported original cannot be
    obtained from the office of any clerk, recorder or register
    of public documents, or public records custodian in this or
    another state, territory or possession, or the federal
    government of the United States or another nation; and,

4.  The production of a facsimile, preparation of a copy, or
    certification of a copy of the document does not violate
    any state or federal law.

                                   ........................................
                                   Signature of Affiant
                                   ........................................
                                   Printed Name of Affiant


Sworn to and subscribed before me
on this ........ day of ........, 200..  .

...............................                 (NOTARY OFFICIAL
Signature of Notary Public                       EMBOSSING SEAL
                                                IMPRESSION BELOW)

[STATEMENT OF AUTHORITY BELOW]
```

While this form of certificate may not necessarily permit the copy of the paper to be read in evidence in some courts or at a hearing, it might be accepted by certain persons as sufficient proof of the correctness of the copy.

For example, medical records which are sent to the courts often are referred to as "certified." In a hospital, an employee who is a notary public in the medical records department, when necessary, will make a photocopy of a medical record chart. The notary public will often attach a certificate to the medical record copy attesting to the fact that the photocopy is a true, correct and complete copy of the original medical chart. This is sometimes referred to as a sworn copy.

A strongly recommended protocol for a notary public to issue an attested copy or copy certification of a document is as follows:

1. The purported original of the document is exhibited and (temporarily) surrendered to the notary public for inspection;
2. the requester of the attested copy completes, signs and swears to an "affidavit and request for an attested copy" which the notary public retains;
3. unless personally known to the notary public, the requester produces suitable identification;
4. the requester signs the notary public register;
5. the requester pays the lawful fee, if desired by the notary public;
6. the notary public proceeds to make a photocopy of the purported original document, then affixes, completes and signs the attested copy certificate to the now attested copy; and
7. the notary public returns the purported original, attested copy, and receipt for notarial services to the requester.

Unless otherwise directed by law, the following certificate language meets most legal requirements for a notary to issue an attest copy or copy certification

STATE OF NEW YORK	ss.:	**COPY**
COUNTY OF		**CERTIFICATION**

On this (date) day of (month), (year), I, (name of notary public), a notary public, attest that the preceding or attached document consisting of (number) page(s) is a true, exact, complete and unaltered photocopy made by me of (description of document), presented to me by the document's custodian, (name of custodian), and, to the best of my knowledge and belief, that the photocopied document is neither a public record nor publicly recordable document, of which certified copies are available from an official source other than a notary public.
EACH PAGE HAS BEEN EMBOSSED WITH MY OFFICIAL SEAL. THE INK COLOR OF THIS CERTIFICATION IS GREEN.

____

Signature of Notary Public

To facilitate service requests, it would be advisable to have an adequate supply of request forms and certificates of attested copy or copy certification. Notaries are strongly encouraged to have the certificate of attested copy form created as a rubber stamp which would allow the application of the certification text directly upon the facsimile copy; on multiple-page documents, the certification should be affixed to the top page. The ink color should not be black to discourage and hamper unauthorized reproduction of attested copies. If possible, green ink is ideal, and can be easily accomplished with a pre-inked or self-inking rubber stamp. Loose certificates which are typically awkward-sized slips of paper requiring attachment by staple are strongly discouraged. The application of the certificate of attested copy or copy certification by rubber stamp creates a permanent, indelible impression which is virtually tamper-proof without detection, lowers cost and greatly reduces the time required to perform the service.

Chapter 11 Questions

1. Is it legally necessary for a notary public to be involved in the execution of a last will and testament? Explain why.
2. Define "testator" and "testatrix".
3. What is a "subscribing witness"? What other legal terms are given to these people?
4. What is a "decedent"?
5. In what unusual situation might a notary public be called upon to take a last will and testament? What other legal term is sometimes given to this type of last will? Is it legal for the notary public to do?
6. What is a "holographic will"? Are these documents legally acceptable, and under what circumstances?
7. Can a notary public ever serve as a witness to a last will and testament? Describe a possible scenario in which this might occur.
8. Define "probate" and "surrogate".
9. Explain what is meant by the term "self-prove" in a last will and testament. Why is it commonly employed?
10. Name two additional legal terms for the document evidencing the "self-prove" of a last will and testament.
11. What is a special commissioner and explain how one might be employed in a probate case in which the subscribing witnesses cannot conveniently appear to testify before the court?
12. What legal terms are used to describe the person(s) selected by the decedent and named in his or her last will and testament to manage the estate?

13. In the event that the decedent fails to designate a person to handle the estate, or the designee is unable or unsuitable to handle the estate, what legal terms describe the person(s) selected by the court to manage the estate?
14. What is the legal document issued as identification to the person(s) approved by the court to execute documents on behalf of a decedent?
15. Define a "living will".
16. How does a health care proxy or medical power of attorney compare to a living will?
17. Explain what is the difference between an ordinary power of attorney and a durable power of attorney.
18. What legal act does a notary public normally employ in connection with a living will? Explain why.
19. What is an attested copy or copy certification issued by a notary public?
20. Under what circumstances may a notary public issue an attested copy or copy certification?
21. Name at least six legal documents which only the government records custodian holding the original record may issue a certified copy.
22. Unless specifically prohibited by state law, why is it desirable for a notary public to issue an attested copy or copy certification of private documents and papers?
23. List the recommended procedure, step-by-step, taken by a notary public to issue an attested copy or copy certification.
24. Which two procedures taken by a notary public can act to lessen legal liability in connection with issuance of an attested copy or copy certification?

Chapter 12

Financial Institutions: Protests and Safe Deposit Boxes

PROTEST

In the event that a bill of exchange (i.e. draft), promissory note, bank check or similar negotiable instrument issued for the payment of money is refused for acceptance or payment by the drawee (i.e. bank), it is the responsibility of the holder to have the instrument "protested." A protest is a solemn declaration and statement in writing, drafted by a notary public at the request of the holder of a bill or note. It is declared that the bill or note described was on a certain day presented for payment (or acceptance) and was refused, stating the reasons given, if any. The notary public protests against all parties to such instrument and declares that they will be held responsible for all loss or damage arising from its dishonor. The purpose of the protest is to set "into motion" the formal process required to start the civil legal proceeding to secure the payment of money.

The subject of protesting negotiable instruments is comprehensive. The following discussion is intended to provide a brief examination of a commonly performed protest. It is strictly intended as attempt to familiarize the notary public with the complex process of protests.

Generally speaking, only those notaries public associated with a financial institution such as a bank will encounter the need to perform a protest. It is the responsibility of all notaries public, however, to become familiar with this essential act.

The *certificate of protest* is the formal, written document of the

PROTEST NOTICE

To ____________________________________

Please Take Notice That a ____________________________________

made by ____

____

in favor of ______________________________________ and by you

endorsed for ____ Dollars

dated ____ being this day

due, demanded and refused, it is delivered to me for protest

by ____

____

The holder, and has been duly protested accordingly, and you

will be looked to for payment, of which you hereby have

notice

____

Notary Public

protest. The original bill or note will be attached to the original certificate of protest. The copies of the certificate of protest will have a copy of the bill or note attached.

A common instance which may require the notary public to perform a protest is when a sight draft (i.e. bank check) is presented for payment to the financial institution on which it is drawn and it is returned for non-sufficient funds (NSF). In other words, the payee (or the payee's bank) presents the check to the issuing bank, and there is not enough money in the account to cover the full payment of the check. *Presentment* is the production of a negotiable instrument to the drawee for acceptance. It is a demand for payment or acceptance made upon the maker, acceptor, drawee or other payor by or on behalf of the holder. For example, many negotiable instruments (such as checks) are informally presented by banks to other banks for payment through the Federal Reserve Bank Clearinghouse System.

Presentment of sight drafts (checks) for acceptance must be made within reasonable time after date or issue, whichever is later.

A "*reasonable time*" to present an uncertified check drawn and payable within the United States, and now drawn by a bank, is presumed to be (1) for liability of the drawer, 30 days after date or issue, whichever is later; or (2) for liability of an endorser, seven days after endorsement.

Presentment at a bank must be during normal business hours.

The refusal to accept or pay a draft or note when presented for payment is termed ***dishonor***. An instrument is dishonored when a necessary (or optional) presentment is properly made and the acceptance or payment is refused. Upon dishonor, notice of dishonor must be given to any endorser, drawer, maker or acceptor. *Notice of dishonor* is a formal notice of the non-acceptance or non-payment of the negotiable instrument.

Notice of dishonor must be sent within the following time limits: By bank, before its midnight deadline; by any other person, before midnight of third business day after dishonor or receipt of dishonor.

Written notice is considered given when *sent,* even if it is not received by the endorser, drawer, maker or acceptor.

Notice of dishonor must be given in any reasonable manner: by sending the negotiable instrument bearing stamp, ticket or writing stating that acceptance or payment has been refused; or by sending notice of debit with respect to instrument; or by sending either oral or written notice.

The notice must clearly identify the instrument and state that it has been dishonored. For example, a bank has given notice of dishonor by returning a "bounced" check with a debit receipt attached deducting the deposit amount as well as returned check costs.

Common reasons for refusal include: non-sufficient funds, account closed, no account, improper signature, etc.

Notice of dishonor may be given to any person who may be liable on the instrument by or on behalf of the holder or any party who has himself received notice, or any other party who can be compelled to pay the instrument.

The following will illustrate the process: Macy's accepts a check in payment for a coat bought by a customer named Smith. Macy's deposits Smith's check into the store's checking account. Macys' bank sends the check to Smith's bank for payment, "*presenting*" the check for payment. At the time of the presentment, Smith does not have enough money in his account to honor the demand for payment. A bank will typically deposit the check a second time as a courtesy to Smith. If funds are still not available, Smith's bank *dishonors* the check and returns the check to Macys' bank, indicating the reason for dishonor as non-sufficient funds (NSF). The check is now returned to Macy's. This phase is termed "*noting the dishonor*" or "*noting for protest*". It may be oral or in writing, as is the case in this example. Upon satisfactory evidence of such notice, the notary public may make a formal protest.

Smith is now contacted by Macy's to "make the check good". If Smith fails to meet the terms of a special arrangement to pay, Macy's now presents the check to Smith's bank (either directly or through their bank) for protest. The notary public now proceeds to complete a *certificate of protest,* utilizing a blank, pre-printed form or creating an original document. The original of the *certificate of protest* is affixed to the actual dishonored instrument (i.e. check), and should be returned to Macy's. Another original certificate of protest should be sent to Smith, along with a copy of the dishonored instrument. In the event that a dishonored instrument has more than one maker, such as on a promissory note, each maker or signer would receive a notice of protest. The notices to the remaining makers and endorsers do not necessarily require a copy of the dishonored instrument.

Certificate of Protest

The suggested form of protest is as follows:

STATE OF NEW YORK } SS.:
COUNTY OF . . . . }

Be it known, that on the (date) day of (month), in the year of our Lord (0000), at the request of (bank), of (city), I, (name), a notary public, duly sworn, residing in the City of (. . .), County of (. . .), and State aforesaid, presented the annexed (instrument type) of (drawer) for $ (amount) . . . at the (drawee), and demanded payment thereof which was refused for (reason). Whereupon, I, the said notary public at the request aforesaid, did protest, and by these presents do solemnly protest against the maker, endorser and all parties whom it may concern, for exchange, reexchange, and all costs, damages, and interest already incurred, or hereafter incurred, by reason of the nonpayment thereof. And I, the said notary do hereby certify, that on the same day and year above written, I deposited, postage-paid in the post office at (city) notice of the foregoing protest, signed by me, addressed to the makers and endorsers thereof, directed to the parties to be charged as follows:

Notice for (Name)	Directed to (Address)
Notice for . . .	Directed to . . .
Notice for . . .	Directed to . . .
Notice for . . .	Directed to . . .

Each of the above named places being the known place of residence of the persons to whom the said notice was directed respectively.

IN WITNESS WHEREOF, I have hereunto subscribed my name and affixed my seal of office.

. . . .
Notary Public

The certificate of protest should be prepared in sufficient number of originals for all makers and endorsers who should receive notice. Each certificate should be *individually* signed and embossed with the official seal of the notary public. A maker or *drawer* of a check is the payor or the party who signs the check (i.e. Smith). The *endorser* is the holder who signs the name on the back of the check to obtain cash or credit represented on the face as payee (i.e. Macy's).

In the previous fictitious example, Macy's would now prepare to pursue the matter by either of two legal approaches. In addition to the civil matter, an instance of passing a bad check can be a *criminal* matter.

Prior to the commencement of any civil or criminal action, the customer (Smith) should be sent a letter (certified mail, return-receipt requested) formally requesting payment in satisfaction of the amount of the bad check, in addition to related costs incurred as a result of the incident. This step will be necessary in order to bring the matter before a police agency or court (civil or criminal).

To activate the civil matter, Macy's would present the protested check and certificate of protest to the appropriate civil court in the jurisdiction where the defendant (Smith) lives or works, or has a place of business. Once a claim is filed with the court clerk, the civil court trial process will now proceed. The state's General Obligations Law provides these remedies. The payee may sue the payor (customer) for a penalty equal to the smaller of twice the value of the check or $400. Should a check be written on a checking account which is non-existent (i.e. closed), the bank will return it and the payee may sue the payor for a penalty equal to the smaller of twice the value of the check or $750. The customer is required to pay these fines in addition to paying the original check. Besides these civil resolutions, criminal penalties are possible. Ordinarily, the claimant (Macy's) will be successful in having the court enter a judgment for the sum of money in question, plus costs to recover. Macy's now presents the judgment to an enforcement officera sheriff, city marshal or constable. The enforcement officer will take a variety of legal measures to recover the money.

In New York, a person who issues or passes a check (or similar sight order) for the payment of money, knowing that it will not be honored by the drawee (bank), commits a criminal act.

CERTIFICATE OF PROTEST

STATE OF__________ COUNTY OF__________ss.

BE IT KNOWN, that I, a duly empowered Notary Public, at the request of

____
Financial Institution Address

did duly present on__________ the attached__________for
Date

$__________dated__________signed by__________

____________________payable

to____________________the time limit having elapsed

and demanded payment thereof, which was refused;

Whereupon I solemnly PROTESTED, and by these presents do publicly and solemnly protest the said instrument as against all parties whom it may concern, for exchange, re-exchange, and all costs, damages and interest already incurred, or hereafter incurred, by reason of the non-payment thereof; and I hereby certify that on the same day, I gave due notice to the makers and endorsers thereof by depositing in the Post Office at__________ postage prepaid, notices thereof directed to the parties to be charged as follows:

NAME	DIRECTED TO
One for__________	__________
One for__________	__________
One for__________	__________
One for__________	__________
One for__________	__________
One for__________	__________

Each notice being directed to the person for whom it was intended at the above address.

Reason for protest__________

IN WITNESS WHEREOF, I have hereunto set my hand and affixed my Seal of Office

__________Notary Public

My Commission Expires__________

AMOUNT		
INTEREST		
PROTEST		
NOTICES		
POSTAGE		
TOTAL		

Form N-1 Rev. 2/78 DeLANO SERVICE, ALLEGAN, MICHIGAN 49010

For these purposes, as well as in any prosecution for theft committed by a check, an issuer is presumed to know that the check (or money order) would not be paid, if: (a) the issuer had no account with the drawee at the time the check or order was issued; or (b) payment was refused by the drawee for lack of funds, upon presentation within 30 days after issue, and the issuer failed to make good within 10 days after receiving notice of that refusal, or after notice has been sent to the issuer's last known address. *Notice of refusal* may be given to the issuer orally or in writing in any reasonable manner by any person. However, in order to successfully prosecute a case, it is strongly recommended to send notice in written form by certified mail, return receipt requested, to serve as proof of notice.

To engage the criminal action, Macy's would present the protested check and certificate of protest to a police agency in the jurisdiction where the check was passed.

In addition to the certificate of protest and the dishonored negotiable instrument, the police agency should be presented with a copy of the notice letter, U.S.P.S. certified mail receipt and (signed) return-receipt. The complainant (Macy's) should retain a photo-copy of all documentation surrendered to police. An evidence receipt should be requested from the police official taking custody of these vital pieces of evidence.

After a sworn complaint is taken, the police will arrest the defendant (Smith). Under New York Penal Law, the crime of issuing a bad check can be designated a misdemeanor. In the Macy's example, the defendant has also committed larceny.

Petit larceny, a misdemeanor, is committed if a person is guilty of stealing property (less than $1000). Grand larceny, a felony, has been committed if the value of the property exceeds $1000.

In review, if a person "bounces" a check, the payee begins to recover the money by obtaining a protest from a notary public. The notary public notifies the customer that legal action is starting.

SIGNATURE GUARANTEE

A signature guarantee is quite different from any of the legal acts performed by a notary public. The confusion is frequently compounded because many persons authorized to guarantee signatures are also notaries public. The primary function of a signature guarantee is to serve as a certification that a signature is truly legitimate. The certification is issued by an officer of a financial institution or bona fide stock brokerage house. The act is referred to as a "guarantee" because the person making the guarantee is creating an obligation, as an agent of the financial institution or brokerage house. In the event that the signature is not genuine and an innocent party is damaged by reliance upon the forgery, the financial institution or brokerage house can be held liable for damages to an innocent party who reasonably relied upon the signature guarantee. It is similar to the warranty of endorser or transferor in check transactions. A person who endorses a check generally gives an engagement to honor the instrument should it be dishonored and properly protested. The signature guarantee is commonly invoked in the transfer of stock securities and sometimes for the execution of mortgages or other loan transactions.

The Uniform Commercial Code (UCC) is the authority source for these related commercial matters. According to the UCC, any person guaranteeing a signature (the guarantor) of an endorser of a certified security, warrants the following at the time of signing: The signature was genuine; the signer was an appropriate person to endorse; and the signer had legal capacity to sign. The UCC further declares that the warranties (or guarantees) are made to any person taking or dealing with the security in reliance on the guarantee, and the guarantor is liable to the person for any loss resulting from breach of the warranties.

Although a notary public takes reasonable and common sense approaches to identification of parties in an acknowledgment matter, the notary public is generally not held liable for a forgery or an impostor, provided there was no evidence of negligence. In a signature guarantee matter, even though a financial institution officer or broker may take the same (or increased) measures as the notary public, the financial institution or brokerage house will generally be held liable for a forgery or an impostor.

In 1989 a New York Law was proposed which would have allowed a certificate of acknowledgment furnished by a notary public to be considered sufficient guarantee of the signature, and no other assurance or requirement in place of, or in addition to, such acknowledgment be required. The premise behind the bill was to alleviate the cost or burden of a consumer (transferor) needing to going through a securities broker every time the transferor wished to transfer stock. A transferor is required to report to a financial institution officer or authorized broker at a brokerage house, even though the transferor does not have a business relationship with either institution. The rationale for amending the law included the economy of notary service (relative to a financial institution or brokerage house guarantee), and the availability and accessibility of notaries public. Although the law was well-intentioned, it would have placed an enormous responsibility upon notaries public, and potentially created an enormous breach of the integrity of the securities industry.

Marine Protest

The notary public should be aware of another form of protest. In maritime law, a protest is a written statement by the master of a vessel, attested by a notary public, swearing that damage suffered by the ship and/or cargo on her voyage was caused by storms or other dangers of the sea beyond his control (without negligence or misconduct). If, for example, an unscheduled port call has to be made to repair damage to the ship, the master of the vessel is required to prepare a sworn statement which justifies the reasons.

Banks and Notaries Public

New York State Archive records of correspondence from the late nineteenth century (circa 1895) show that notaries public have a long-standing, deep-rooted association with the banking industry. Copies of correspondence issued from the governor's office prove the status and importance placed upon appointment as a notary public. At that time, each application was reviewed by the governor who made appointments based upon the approval of the state senate. A refusal was not uncommon, even for political reasons.

Each banking institution was allowed a certain number of appointments which were closely monitored. If a banker left the financial institution, the president of the bank was required to nominate a successor pending gubernatorial and senate approval. The reason for such prestige is the fact that many of the notarial duties are essential to the banking and financial industries, particularly with reference to negotiable instruments.

Since banks were known to have notaries public, citizens became accustomed to bringing their documents (in addition to financial) to these community institutions. Because the contemporary

Photograph credit: Penobscot Marine Museum, Searsport, ME.

(Form No. 37.)

MARINE NOTE OF PROTEST.

Consulate of the United States of America,

Port of Hiogo, Japan
June 8th, 1885

On this 8th day of June, in the year of our Lord eighteen hundred and eighty-five before me, T. McF. Patton Consul of the United States of America for Osaka & Hiogo, Japan and the dependencies thereof, personally appeared Leroy Dow, Master of the ship or vessel called the "Clarissa B. Carver", of Searsport, of the burden of 1144.14 tons or thereabout, and declared that on the 2d day of June, 1885 last past he sailed in and with the said ship from the port of Yokohama, laden with Rags and General Cargo and ~~arrived in the ship at~~ was wrecked in collision with the British S.S. "Glamorganshire" June 7, 1885 near Hiogo, and having experienced boisterous weather on the voyage and received damage to his said ship and cargo

hereby enters this Note of Protest accordingly, to serve and avail him hereafter if found necessary.

Leroy Dow
Master.

Attested: T. McF. Patton
U.S. *Consul.*

Here insert the day and hour.

MARITIME PROTEST

UNITED STATES OF AMERICA)
STATE OF NEW YORK) ss.:
COUNTY OF [county name])

BEFORE ME, the undersigned authority, a Notary Public in and for the state of New York, personally came and appeared: [Master name], a person of full age of majority and a resident of [city, state, country], who, after first being duly sworn by me, did depose and say that:

1. He is the Master of M/V [vessel name], a [country] flag vessel, home port of [city, state], of [number] feet breadth and depth of [number] feet;

2. By this public instrument be it known, unto all whom it may concern, that on this [date] day of [month] in the year of our Lord [year] A.D., the said M/V [vessel name] is located at approximately [geographical position] and said vessel departed from the port of [city name] as heretofore described. Having, in due prosecution of the voyage encountered:

[Master statement].

WHEREFORE, the said affiant, [Master name], Master of the said M/V [vessel name], has requested me to protest, and I, the Notary, at such request, have protested, and by these presents do publicly and solemnly protest against all and every person and persons whom it doth, shall, or may concern, and against all and singular, the accidents, casualties and circumstances already set forth in the foregoing declaration, on oath, for all manner of losses, costs, damages, charges, expenses, and injuries whatsoever which said ship and her cargo on board, and the freight by her earned, or to be earned, or either of them, or any part thereof, have already sustained, or may hereinafter sustain, by reason or means of the foregoing premises.

Thus done and protested, in the City of [city name], this [date] day of [month] in the year of our Lord [year] A.D.

IN TESTIMONY WHEREOF, I, the aforementioned authority, have hereunto my hand affixed my notarial seal.

[Master signature]

SWORN TO & SUBSCRIBED BEFORE
ME THIS [DATE]

[Notary signature]

[Statement of authority]

WITNESSES:
[(Two) name, signature & address]

MARITIME NOTE OF PROTEST

On this Eighteenth day of July, in the year of our Lord Two Thousand, personally appeared and presented himself before me, Alexander Hamilton, a Notary Public in and for the State of New York at New York, Alfred E. Piombino, Master of the Motor-Vessel "CHAMPION", which sailed from Halifax, Nova Scotia, Canada, on or about the Tenth day of July, 2000, carrying General Cargo bound for Norfolk, Virginia via Portland, Maine, and arrived at New York on the Eighteenth day of July, 2000, and fearing loss or damage owing to:

> encountering high winds and tempestuous seas which caused the vessel to roll and pitch heavily and ship water over-all, particularly on the Tenth, Eleventh and Twelfth days of July, 2000, when winds reached force 9 Northeasterly,

during the voyage, the said Master hereby notes his protest against all losses, damages, costs and expenses, reserving the right to extend the same at time and place convenient.

s/ ALEXANDER HAMILTON Notary Public State of New York Qualified in New York County Commission Expires 10-10-2001	s/ Master

---

UNITED STATES OF AMERICA)
STATE OF NEW YORK) ss.:
COUNTY OF NEW YORK)

I, Alexander Hamilton, a Notary Public duly commissioned, sworn and qualified in County of New York, State of New York, DO HEREBY CERTIFY:

THAT the foregoing Note of Protest is a true copy of the Protest noted by Alfred E. Piombino, Master of the Motor-Vessel "CHAMPION", on the Eighteenth day of July, A.D. 2000, the original of which is on file in my office, located at 357 Canal Street, New York, New York.

DATED at New York, New York, this Eighteenth day of July, A.D. 2000.

s/
ALEXANDER HAMILTON
Notary Public State of New York
Qualified in New York County
Commission Expires 10-10-2001

appointment process and regulations concerning notaries public have been significantly relaxed, notaries are more widely available. Many constituents, however, still rely on their community banking institutions for their notarial service needs. Consequently, the banks and similar firms are sometimes annoyed at the non-bank customers "monopolizing" their bank employees' services.

While it may appear that an unfair focus has been placed upon the banking industry, it should be recognized that all organizations may be practicing policies which do not comply with the state law and/or ethical practices of notaries public. Because the banking industry has a significant impact upon our general economy and personal lives in so many ways, it is probably one of the most influential, essential and widely-used public service institutions in any community. Accordingly, each banking center has a moral obligation to respond to the needs of the public, particularly those requiring the services of a notary public.

It is *inappropriate* for a notary public, employed by a bank or other private firm, to refuse to perform an official notarial act for a non-bank or firm patron. A bank or company policy that requires such action is violating the separation of private and public duties. So called "company" notaries public, who refuse to perform notarial acts for non-business related persons, are subject to both criminal and civil penalties, in addition to possible removal from office. Equally unacceptable is a private company or other organization which attempts to manipulate a trusted public office for private interests.

The notary public is legally obligated to serve the general public from whom he receives his authority. Therefore, to charge non-bank or business constituents while waiving fees for bank or firm patrons is inappropriate. Such actions may lead to civil actions against the notary public. Furthermore, it is *illegal* for a bank, company or organization to require a notary public to collect more than the lawful statutory fee for a notarial act. It is important that both the employer and notary public recognize and respect this distinction. The notary public is not a mere *agent* or *servant* of the bank, but a *public officer* sworn to discharge office duties properly. The notary public is under a higher control than that of the employer. The notary public owes duties to the public and must adhere to the law first and foremost. Therefore, when the notary is acting in an official capacity, he is not acting as an employee of the bank and the bank cannot direct how the duties of the officer should be performed.

If the notary public is guilty of wrong doing or *malfeasance* in the performance of an official act, the bank will not generally be held liable. It is the individual notary public who will be held responsible and accountable to the people of the State of New York for any violation of trust. It is the notary public (personally) who faces imprisonment, fines, removal from office, or all of these penalties for misconduct. The highest degree of ethical standards is crucial.

While the notary public is an employee and agent of the bank or firm, the separation of duties is clear. When the notary public is engaged in the performance of an official act of public (governmental) service, the private service is suspended until the official act is completed. Many banks and other companies use their own employees (who are notaries public) for internal notarial requirements. However, a growing number of financial institutions and firms are adopting a policy in which they utilize notaries public from other banks and firms for a variety of notarial acts. These organizations institute such a policy to reduce their potential exposure to legal liability and subsequent legal actions by parties challenging the notarial act, claiming misconduct, collusion (conspiracy) or conflict of interest.

The notary public commission is issued strictly to the *individual.* If the employer elects to pay costs, reimburse or otherwise underwrite the costs to the employee or agent for the application fee, filing fees, equipment and supply costs, it should be clear that this does not obligate the notary public to the employer. Certainly the bank or company may enjoy the privilege of utilizing the services of the "resident" notary public, but it also bears the accompanying responsibility for such an arrangement.

Safe Deposit Boxes

New York State law permits banks to force open safe deposit boxes if the customer does not pay the box rent for a period of one year, or if they do not remove the contents within 30 days of termination of the safe deposit box lease. The bank will send a letter (either certified or registered mail, return-receipt requested) informing the customer that, if the past-due rent is not paid within 30 days or the customer property is not removed from the box, the deposit box will be forced open and the contents removed and inventoried. After 30 days from written notification, the bank may have a locksmith force open the deposit box. The bank will inventory the contents in the presence of a notary public and designated bank officer.

PROCEDURE SUMMARY
FORCED OPENING OF SAFE DEPOSIT BOX
PURSUANT TO BANKING LAW §335

CONDITIONS: Non-payment of box rent for 1 year *or* failure to vacate box within 30 days of termination of lease.

PROCEDURES: Lessor sends letter to lessee, warning opening of box if lessee fails to pay rent/vacate box within 30 days of letter.

If unresolved, lessor forces open box in presence of notary public, who files a certificate with lessor noting date, name of customer and list of contents, if any.

Lessee sent copy of notary certificate/inventory within 10 days of box opening. Lessee is informed that lessor will store contents for 2 years.

If still unresolved after 2 years, lessor sends customer notice of intent to sell valuable contents, noting auction date, time, place and total amount due. Notice must be sent 30 days in advance of auction.

Notice of auction must be published 10 days prior to auction date in newspaper (locale of auction).

All related, accrued costs are deductible from sale proceeds/cash in box.

After 3 years, sale proceeds/cash in box become abandoned property, subject to handling pursuant to Abandoned Property Law.

Documents, personal papers, and articles of no value are retained for 10 years before destruction.

The bank will hold the contents for two years. Rent continues to be billed for the safe keeping of the property. The notary public in attendance will file a certificate with the bank, indicating the date of the box opening, name of lessee and list of the deposit box contents (if any). The lessee must be sent (either certified or registered

Bank Notary's Certificate of
Safe Deposit Box Inventory

STATE OF NEW YORK) ss.:
COUNTY OF ....)

KNOW ALL MEN BY THESE PRESENTS THAT:

1. I, ... , the undersigned notary public in and for the State of New York, duly appointed, commissioned and sworn, and in the employ of .... ;

2. On the .... day of .... in the year A.D. 200.. , at approximately .... a.m./p.m., in my presence, and in the presence of ...., as both witness and a .... of .... , said bank caused to be opened Safe Deposit Box No. .... in the vault of said bank located at .... in the City/Town/Village of .... , County of ...., State of New York, standing in the name/s of the lessee/s, namely ....

3.. The contents of said safe deposit box were thereupon removed and consisted of the following: ....

The estimated value thereof is approximately $ ....

4. The aforesaid contents of said safe deposit box were then placed by me in a package which I immediately sealed and upon which I endorsed the following:

(a) The name/s of the person/s or corporation in whose name said safe deposit box was registered and the number of said safe deposit box, and
(b) the estimated value of such contents, viz: $ .... and the package so sealed and marked was in my presence then placed in one of the general safes in the vault of above captioned bank.

WITNESS my hand and seal of office this .... day of .... in the year A.D. 200..

....	....
Signature of Notary Public	Signature of Bank Witness
....	....
Printed Name of Notary Public	Printed Name of Bank Witness
Commission Expires	
NOTARY PUBLIC STAMP/SEAL BELOW (If applicable)	(NOTARY OFFICIAL EMBOSSING SEAL IMPRESSION BELOW)

Independent Notary's Certificate of
Safe Deposit Box Inventory

STATE OF NEW YORK) ss.:
COUNTY OF ....)

KNOW ALL MEN BY THESE PRESENTS THAT:

1. I, ... , the undersigned notary public in and for the State of New York duly appointed, commissioned and sworn, and not in the employ of .... ;

2. On the .... day of .... in the year A.D. 200.. , at approximately .... a.m./p.m., in my presence, and in the presence of ...., as both witness and a .... of .... , said bank caused to be opened Safe Deposit Box No. .... in the vault of said bank located at .... in the City/Town/Village of .... , County of ...., State of New York, standing in the name/s of the lessee/s, namely ....

3.. The contents of said safe deposit box were thereupon removed and consisted of the following: ....

The estimated value thereof is approximately $ ....

4. The aforesaid contents of said safe deposit box were then placed by me in a package which I immediately sealed and upon which I endorsed the following:

(a) The name/s of the person/s or corporation in whose name said safe deposit box was registered and the number of said safe deposit box, and
(b) the estimated value of such contents, viz: $ .... and the package so sealed and marked was in my presence then placed in one of the general safes in the vault of above captioned bank.

WITNESS my hand and seal of office this .... day of .... in the year A.D. 200..

....	....
Signature of Notary Public	Signature of Bank Witness
....	....
Printed Name of Notary Public	Printed Name of Bank Witness
Commission Expires	
NOTARY PUBLIC STAMP/SEAL BELOW (If applicable)	(NOTARY OFFICIAL EMBOSSING SEAL IMPRESSION BELOW)

mail, return-receipt requested) a copy of the notarial certificate, including the inventory, within ten days after opening the box. Notice of intention to store the property at the expense of the lessee for not more than two years is required.

The contents will be delivered to the lessee, upon the payment of delinquent rental fees, box opening costs (including locksmith services), notary public fees and storage service.

After two years, the lessor (bank) may inform the customer by mail (either certified or registered mail, return-receipt requested) of intent to sell the deposit box contents (property or articles of value), indicating the time and place of sale. The notice must be 30 days in advance of the sale and indicate the total charges accumulated to date. The advertising (legal notice) costs regarding the box are the responsibility of the lessee.

Unless the lessee settles the account with the lessor (on or before the date indicated in the letter of notice), the deposit box contents will be sold at a public auction. Ten days prior to the public auction, notice must be published (in the locale of the slated sale).

All accumulated costs may be deducted from the sale cash proceeds. The remaining balance may be drawn upon in the future to satisfy costs, charges and fees. United States coin or currency may be directly applied to the payment of charges, costs and fees. After three years from the forced box opening, the remaining balance (of the sale proceeds) becomes abandoned property and may be disposed of by the lessor in accordance with the New York Abandoned Property Law.

Documents, letters, personal papers and articles of no apparent value will not be sold. The lessor must retain such items for ten years from the date of the forced box opening. After ten years, this property may be destroyed.

Chapter 12 Questions

1. What is the legal definition of a notarial protest?
2. Describe a notarial protest in your own words. Use a fictitious example in your response.
3. In what two U.S. jurisdictions are notarial protests routinely performed and an integral component of the legal systems? Explain in what two legal situations they would be employed.
4. As a general rule, where will a notarial protest be performed and by whom? Explain why.

5. Compare how a certificate of protest differs from a notice of dishonor. Explain why both are necessary.
6. What is an example of a dishonored negotiable instrument?
7. Define "dishonor".
8. Define "notice of dishonor".
9. Name four common reasons for dishonor.
10. What are two common terms for a "sight draft"?
11. Explain when a sight draft is payable and why.
12. Define "maker", "drawer", "drawee", and "endorser".
13. Explain why it is critical for notaries public in states where protests are not routinely performed to understand the basic process, and if requested, be able to issue notarial protests.
14. Define a maritime protest. Explain some common incidents in which such protests are employed.
15. Explain why banks and notaries public have been historically closely linked.
16. Discuss the legal issues associated with a corporate policy to refuse notarial services to non-bank patrons.
17. What legal liability does a notary public employed by a bank risk as the result of inappropriately refusing to provide notarial services?
18. Explain the customary employee-employer legal relationship. How does this relationship shift when the employee/notary public provides notarial services to a person?
19. Discuss employee/employer contracts stipulating fee arrangements for notarial services.
20. What is a signature guarantee?
21. How does a signature guarantee differ from an act by a notary public? Are these acts legally interchangeable?
22. Why does the financial community consider the signature guarantee more reliable than an act by a notary public?
23. Who performs signature guarantees and at what fee?
24. How does a signature guarantor obtain the right to issue signature guarantees?
25. Why does confusion exist between signature guarantees and notarial acts, especially in banks and other financial institutions?
26. Explain the possible impact to the American Stock Market in the event that signatures guarantees were legally equivalent to notarial acts.
27. Name three common financial-type transactions in which a signature guarantee might be required.
28. What body of law is the basis for signature guarantees?
29. Explain what role a notary public serves in the forced opening of an abandoned safe deposit box.
30. Describe the process, step-by-step, taken by a notary public in the supervision of the forced opening of an abandoned safe deposit box.

31. Outline the essential elements of the notary public report documenting the forced opening and inventory of an abandoned safe deposit box.
32. Is it legally permissible for a bank or safe deposit box company to utilize an employee/notary public to preside over an abandoned safe deposit box ceremony? Explain the advantages and disadvantages of this situation.
33. Why is it considered prudent risk management for a financial institution standard operating procedure to incorporate the use of a non-employee/notary public, even in jurisdictions where the law doesn't require such, in supervising forced opening of abandoned safe deposit boxes?

Glossary

ABETTING: To help or urge.

ABSCOND: To hide or conceal with intent to escape the law.

ACCEDE: To consent or agree.

ACCOST: To approach and speak to.

ACCRUE: To increase.

ACKNOWLEDGE: To own or admit as true and accept responsibility.

ACKNOWLEDGMENT: Formal declaration before an authorized officer (e.g. notary public) by the person who executed an instrument, orally stating that it was done freely. The taking of an acknowledgment of the execution of a written instrument is legally different from the acknowledgment component of the execution of a last and will testament. (See proof of execution and subscribing witness)

ACT: A doing, a public act is one which has public authority, been made before a public officer and is authorized by a public seal.

ACTION: A lawsuit; a formal complaint within the jurisdiction of a court of law.

A.D.: The abbreviation for the Latin *Anno Domini* meaning "in the year of our Lord."

ADJUDGE: To decide or settle by law.

ADMINISTER: To discharge the duties of an office; to give.

ADMINISTRATOR: A person appointed by the court to manage the estate of a deceased person who did not leave a will.

ADMINISTRATRIX: A female administrator.

ADMISSIBLE: Appropriate to be considered in reaching a decision (i.e. admissible evidence is acceptable to the court or judge).

ADMONISH: To warn or advise.

ADVERSE PARTY: A party in a hearing or trial whose interests are opposed to the interests of another party in a matter.

AFFIANT: The person who makes and signs an affidavit.

AFFIDAVIT: A sworn written or printed declaration or statement of facts, made voluntarily and confirmed by the oath or affirmation of the party making it, before a notary public or other authorized officer.

AFFIRM: To confirm or verify.

AFFIRMANT: A person who testifies on affirmation or who affirms instead of taking an oath.

AFFIRMATION: A solemn, formal declaration (made under the penalty of perjury) by a person who refuses or declines to take an oath; it is legally equivalent to an oath.

AFFIX: To attach physically or inscribe/impress, as a signature or seal.

AGGRIEVED: Injured; having suffered a loss or injury.

AGNOSTIC: An individual who denies the possibility of knowing the existence of God.

ALLEGATION: The claim, declaration or statement of a party to an action; a charge.

ALLEGE: To state, assert or charge.

AMEND: To change.

ANNEX: To attach to.

ANNOTATION: A note or case summary.

ANNUL: To make void or nullify.

APOSTILLE: NYS Department of State certification attached to a document signed by a NYS notary public for possible international use. This state certificate is recognized by foreign countries who have signed the Hague Convention (treaty) abolishing the requirement for legalization for foreign public documents. It is a declaration by the NYS Secretary of State of the genuineness of the accompanying certificate issued by a NYS county clerk (who previously made a certification as to the authenticity and authority of the signing NYS notary public).

APPELLATE COURT: Generally a reviewing, not trial court; appellate division; however, has trial jurisdiction.

ARBITRATION: Referring a dispute to an impartial (third) person, chosen by the parties involved (or judge) who agree in advance to accept the decision of the arbitrator.

ASSENT: Compliance or approval.

ATHIEST: An individual who unequivocally denies the existence of God.

ATTEST: To witness or affirm to be true.

ATTESTATION: The witnessing of an instrument in writing at the request of the party making and signing it as a witness.

AUTHENTICATION: Giving legal authority to a record or other written document, causing it to be legally admissible in evidence, by certification issued by a clerk, state or federal authority.

BAILEE: One to whom goods are entrusted by a bailor.

BAILIWICK: A territorial segment over which a bailiff or sheriff has jurisdiction, similar to the contemporary

BAILIFF: A court officer who has charge of a court session in the matter of keeping order, custody of the jury, and prisoners while court is in session; sometimes assists the sheriff in executing writs and making arrests.

BAILOR: The transferor of goods under a bailment; the party who bails or delivers goods to another (bailee) in the contract of bailment.

BAILMENT: A delivery of goods by one person (bailor) to another (bailee) in "trust" for the execution of some act, with the eventual redelivery of the goods to the bailor. A pawn is an example of a bailment.

BEARER: The person in possession of an instrument, document of title or security, payable to the bearer or endorsed in blank (no payee indicated).

BENEFIT: Any tangible or intangible gain or advantage.

BILL OF SALE: A written document given to pass title (ownership) of personal property from vendor to vendee (seller to purchaser).

BONA FIDE: In good faith without fraud.

BREACH: The breaking or violating of a law, right, obligation or duty.

CANCELLED CHECK: A check which bears the notation of cancellation of the drawee bank as having been paid and charged to the drawer.

CANON LAW: A body of Roman church jurisprudence or law compiled in the twelfth, thirteenth and fourteenth centuries from the opinions of the ancient Latin fathers, the decrees of General Councils and the Holy See.

CAPACITY: Legal competence or power.

CERTIFICATE OF GOOD CONDUCT: A document, issued by the NYS board of parole, to an eligible convicted offender which removes civil disabilities, imposed by law, prohibiting certain types of employment and licenses for individuals who have been convicted of two or more felonies. It also may restore the right to hold public office. For consideration, certain minimum periods of good conduct in the community are necessary: one year for a misdemeanor; three years for a class c, d or e felony; and five years for a class a or b felony.

CERTIFICATE OF RELIEF FROM DISABILITIES: Commonly referred to as a certificate of relief, it is a document, issued upon release from imprisonment (if any) by the sentencing court or NYS board of parole, to an eligible convicted offender which removes civil disabilities, imposed by law, prohibiting certain types of employment and licenses for individuals who have been convicted of a misdemeanors or a maximum of one felony. It does not restore the right to hold public office. A certificate applies only to one criminal incident, not an entire criminal history.

CERTIFIED CHECK: The check of a depositor drawn on a bank on the face of which the bank has written or stamped the words "certified" or "accepted" with the date and signature of a bank official; it means that bank holds money to pay the check and is liable to pay the proper party.

CERTIFIED COPY: A copy of a document or record, signed and certified as a true copy by the public officer who keeps the original.

CHAMBERLAIN: A city officer similar to a treasurer; may serve as city clerk and custodian of public city records.

CHATTEL: Movable, personal property such as household fixtures or goods (i.e.: a car, television, etc.).

CHATTEL PAPER: A document which indicates both a monetary obligation and a security interest in a lease of (chattel) goods.

CHECK: A draft drawn upon a bank and payable on demand, signed by the maker or drawer, containing an unconditional promise to pay a certain sum (in money) to the order of the payee.

CHECK KITING: Writing a check against a bank account without enough money to cover it, expecting that the funds will be deposited before the check is cashed.

CIVIL ACTION: A lawsuit based on a private wrong, as distinguished from a crime, or to enforce rights (through remedies) of a private or non-penal nature (i.e. breach of contract, divorce, etc. compared to robbery, forgery, etc.).

CIVIL LAW: The collection of law which every nation, state, commonwealth or local municipality has established specifically for itself; "municipal law." Laws concerned with civil or private rights and remedies, as compared to criminal law.

CODICIL: A supplement or addition to a will.

COERCE: Force to compliance.

COLLUSION: A secret agreement between two or more persons to defraud another person of his rights (using the law), or to obtain an object forbidden by law; conspiracy.

COMMISSION: Authority issued from the government, one of its departments or a court, authorizing a person to perform specific acts or exercise the authority of a public office.

COMMISSIONER: A person to whom a commission is directed by the government or a court (e.g. commissioner of deeds or court commissioner).

COMMON KNOWLEDGE: Knowledge that every reasonably intelligent person has including learning, experience, history and facts.

COMMON LAW: The collection of law based upon custom, court decisions and common usage.

COMPEL: To force or get by force.

COMPETENT: Capable, qualified and meeting all requirements; having sufficient ability or authority; being of a certain age and mental ability.

CONSENT: Agreement.

CONSIDERATION: Something of value which is the reason a person enters into a contract, including money, a right, interest, personal services and love/affection.

CONSTITUENT: A person who is served or represented by a public officer.

CONTEMPT: A willful disregard or disobedience of public authority (e.g. a court).

CONTEMPT OF COURT: Any act which is intended to embarrass or obstruct the court in the administration of justice or lessen its authority or dignity.

CONTRACT: An agreement between two or more persons which creates an obligation to do or not to do a particular thing.

CONVEYANCE: A document by which some estate or interest in real property is transferred from one person to another.

COUNSEL/COUNSELLOR: An attorney at law; a lawyer.

COVENANT: Agreements written into deeds and other documents promising performance or non-performance of certain acts; specifying certain uses or non-uses of a property.

CRIME: A misdemeanor or a felony.

CULPA: Fault, neglect or negligence.

CURSORY EXAMINATION: A rapid inspection for visible flaws, determined by ordinary examination (i.e. skimming).

DAMAGES: The sum of money awarded to a person injured by the wrongful act or omission of another.

DBA: "Doing business as." An assumed business name or use of a trade name. In NYS, a person forming a sole proprietorship will complete and execute a business certificate, commonly referred to as a "DBA" which must be acknowledged before a notary public prior to recording at the county clerk's office.

DE BENE ESSE DEPOSITION: A sworn verbal examination of a witness whose testimony is considered important to a matter, but might otherwise be lost.

DECLARATION: An unsworn statement or narration of facts made by a party to the transaction, or by one who has an interest in the existence of the facts recounted. Also, similar statments made by a person since deceased, which are admissible in some cases, contrary to the hearsay rule (e.g. dying declarations).

DECLARANT: A person who makes a declaration.

DECLARE: To announce openly and formally; to say emphatically.

DECREE: An order or decision issued by a legal authority (i.e. courts).

DEEM: To hold to be true or consider.

DE FACTO: Actually existing, but not officially approved.

DEFENDANT: The party against whom a civil or criminal action is brought.

DE JURE: Legitimate or lawful.

DEPONENT: A person who testifies to the truth of certain facts or gives testimony under oath which is transcribed to a written statement.

DEPOSE: To make a deposition; to give evidence in the form of a deposition.

DEPOSITION: The testimony of a witness taken out of court or a hearing, under oath or affirmation, which is intended to be used at a judicial hearing or trial.

DEPRAVE: Corrupt; to make morally bad.

DISCOVERY DEPOSITION: A sworn verbal examination of a witness taken to extract facts from those individuals involved in a dispute, prior to a formal trial.

DOCUMENT: Anything printed or written which is relied upon to record or prove something.

DOWER: The provision which the law makes for a widow out of the lands of her husband. Dower has been abolished in most jurisdictions.

DRAFT: A written order of the first party (drawer) instructing a second party (drawee - i.e. bank), to pay a third party (payee).

DRAWEE: The person on whom a bill or draft is drawn. The drawee of a check is the bank on which it is drawn.

DRAWER: The person who draws a bill or draft. The drawer of a check is the person who signs it.

DUE DILIGENCE: To give proper attention to a matter on a timely basis.

DULY: In proper form or manner; according to legal requirements.

DURABLE POWER OF ATTORNEY: A signed and witnessed document which permits an individual to act for another in case of incapacitation, to make financial and accounting decisions for the principal.

DURESS: Unlawful restraint or action placed upon a person by which the person is forced to perform an act against his or her free will (i.e. a person threatening to injure another if something is not done).

E.G.: Latin abbreviation for the Latin *exempli gratia*; for the sake of an example.

ELEEMOSYNARY: Charity.

EMPOWER: Grant authority to.

ENDORSEE: The person to whom a negotiable instrument, promissory note or similar instrument is assigned, by endorsement (i.e. the party to whom a check is made payable).

ENDORSEMENT: The action of a payee, drawee, endorser or holder of a bill, note, check or other negotiable instrument, in writing his name upon the back of it, assigning and transferring the instrument (i.e. signing the back of a check to obtain the money).

ENDORSER: He who endorses (i.e. a person who signs his name as payee on the back of the check to obtain the cash or credit indicated on the front).

ENJOIN: To require a person by court order to perform or not perform some action.

ENTITY: An organization or person.

ESCROW: The status of a writing, deed, sum of money, stock or other property, put in the care of a third party until certain conditions are fulfilled.

ESTATE: The total of all real property (i.e. real estate), personal property and money owned by a person.

ET AL.: An abbreviation for the Latin *et alii* meaning "and others."

EXECUTE: To complete, perform or make; to sign.

EXECUTOR: A person appointed by a testator to carry out the directions and requests in his will and to dispose of his property according to the provisions of the last will and testament.

EXECUTRIX: A female executor.

EX OFFICIO: From office; by virtue of the office. Powers may be exercised by an officer which are not specifically given to him, but are implied in his office.

EX PARTE: On one side only; by or for one party.

EX-POST FACTO: After the fact.

EXTORTION: The obtaining of property from another by the wrongful use of actual or threatened force or violence, or under the pretense of an official right.

FELONY: Any offense punishable by death or imprisonment for a term exceeding one year; may also be punishable by fine.

FIDUCIARY: Relating to trust, confidence and good faith.

FLAGGED: A common term which refers to the fact that a document signed by a notary public has a certificate of authentication attached to it.

FOR CAUSE: For reasons that law and public policy recognize as sufficient for action.

FORGE: To create by false imitation or altering.

FORMA: Latin for "form"; the directed form of judicial and legal proceedings.

FRAUD: Intentionally distorting the truth. A deceptive practice intended to cause a person to give up a lawful right or property.

FRAUD, STATUTE OF: Law which requires that certain contracts must be in writing to be enforceable. The object of the law is to reduce the potential temptation for fraud, perjury and deception (at a later time) by forcing contracting parties to make certain agreements in writing at the moment in time that the deal is actually transacted.

FREEHOLD: An estate for life or in fee.

FREEHOLDER: One having title to realty.

GRANTEE: A person who receives the deed of real property from the grantor.

GUARDIAN: A person who is legally in charge of either a minor or someone incapable of taking care of his own affairs.

GRANTOR: The person transferring title to or an interest in real property to a grantee.

HEIR: The person appointed by law to inherit real or personal property of another person.

HEREDITAMENTS: Things capable of being inherited.

HOLOGRAPHIC WILL: A will written in the personal handwriting of the testator.

I.E., Latin abbreviation for *id est*; that is.

INCOMPETENT: A person without adequate ability or knowledge who is unable to manage his own affairs.

INC.: Incorporated.

INDEMNIFY: To make good or compensate.

INDICTMENT: A written accusation presented by a grand jury charging a person with a criminal act or omission.

INFRA: Below; opposite of supra; often used in affidavits.

IN LIEU OF: Instead of; in place of.

IN MALAM PARTEM: In a bad sense; evil.

INSOLVENCY: Inability or lack of means to pay one's debts.

INSTRUMENT: A written document; a formal or legal document in writing, such as a contract, deed, bond, will or lease.

INTEGRITY: Moral principle and character; honesty.

INTERROGATORIES: Formal written questions used in the judicial examination of a person, who must provide written answers under oath.

INTESTATE: Dying without making a will.

IN TOTO: In the whole; entirely.

INTRA VIRES: An act within the power of a person or corporation when it is within the scope of his or its power or authority.

IPSO FACTO: By the fact itself; by the mere fact.

J.D.: Abbreviation for "Juris Doctor" or "Doctor of Jurisprudence"; equivalent to "LL.B."; the university degree required to practice law.

JOSTLE: To shove or push roughly.

JUDGE: A public officer appointed to preside and administer the law in a court of justice. "Judge," "justice" and "court" are used interchangeably.

JUDGEMENT: The final decision of the court settling a dispute and determining the rights and obligations of the parties.

JURAT: The statement of an officer before whom a statement was sworn to.

JURIS: Of law.

JURISDICTION: Areas of authority; the geographic area in which a court has power or types of cases it has authority to hear.

JURISPRUDENCE: The philosophy of law.

JUST: Right; fair; lawful.

JUST CAUSE: A reason based on fair and honest grounds.

JUSTICE COURT: An inferior court (not of record) with limited civil and criminal jurisdiction, held by justices of the peace.

JUSTICE OF THE PEACE: A judicial magistrate of English origin, not of superior rank, having jurisdiction limited to civil duties (e.g., performance of marriages) and sometimes minor criminal matters. Each NYS town and village has a court, commonly referred to as a justice court. The court hears any criminal matter (including traffic violations), except felonies; however, felony arraignments and preliminary hearings are conducted. Civil cases are limited to claims of $6,000, except in small claims part where cases are limited up to claims of $2,000.

LACHES: The delay or negligence in claiming one's legal rights.

LACHES, ESTOPPEL BY: A failure to do something which should have been done; failure to claim or enforce a right at a proper time.

LAWFUL AGE: Full or legal age.

LEASE: An agreement outlining the relationship of landlord and tenant (lessor and lessee).

LEGALIZATION: The act of making certain documents which have been signed by a notary public or certified by another public officer (i.e. a certified copy of a birth, death or marriage certificate) suitable for use in another jurisdiction. See authentication; see also, apostille.

LESSEE: A person who rents property from another.

LESSOR: A person who rents property to another; landlord.

LETTERS ROGATORY: One court requesting another court (in another, independent jurisdiction) to examine a witness with written questions or interrogatories, sent with the request.

LEWD: Indecent; lustful; obscene.

LIBER: A book.

LIEN: A legal right or security attached to real (estate) or personal property until the payment of some debt, obligation or duty.

LIS PENDENS: The doctrine that pending legal action is notice to all interested parties, so that if any right is acquired from a party to such action, the transferee takes that right, subject to the outcome of the pending action. It acts to warn potential purchasers and lenders that the title to a parcel of real estate is in litigation.

LITIGATION: A lawsuit or legal action.

LITIGANT: A person involved in a lawsuit.

LIVING WILL: A signed, dated and witnessed document allowing a person to make his wishes about life-sustaining treatment known to others, in case of incapacity or inability to communicate.

LL.M. and LL.D.: Academic degrees in law—master and doctor of laws.

L.L.C.: Limited liability company.

L.L.P.: Limited liability partnership.

LOAN: One party transfers a sum of money to another, with an agreement to repay it with or without interest.

LOCUS SIGILLI: In place of the seal; the place occupied by the seal of written instruments. It is abbreviated L.S. on documents.

LOWER COURT: A NYS court with authority to try misdemeanor cases and cases of lesser severity. Examples are: village and town justice courts, police courts, city courts and district courts.

LUCID: Clear; rational; sane.

LTD.: A notation following a corporate business name, indicating its corporate status; although found in use in America, it is more commonly found in British and Canadian corporate names.

MAGISTRATE: A public civil officer empowered with limited judicial or executive power (i.e. justice of the peace).

MAJORITY: Full or legal age.

MAKER: One who makes or executes (i.e. signs a check or a note to borrow).

MAL: Bad.

MALA: Evil, wrongful or bad.

MALA IN SE: Acts morally wrong, contrary to the fundamental sense of a civilized society, such as bribery.

MALA PROHIBITA: Acts wrong, not because they are inherently evil, but for the convenience of society, such as a parking fine scofflaw.

MALFEASANCE: Evil doing or ill conduct.

MALICE: The intentional doing of a wrongful act without just cause or excuse, with an intent to inflict an injury.

MALPRACTICE: Professional misconduct or unreasonable lack of skill.

MALUM IN SE: A wrong in itself; an illegal act, based upon principles of natural, moral and public law.

MARSHAL: Federal officers who execute lawful writs, process and orders issued under the authority of the United States. U.S. Marshals may exercise the same powers in a state as a sheriff of that state. In NYS, city marshals are appointed in the City of New York and also other cities upstate. City marshals are independent public officers, not employees, similar to notaries. City marshals are compensated by fees collected for official services. City marshals execute court money judgments by locating and "marshaling" assets of debtors subject to seizure and sale at a public auction.

MERCANTILE LAW: Commercial law.

MERCANTILE PAPER: Commercial paper.

MINISTERIAL: Activities which require obedience to instructions and demand no special discretion, judgment or skill.

MINISTERIAL OFFICER: One whose duties are purely ministerial, as distinguished from executive, legislative or judicial functions.

MISCONDUCT: Neglect of duty; willful illegal behavior.

MISDEMEANOR: Any offense other than a felony, generally punishable by fine or jail, or both.

MISFEASANCE: The improper performance of a lawful act.

MORAL TURPITUDE: Shameful wickedness; anything opposed to justice, honesty, modesty or good morals.

MORTGAGE: A conditional transfer or pledge of real estate as security for the payment of a debt.

MORTGAGEE: A lender in a mortgage loan transaction.

MORTGAGOR: A borrower who transfers his or her property as security for a loan; the holder of a mortgage.

MOTION: A request made to a court or judge for obtaining some action to be done in favor of the applicant.

MUNICIPAL: Associated with a local government unit such as a city, town or village.

N.A.: An abbreviation for not applicable or not available.

N.B.: An abbreviation for the Latin *nota bene,* meaning "note well" or "mark well."

NEGLIGENCE: The omission to do something which a reasonable person would do or not do.

NEGOTIABLE: Legally capable of being transferred by endorsement or delivery; usually refers to checks, notes, bonds and stocks.

NEGOTIATE: To discuss with a view of reaching agreement; to settle, transfer or sell.

NIL: Nothing.

NOMINAL DAMAGES: Award of an insignificant sum in which no substantial injury was proved to have occurred.

NONFEASANCE: Nonperformance of some act which ought to be performed; omission to perform a required duty at all or total neglect of duty.

NOTARIAL: Taken by a notary; performed by a notary in his official capacity; belonging to a notary and proving his official character, such as a notarial seal.

NOTARIAL ACTS: Official acts of a notary public.

NOTE: A document containing a promise of signer (i.e. maker) to pay a specified person or bearer a definite sum of money at a specified time.

NOTE OF PROTEST: A brief written statement of the fact of a protest, signed by the notary public on the bill, which will be transcribed into proper form at a later time.

NOTICE: Information; knowledge of the existence of a fact or state of affairs; a written warning intended to inform a person of some hearing or trial in which his interests are involved.

NULL: Of no validity or effect; void.

OATH: An outward, oral pledge given by the person taking it that his promise is made under an immediate sense of his responsibility to God; a solemn invocation or call for the punishment of God upon the oath taker (affiant, deponent or witness) if he does not declare the whole truth.

OBLIGEE: Receiver of a promise.

OBLIGOR: A person who makes a promise.

OFFENSE: A felony or misdemeanor; a breach of the criminal laws.

OFFER: A proposal to do a thing or pay an amount, usually accompanied by an expected acceptance, counter-offer, return promise or act.

OFFEREE: The receiver of an offer.

OFFEROR: In contracts, the party who makes the offer and looks for acceptance from the offeree.

OMBUDSMAN: A Swedish word meaning "representative" or "attorney"; an official state office which receives citizens' complaints connected with the government. The ombudsman represents the citizen and acts before government on his/her behalf.

OMISSION: The intentional or unintentional neglect to perform what is required.

ORAL CONTRACT: An agreement which is partly written and partly depends on spoken words, or is totally unwritten.

ORDER: A mandate, rule or regulation; command or direction given by an authority.

ORDINANCE: A written law or statute created by the legislative body of a municipality (i.e. a city council).

ORDINARY POWER OF ATTORNEY: A signed and dated (and usually acknowledged) document authorizing another person to make decisions for a principal. This lapses if the principal becomes incompetent.

OVERDRAFT: A check written on a checking account containing less funds than the amount written on the face of the check.

OVERT: Public; open.

PACT: A bargain or agreement.

PAR: Equal; equity.

PARALEGAL: A person with legal skills, but who is not an attorney and who works under the supervision of a lawyer.

PARDON: To release from further punishment and forgive an offense; an official document granting a pardon.

PAROL: Oral or verbal.

PAROL CONTRACT: An oral contract as distinguished from a written or formal contract.

PAROL EVIDENCE: Oral or verbal evidence.

PAROLE: The procedure in which a convict is released from jail, prison or other confinement on good behavior, after serving part of his term, but before the expiration of his sentence.

PATENT: Open; obvious; evident.

PAYEE: The person to whom a bill, note or check is made or drawn.

PAYOR: The person who has drawn a note.

PECULATION: The unlawful granting of property; falsely granting entrusted money or goods to oneself.

PECUNIARY: Monetary; relating to money; financial.

PENAL: Punishable; inflicting a punishment; containing a penalty.

PENALTY: Punishment, civil or criminal; a financial punishment.

PEREMPTORY: Final; decisive; absolute.

PERFORMANCE: The fulfillment or accomplishment of a promise, contract or other obligation according to its terms.

PERIL: Risk or hazard.

PERJURY: Making a false statement under oath (or affirmation), swearing or affirming its truth, when the statement is not believed to be true.

PER SE: By itself; simply as such.

PERSON: A natural, human being; also any corporation, joint stock company, estate, general partnership (including a limited liability partnership or foreign limited liability partnership), limited liability company (including a foreign professional service limited liability company), foreign limited liability company (including a foreign professional service limited liability company), joint venture, limited partnership, attorney in fact, real estate investment trust, business trust, custodian, nominee, or any other individual or entity in its own or any representative capacity.

PETITION: A formal written document requesting court action on a certain matter.

PETITIONER: One who presents a request to a court, officer or legislative body.

PETTY: Small; minor.

PETTY OFFENSE: A crime with a maximum punishment of a fine or short term in a jail or house of correction. Any misdemeanor in which the penalty does not exceed imprisonment for a period of six months or a maximum fine of $500, or both.

P.L.: An abbreviation for "Public Laws."

PLAINTIFF: A person who starts a lawsuit.

PLEA: The defendant's answer to charges against him.

PLEADINGS: The formal charges or responses by the parties in a lawsuit of their respective claims and defenses.

POST-DATED CHECK: A draft (check) presented before the date written on it.

POWER OF ATTORNEY: An instrument authorizing another to act as one's agent or attorney. His power is legally revoked upon the death of the principal; an ordinary power of attorney.

PRESCRIBE: To direct.

PRESENTS: Now existing; at hand; relating to the present time. The body of many legal documents begins with the phrase "Know all men by these presents."

PRESENTER: Any person presenting a draft or demand for payment for honor under a credit.

PRESENTMENT: The production of a negotiable instrument to the drawee for his acceptance or to the drawer or acceptor for payment.

PRIMA FACIE: Presumable; a fact thought to be true unless disproved by evidence.

PRIMA FACIE EVIDENCE: Evidence sufficient to establish a fact, unless disproved by other evidence.

PRINCIPAL: A person who has permitted or directed another to act for his benefit.

PROBABLE CAUSE: Reasonable cause.

PROBATE: Court procedure by which a will is proved to be valid or invalid.

PROBATION: Allowing a person convicted of a minor offense to go free under a conditional suspension of sentence, during good behavior, generally under the supervision of a probation officer.

PRO BONO PUBLICO: For the public good.

PROCEEDING: The form and manner of conducting judicial business before a court or judicial officer.

PROCESS: Any method used by the court to get or use its jurisdiction over a person or a specific property; the summons or notice of the beginning of a lawsuit.

PROCUREMENT: Obtaining.

PRO FACTO: For the fact; as a fact.

PRO FORMA: As a matter of form or for the sake of form.

PROMISSORY: Containing or consisting of a promise.

PROMISSORY ESTOPPEL: A promise given by a party that induces another party to act and which may be enforceable (without consideration). The promise is enforced by refusing to allow the promisor to establish the defense of no consideration; the promisor is "estopped" from asserting the lack of consideration.

PROMISSORY NOTE: A written promise made by one or more persons to pay a specific amount of money (or other items of value) to a named person.

PROMULGATE: To officially announce.

PROOF OF EXECUTION: A formal declaration made by a subscribing witness to the execution of an instrument or document.

PROPER CARE: The degree of care which a cautious person would use under similar circumstances.

PROPRIETOR: One who has the legal right or exclusive title to anything; an owner.

PRO RATA: Proportionately.

PROSECUTE: To file criminal proceedings against a person.

PROTEST: A formal written statement by a notary public (under seal) that a specific bill of exchange or promissory note was presented on a certain day for payment or acceptance and was refused; in maritime law, a written statement sworn to by the master of a vessel before a notary public, verifying that damage suffered by the ship and/or cargo on her voyage was caused by storms or other dangers of the sea beyond his control (without negligence or misconduct).

PROTHONOTARY: The title given (e.g. in Pennsylvania) to an officer who officiates as principal clerk of some courts.

PROTONOTARY: Originally a chief ecclesiastical notary, later a member of the college of protonotaries apostolic of the Roman curia; also an honorary title conferred by the Pope granting certain privileges to the bearer.

PROVISO: A condition, stipulation, limitation or provision included in a deed, lease, mortgage or contract that will validate the instrument. It usually begins with the word "provided."

PROXY: A person who is substituted or assigned by another to represent and act for him.

PUBLIC OFFENSE: An act or omission forbidden and punishable by law. It describes a crime as compared to an infringement of private rights.

PUBLIC OFFICIAL: The holder of a public office; not all persons in public employment are public officials.

PUNITIVE: Relating to punishment.

PURPORT: To imply; intend; claim.

PURSUANT: A following after or following out. To carry out in accordance with terms of a contract or by reason of something.

QUALIFIED: Applied to one who has taken all of the steps to prepare himself for an appointment to office, such as taking/filing the oath of office.

QUASH: To make void or vacate.

QUASI: As if.

RATIFY: To approve.

RE: Regarding the matter of (i.e. "In re: . . . ").

REAL ESTATE: Land and anything permanently affixed to the land, such as buildings, fences and items attached to the buildings, such as light, plumbing and heating fixtures (or other items which would be personal property if not attached).

REALTY: A term for real property or real estate.

REASONABLE AND PROBABLE CAUSE: Reasons that justify suspecting a person of a crime and placing him in custody.

REASONABLE CARE: The degree of care which a person of ordinary caution would exercise in the same or similar circumstances.

REASONABLE DOUBT: Doubt that would cause reasonable people to hesitate before acting in matters of importance to themselves.

REBUT: To contradict or oppose.

RECALCITRANT: Stubbornly resistant to authority or guidance.

RECEIVER: A "neutral" person appointed by a court to manage property in litigation or the affairs of a bankrupt.

RECIDIVIST: A habitual criminal; a criminal repeater.

RECIPROCITY: Mutuality. The relationship existing between two states when each of them gives the residents of the other certain privileges, on the condition that its own residents will enjoy the privileges of the other state.

RECOGNIZANCE: An obligation entered into before a court or magistrate in which the recognizer declares that he will do some act required by and specified by law. An obligation undertaken by a person, generally a defendant in a criminal case, to appear in court on a particular day or to keep peace. It may not require a bond.

RECORDER: A public officer of a municipality charged with the duty of keeping the record books required by law to be maintained in his or her office. The recorder receives/copies documents legally entitled to be recorded.

REFEREE: A person to whom a court case is referred (by the court) to take testimony, hear parties and report the results to the court. The person acts as a judicial officer and is an extension of the court for a specific purpose; attorneys are typically appointed.

REGISTER: An officer authorized by law to keep a record called a "register" or "registry."

REGISTRY: A register or book legally authorized or recognized for the recording or registration of facts or documents.

RELATIVE: A person connected with another by either blood or marriage.

RELEASE: The giving up or abandoning of a right or claim to another.

RELEASEE: The person to whom a release is made.

RELEASOR: A person who makes a release.

REMIT: To send.

REPLEVIN: An action in which the owner regains possession of his own goods.

REPUDIATE: To reject a right, duty, obligation or privilege.

RESPONDENT: The party against whom a petition is made in a legal action (i.e. petitioner v. respondent).

RESTRAINING ORDER: A command forbidding the defendant to do a threatened act until a hearing can be held.

RETAINER: A fee paid to engage a professional's service (i.e. a lawyer or accountant).

REVOCATION: The recall of some power, authority or thing granted.

SAFE DEPOSIT BOX: A sturdy container kept by a customer in a bank, in which he deposits papers, securities and other valuable items. Two keys are required to open the box; one is retained by the bank and the other by the customer.

SALE: A contract between two parties, seller and buyer, in which the seller, for payment or promise of payment of a certain price in money, transfers to the buyer, the title and possession of property.

SANCTION: The penalty that will be given to a wrongdoer for breaking the law.

SEAL: An impression upon wax, wafer or other moldable material capable of being impressed. In current practice, a particular sign (i.e. "L.S.") or the word "seal" is sometimes made instead of an actual seal to attest the execution of the instrument.

SEALED: Authenticated by a seal; executed by the affixing of a seal.

SELF-PROVE: In self-proving a will, the testator and witnesses will swear to and sign an affidavit before a notary public declaring that the document is truly the testator's will and that it was lawfully executed. The affidavit of execution is attached to the will, but is not a part of the actual will document.

SELLER: Vendor; a person who has contracted to sell goods or property.

SETTLEMENT: An agreement.

SHAM: Something false or fake.

SHERIFF: A county officer chosen by popular election (except in New York City, Long Island and Westchester County) whose principal duties are to aid criminal and civil courts. The sheriff is the chief preserver of the peace who serves processes, summons juries, executes judgments and holds judicial sales.

SHOW CAUSE ORDER: An order to appear (in court) and present reasons as to why a particular order should not be confirmed, take effect or be executed.

SHYSTER: A dishonest or deceitful business or professional person.

SIGHT DRAFT: An instrument payable on presentation (i.e. check).

SIGILLUM: Latin for "a seal"; originally a seal impressed upon wax.

SIGLA: Latin for "marks or signs of abbreviation" used in writing.

SIGNATURE: The action of putting one's name at the end of an document to certify its validity. A signature may be written by hand, printed, or stamped. Whatever mark, symbol or device a person may choose to represent himself. A signature may be made by using any name, including any trade or assumed name or by a word or mark instead of a written signature, including a fingerprint.

SIGNATURE CARD: A card which a bank or other financial institution requires from its customers on which they put their signatures and other data.

SILENCE: The state of a person who does not speak or refrains from speaking. In the law of estoppel, "silence" implies knowledge and an opportunity to act upon it.

SILENCE, ESTOPPEL BY: A person is under a duty to another to speak; failure to speak is not appropriate during honest dealings.

SMALL CLAIMS COURT: A special court which provides quick, informal and inexpensive settling of small claims; limited to small debts, accounts and other matters up to $2,000.00 in New York.

SPECIAL COURT: A NYS court with authority to hear matters on specific subject matters. Examples are: county surrogate court and county family court.

SS.: An abbreviation used in a record, pleading or affidavit called the "statement of venue." A contraction of the Latin *scilicet.*

STALE CHECK: A check which is dated much earlier than the date of its presentation or negotiation. In New York, a personal or business check is "stale" after six months; a federal social security check after 12 months.

STANDARD OF CARE: The degree of care which a reasonably prudent person would exercise under similar conditions.

STARE DECISIS: Latin for "let the decision stand." The principle that the decisions of the court should stand as guidance for future cases; basis of common law.

STATUTE: The written law as opposed to the unwritten or common law.

STATUTE OF FRAUDS: The law that requires certain contracts to be written or partially complied with, in order to be legally enforceable.

STATUTE OF LIMITATIONS: The time limit that legal action must take place or rights be enforced. After the time period set by law, no legal action can be brought, regardless of whether any cause of action existed.

STATUTORY: Relating to a statute.

STAY: A stopping; the act of stopping a judicial proceedings by the order of a court.

STIPULATE: Arrange or settle.

SUBORDINATION CLAUSE: A clause or statement which permits the placing of a mortgage at a later date, taking priority over an existing mortgage.

SUBORN PERJURY: The offense of securing a sworn statement or testimony which was known to be false (e.g., a notary knowingly notarizes a false statement and was responsible for suggesting that the attesting person make a false statement under oath).

SUBPOENA AD TESTIFICANDUM: A command requiring a witness to appear at a certain time and place to give testimony before a court or magistrate; ordinary subpoena.

SUBPOENA DUCES TECUM: A command which requires a witness to produce certain documents or records in a trial or hearing.

SUBSCRIBE: To write underneath (i.e. name) at the end of a document.

SUBSCRIBER: A person who adds his signature to any document.

SUBSTANTIAL: Of considerable value.

SUBVERSION: The act or process of overthrowing, destroying or corrupting.

SUE: To start, continue and carry out legal action against another.

SUFFICIENT CAUSE: Cause of a substantial nature directly affecting the public's rights and interests, concerning an officer's qualifications or performance of duties, showing that he is not fit or proper to hold office.

SUMMONS: A document issued and served to a defendant in a civil suit informing him of the action and that he is required to appear in court.

SUPERIOR COURT: A NYS court with authority to try felony cases and hear appeals of lower court case judgments or decisions. Examples are: supreme court (New York City) and county courts (outside New York City).

SUPERSEDE: Set aside, annul or replace.

SUPRA: Above (i.e. found in superseding text of document).

SURETY: A person responsible for the debt or promise of another.

SURROGATE: The title given to the NYS judge who has jurisdiction over the administration of probate matters (wills) and guardianships.

SUSTAIN: To affirm or approve; to support.

SWEAR: To put under oath; to administer an oath to a person; to take an oath.

SWINDLE: To defraud (another) of money or property; cheat.

SWORN: Verified.

SYNOPSIS: A brief or partial statement; a summary.

TAMPER To alter, especially to make illegal.

TANGIBLE: Having physical form.

TENANT: One who holds lands of another; a renter.

TENDER: An offer of money.

TENEMENTS: At common law, included lands, or other inheritances, capable of being held in freehold, and rents.

TERM: A fixed and definite period of time during which the law prescribes that an officer may hold an office.

TESTABLE: Having the legal capacity of making a will.

TESTACY: Leaving a will at one's death.

TESTAMENT: The disposition of personal property by will.

TESTAMENTUM: A will or last will.

TESTATION: Witness; evidence.

TESTATOR: The person who makes (or had made) a valid will.

TESTATRIX: A woman who makes (or had made) a valid will.

TESTES: Witnesses to the signing of a will.

TESTIFY: To give evidence as a witness. To make a solemn declaration under oath or affirmation.

TESTIMONIUM CLAUSE: The clause of a document that ends with "In witness whereof, the parties to these presents have hereunto set their hands and seals."

TESTIMONY: Evidence given by a competent witness under oath or affirmation.

THREAT: A communicated intent to inflict physical or other harm on any person or property.

TITLE: The certificate which acts as evidence of ownership.

TORT: A civil or private wrong/injury, either with or without force, against the person or property of another, for which the court will provide a remedy (in damages). It does not include breach of contract, but it can include interference with a contract (e.g. inducing a breach).

TORTIOUS: Wrongful.

TRAFFIC INFRACTION: The violation of a vehicle and traffic law not declared to be a misdemeanor or felony. A traffic infraction is not a crime and the punishment given may not be considered penal or criminal punishment; conviction will not impair his credibility as a witness.

TRANSACT: To negotiate; to carry on business; perform.

TRANSCRIPT: An official copy of a document or writing; usually refers to the record of a trial or hearing.

TREBLE DAMAGES: Damages given by law in certain cases, consisting of the award of damages (which are tripled in amount) found by the jury.

TRIBUNAL: The seat of a judge; the place where the judge administers justice.

TRUE COPY: Not an absolutely exact copy, but an accurate replica of the original (in content).

TRUST: A right of property, real or personal, held by one party for the benefit of another.

TRUSTEE: A person holding property in trust for another (e.g. a lawyer, bank, group, etc.).

TRUST FUND: Money or property set aside as a trust for the benefit of another and held by a trustee.

TRUSTOR: One who creates a trust.

ULTERIOR: Intentionally kept concealed or hidden.

UNDUE INFLUENCE: Whatever destroys free will and causes a person to do something he would not do if left to his own free decision.

ULTRA VIRES: Actions which are beyond the power of a person or corporation when it is not within the scope of his or its power or authority.

USURY: The practice of lending money at an excessive or illegal rate of interest.

UTTER: To put or send into circulation; to publish or offer.

VACATE: To put an end to; to make empty or vacant.

VAGRANT: Wandering or going from place to place by an idle person who has no lawful or visible means of support and who survives on charity and does not work, although capable.

VEND: To sell.

VENDEE: A purchaser or buyer.

VENDOR: The person who sells property.

VENUE: The particular municipality in which a court with jurisdiction may hear and determine the case; it also refers to the actual location where an official act takes place (i.e. an acknowledgment).

VERDICT: The formal and unanimous decision or finding made by a jury, reported to the court and accepted by it.

VERIFIED COPY: Copy of a document which is proved by independent evidence to be true.

VERIFY: To confirm or substantiate by oath of affidavit. Particularly used of making formal oath to accounts, court petitions or pleadings, or other papers. In NYS, it is frequently used interchangeably with "sworn."

VERILY: In very truth; beyond doubt or question; in fact; certainly; truly; confidently.

VIGILANCE: Watchfulness; precaution.

VILE: Morally evil; wicked.

VINCINAGE: The county where a trial is had or a crime has been committed.

VINDICATE: To clear of suspicion, blame or doubt.

VOID: Null; having no legal force or binding effect.

V.: An abbreviation for versus (against), commonly used in legal proceedings and entitling cases; may also appear as (vs.).

WAIVE: To abandon; throw away; surrender a claim privilege or right.

WAIVER: The voluntary and intentional surrender of a known right.

WANTON: Reckless; malicious.

WARRANT: A written order based upon a complaint issued according to law and/or court rule which requires law enforcement officers to arrest a person and bring him before a magistrate or judge.

WILL: A legal document directing the disposal of one's property after death.

WITNESS: To write one's name to a deed, last will or other document for the purpose of declaring its authenticity and proving its execution.

WRIT: An order issued by a court requiring the performance of a specified act or giving authority to do it.

Sample Examinations

The following four sample examinations are provided *strictly* for study and review purposes.

For those preparing to take their pre-appointment examination, it is recommended that the "practice exam period" be limited to a maximum of 60 minutes in order to simulate the actual time constraint of the official state examination.

Commissioned notaries public will find the sample examinations helpful for reviewing, refreshing and testing their knowledge.

EXAMINATION ADVICE

1. Make a study plan early. Pick a target examination date that fits into your personal schedule and set time aside to read, study and review. The ideal study plan is to allow at least a few weeks for preparation.
2. Select a quiet and comfortable study site. If your home is not desirable for study, consider alternative places to study. Visit your local public or university library. Construct a study plan with your calendar. Make a mini-lesson plan for each study session. Don't attempt to accomplish too much in each study session.
3. Get a good night's sleep the night prior to the exam. If you live a considerable distance from the examination city, consider traveling to the examination city the night before and stay at a local motel or hotel. If you are not familiar with the examination site, take a practice drive to the area the night before to check out the building, best places to park, etc. Avoid late night study and consuming too much caffeine.
4. Eat a good breakfast on the morning of the examination. Arrive early—at least 30 minutes prior to the examination. It is not uncommon for test sites to fill to capacity 30–45 minutes before the scheduled start time. Once the examination room is full, you will likely be turned away and have to return on another day. If possible, avoid stressful situations on the evening before and the morning before the examination. If you have the flexibility, it might be helpful to avoid going into the office, even for a little while, before your examination. Consider taking a vacation or personal day on the examination day to reduce stress and help to keep your mind clear.
5. Don't be pressured by proctors. You have paid for the entire examination time allotted. Even if you are the last examinee to leave and the proctors are checking their watches, looking at you, talking with one another about an early lunch, etc., do not be intimidated. You will also notice a few people who will race through the examination, leaving remarkably early. Don't get distracted by these people. Keep focused on your test. Remember, if you take about a minute to carefully read, think about and select an answer for each question, it should take approximately 30–40 minutes. If you take a few more minutes to double-check your work, comparing the ques-

tions with your answer sheet, it should take nearly the entire hour period.

6. Upon being instructed to start your examination by the proctors, look through the entire examination from start to finish. Make sure it has the required number of pages and the pages do not contain any printer errors. Quickly scan each question to get a general sense of the entire test. You'll start to feel much better after you notice a few questions that you are familiar with and know the answers.
7. Don't waste time agonizing over a confusing question. Read the question again, slowly. If you don't know it, skip it and return to it later. It is possible that as you relax a little and begin to focus on your work, you'll start to remember more than you thought you knew. In addition, some later questions may jog your memory and enable you to recall some helpful facts that you forgot you knew.
8. Re-check your work. Make sure you correctly marked your answer sheet with the intended selection. Remember, a wrong answer is wrong forever. Make sure that you don't leave any questions unanswered. Try to read through each question and eliminate answers which are clearly incorrect.
9. Don't walk out of the examination center and start to compare answers with your fellow examinees. This can be very frustrating and even serve to discourage you needlessly. In fact, you may have answered some questions differently from your fellow examinees, but that doesn't mean you won't be successful in passing your examination. There will likely be several different versions of examinations being distributed at your examination site.

Suggested Study Action Plan

1. Attend a notary public class. Contact your local community college or university continuing and adult education department and register for a notary public class designed for individuals preparing to take the New York State pre-appointment notary public examination.
2. This book contains four, all-new and completely revised practice examinations. Each examination is styled after the official New York State examination style. Each practice examination is entirely multiple-choice. At the conclusion of the practice

examinations, the answer key for each practice examination is provided. The correct answer is supplied along with a detailed explanation about the correct answer as well as the incorrect answers. Choose a practice examination. Under simulated, closed-book test conditions (quiet place, no unnecessary interruptions, no references, no checking the answer key), take a practice examination. Rather than write your answers in the book, mark your answers down on a separate sheet of paper. After you finish your examination and correct your work, you will likely surprise yourself with how much you already know. If you don't know as much as you would like to know, don't worry. You certainly will score progressively better on the next three practice examinations.

3. Read this book at a comfortable pace. The chapters are short and there are numerous illustrations to help illuminate the concepts. Do not skip the glossary. Pay special attention to the glossary. Make certain that you are familiar with the unique and unusual legal jargon. The state examination will be filled with this legal jargon. In order to better understand each question and pick the correct answer, your thorough command of legal terminology is essential. You will likely be pleasantly surprised about how many legal terms you already know. One of the most important parts of this book is the glossary. Your command of this legal vocabulary will not only assist you with passing the examination, but greatly enhance your future experience as a notary public. Many of the terms and concepts that you will read in this book will also assist you in your personal life and employment career.
4. After—but not before—you have carefully and thoroughly read and studied all of the chapters and the glossary of this book, now proceed to read appendix c—the New York State Department of State Examination Study Material. The material contained in appendix c is provided strictly for your convenience. The material is printed verbatim from the state source; no editing has been performed by the author. Although most readers do not find this appendix reading assignment very enjoyable, or even helpful, your prior preparation will help you navigate successfully through this material. It is essential that you read through this appendix—after you have thoroughly read through this book up to and including the glossary.

5. Now you are ready to proceed to challenge yourself and advance to taking and passing the three remaining practice examinations. Do not skip any one examination. So that your examination preparation is complete, it is vital that you work through all of the examinations—twice. By reading and answering all four examinations—twice, you will have reviewed all of the concepts, principles, laws and legal terminology required for success on your actual examination and also as a practicing notary.

   All the best!

SAMPLE EXAMINATION A

1. Prior to receiving a suspension of his commission as a notary public by the secretary of state, the accused person shall be entitled to which of the following?
   A. A hearing before a judge of a court of record.
   B. A hearing before an administrative law judge.
   C. A hearing before a city judge or a town or village judge or justice.
   D. A writ of certiorari.

2. A safe deposit box lessor may force open a safe deposit box if the lessee does not pay the box rent due for one year, or if he does not remove the contents within (. . .) days of termination of the box lease.
   A. 30.
   B. 45.
   C. 60.
   D. 90.

3. A law established by an act of the state legislature is a(n):
   A. ordinance.
   B. statute.
   C. rule.
   D. bylaw.

4. Executive law section 130 states that no person shall be appointed as a notary public under this article who has been convicted, in this state or any other state or territory, of a felony . . ., and who has not subsequent to such conviction received a(n):
   A. executive pardon therefore or a certificate of good conduct from the state parole board.
   B. executive pardon therefore or a certificate of relief from disabilities from the state parole board or court.
   C. commutation.
   D. reprieve from the governor.

5. A notary public is presented with a business contract for a corporation. After scanning the document, the notary observes that a corporation acknowledgment certificate is

printed at the conclusion of the document. The contract is presented by a person who claims to be a corporation officer. Which of the following duties is not legally required and would be inappropriate for the notary to perform?

A. Request corporate identification documentation.
B. Request personal identification credentials.
C. Have the person swear to the information contained in the acknowledgment certificate.
D. Review the acknowledgment certificate to assure, if described in the acknowledgment recitals, that the seal of the corporation has been affixed to the contract.

6. Any form of attestation by which a person signifies that he is bound to perform an act faithfully and truthfully is a(n):
   A. acknowledgment.
   B. oath.
   C. testation.
   D. decree.

7. Real property law, section 298, acknowledgments and proofs within the state, provides that an acknowledgment or proof, within this state, of a conveyance of real property situate in this state, may be made at any place before:
   A. (a) a justice of the supreme court; (b) an official examiner of title; (c) an official referee; or (d) a notary public.
   B. (a) a justice of the court of appeals; (b) a county court judge; (c) a town clerk; or (d) a notary public.
   C. (a) a justice of the peace; (b) a surrogate; (c) a town judge; or (d) a notary public.
   D. (a) a justice of the peace; (b) a court of claims judge; (c) a district court judge; or (d) a notary public.

8. The term of office that a notary public is appointed for is:
   A. ten years.
   B. two years.
   C. three years.
   D. four years.

9. According to the New York State Supreme Court case, *Bookman v. City of New York,* which of the following is the simplest form in which an oath may be administered?

A. "Is this true?"
B. "Do you solemnly swear that the content of this affidavit subscribed by you is true and correct?"
C. "Are you familiar with the content of this document?"
D. "Do you acknowledge that this is your signature?"

10. The state crime of issuing a false certificate is classified as a:
A. class b felony.
B. class c felony.
C. class d felony.
D. class e felony.

11. Executive law section 130 provides that the secretary of state may suspend or remove from office, for misconduct, any notary public appointed by him but no such removal shall be made unless the person who is sought to be removed shall:
A. have been mailed a copy of the charges against him and have an opportunity to respond in writing by mail.
B. have been served with a copy of the charges against him and have an opportunity of being heard.
C. have been properly arrested, orally informed of his constitutional rights and arraigned before a judge of a court of record.
D. have been contacted by telegram with a copy of the charges against him and have an opportunity to respond in writing by mail.

12. To qualify for the office of notary public, the required minimum length of state residency is:
A. two years.
B. six months.
C. thirty days.
D. one day.

13. According to executive law, the secretary of state may appoint and commission as many notaries public for the state of New York as in his judgment may be deemed best, whose jurisdiction shall:
A. extend to the borders of the city of New York, if he resides or is employed in the city.
B. extend to the borders of the state.

C. extend to the borders of the county in which the applicant resides.
D. extend to the borders of the judicial district in which the applicant resides.

14. The state penal law provides that an officer before whom an oath or affidavit may be taken is bound to administer it when requested. A refusal by the officer to comply is a crime, specifically a misdemeanor, carrying a maximum jail sentence of:
A. thirty days.
B. ten days.
C. six months.
D. any term less than one year.

15. A notary public is presented with a pre-printed legal form by a person for notarial service. Upon reviewing the form, the notary detects an individual acknowledgment certificate at the conclusion of the form. However, the person has not yet completed the document, which is "essentially in blank". Therefore, the notary should decline to proceed to officiate until:
A. the person presents satisfactory identification.
B. the person swears that he has signed the form.
C. the person fully completes and executes the form.
D. he is positive that the signature is that of the person before him.

16. In the state of New York, the criminal offense of the practice of law without a license is a:
A. misdemeanor.
B. felony.
C. infraction.
D. violation.

17. A notary public has a co-worker present him with an affidavit in connection with a traffic court trial. The co-worker is personally known to the notary. In addition to correctly marking the venue, the notary is legally required to perform all of the following, except:
A. administer an oral oath to the affiant.

B. require personal identification from the affiant.
C. attach and execute a jurat.
D. require execution of the affidavit in his presence.

18. Of the following public offices, which one is not compatible with an appointment to the office of notary public?
    A. Commissioner of elections.
    B. Inspector of elections.
    C. Sheriff.
    D. State legislator.

19. In the event that a notary public willfully fails to mark the venue upon a document, which of the following is he likely to encounter?
    A. Discipline by the secretary of state.
    B. Court action by the document signer.
    C. Lawsuit by an interested party.
    D. Request for judicial intervention (RJI) by a local bar association.

20. An individual presents a conveyance for real property to a notary public. Beneath his own executing signature, on the reverse side of the conveyance, the following statement is printed: "On the [day] of [month], [year], before me personally came . . . , to me personally known, and known to be one of the individuals described in, and who has executed the foregoing instrument, and duly acknowledged that he executed the same as his free act and deed." The notary should proceed to:
    A. Perform and certify a proof of execution.
    B. Administer an oath.
    C. Take and certify an acknowledgment.
    D. Request that the person sign his name again in his personal presence.

21. A notary public who knowingly makes a false certificate, that a deed or other written instrument was acknowledged by a person, is guilty of the crime of:
    A. forgery in the first degree.
    B. forgery in the second degree.
    C. perjury in the first degree.
    D. perjury in the second degree.

22. Pursuant to state banking law, who must be present at a forced opening of an abandoned safe deposit box?
    A. Bank guard and notary public.
    B. Bank officer and notary public.
    C. Attorney-in-fact and notary public.
    D. Notary public.

23. A notary public who is a resident of New York state changes his residence to another state. Which of the following situations would permit him to retain his appointment to the office of notary public?
    A. Register as a qualified voter in New York.
    B. Hold a bank checking account in New York.
    C. Maintain a place of business or office in New York.
    D. File a certificate of official character in New York.

24. For notarial purposes, a notary public who undergoes a lawful name change may discontinue signing her former name as noted on her notary public identification card:
    A. immediately upon the legal change.
    B. at the conclusion of her current term.
    C. never during in her lifetime.
    D. as soon as she files the notice of change of name with the appropriate fee at the department of state.

25. A useful consequence of taking an acknowledgment in connection with a conveyance for real property is:
    A. verification of the identity of the signer.
    B. description of the property.
    C. proof of an equitable sale.
    D. determination of any lien holder.

26. In the event of a forced safe deposit box opening, how many days prior to the public auction of the contents must the legal notice be published in the local newspaper?
    A. Five.
    B. Ten.
    C. Fifteen.
    D. Sixty.

27. While not explicitly required by state statute, a notary public should purchase and utilize an embossing seal (along with

marking the statement of authority) on all documents because:
A. many federal and state laws strongly imply its use.
B. it assists to deter acts of forgery and fraud.
C. it reinforces the legal importance of the official act being performed by the notary.
D. of all of these reasons.

28. The fee to secure an apostille from the NYS department of state is:
A. $5.
B. $10.
C. $20.
D. $25.

29. Committing a crime other than a felony is a(n):
A. infraction.
B. misdemeanor.
C. tort.
D. breach.

30. In connection with protesting a dishonored negotiable instrument, the maximum fee that may be collected for the certificate of protest is:
A. $.10.
B. $.25.
C. $.75.
D. $2.00.

31. Behavior disrespectful of the authority of a court which disrupts the execution of court orders is:
A. subordination.
B. contempt.
C. insubordination.
D. conspiracy.

32. Which statutory law volume authorizes a deposition to be taken before a notary public in a civil proceeding?
A. Domestic relations law.
B. Election law.
C. Public officers law.
D. Civil practice law and rules.

33. A notary public is presented with an affidavit by an individual who is personally known to him. The notary should proceed to:
   A. administer an oral oath.
   B. administer a written oath.
   C. take an acknowledgment.
   D. take a proof of execution.

34. According to public officers law, each county clerk shall designate from among the members of his or staff at least . . . to be available to serve the public in his office during normal business hours.
   A. five notaries public.
   B. three notaries public.
   C. two notaries public.
   D. one notary public.

35. All of the following identification documents are recommended for reasonable identity purposes, except:
   A. a valid driver's license.
   B. a valid U.S. passport.
   C. an original, sealed birth certificate.
   D. a valid military identification card.

36. Which of the following acts may not be performed on Sunday?
   A. Taking and certifying a civil deposition.
   B. Protesting a dishonored negotiable instrument.
   C. Verifying a civil complaint.
   D. Taking and certifying a criminal deposition.

37. Before issuing to any applicant a commission as notary public, unless he be an attorney and counsellor at law duly admitted to practice in this state, the secretary of state shall satisfy himself that the applicant is of:
   A. good moral character, has the equivalent of a high school education and is familiar with the duties and responsibilities of a notary public.
   B. good moral character, has the equivalent of a common school education and is familiar with the duties and responsibilities of a notary public.

C. good moral character, has the equivalent of a trade school education and is familiar with the duties and responsibilities of a notary public.
D. good moral character, has the equivalent of a middle school education and is familiar with the duties and responsibilities of a notary public.

38. In New York, the source of the official state forms of ceremonies for oaths and affirmations is:
A. executive law.
B. public officers law.
C. penal law.
D. civil practice law and rules.

39. The fee to obtain a certificate of official character for a notary public from a county clerk is:
A. $1.
B. $5.
C. $10.
D. $15.

40. The certification subjoined by a county clerk to any certificate of acknowledgment or proof, or oath certificate, signed by a notary public is a(n):
A. exoneration.
B. nullification.
C. authentication.
D. examination-before-trial.

SAMPLE EXAMINATION B

1. The civil practice law and rules authorize a deposition to be taken before a notary public in a(n):
   A. criminal proceeding.
   B. civil proceeding.
   C. administrative proceeding.
   D. legislative proceeding.

2. A notary public has administered an oath to a person in connection with a deposition, and has collected the lawfully permitted fee. After marking the venue and jurat, and his official signature, statement of authority and seal, the notary is entitled to collect:
   A. $.25.
   B. $.75.
   C. $2.00.
   D. $0.00.

3. The sentence of imprisonment for a class a misdemeanor shall not exceed:
   A. one year.
   B. one and a half years.
   C. two years.
   D. three years.

4. According to domestic relations law, a notary public has no authority to:
   A. administer an oath to a petitioner for divorce.
   B. administer an oath for a man to acknowledge paternity.
   C. take and certify the acknowledgment of parties and witnesses to a pre-nuptial or ante-nuptial contract.
   D. take and certify the acknowledgment of parties and witnesses to a marriage contract.

5. A notary public is often classified as a(n):
   A. ministerial officer.
   B. executive officer.
   C. judicial officer.
   D. legislative officer.

6. Penal law section 195.00, official misconduct, declares a public servant is guilty of official misconduct when, with intent to obtain a benefit or deprive another person of a benefit: (1) he commits an act relating to his office, but constituting an unauthorized exercise of his official functions, knowing that such act is unauthorized; or (2) he knowingly refrains from performing a duty which is imposed upon him by law or is clearly inherent in the nature of his office. Official misconduct is a(n):
   A. infraction.
   B. violation.
   C. class e felony.
   D. class a misdemeanor.

7. A business contract is presented to a notary public by three individuals, all present before the notary. After all parties have executed the contract, had their acknowledgments taken and the notary has completed the acknowledgment certificates, the total fee which the notary may collect is:
   A. $.25.
   B. $.75.
   C. $1.75.
   D. $6.00.

8. When appointed by the secretary of state, the notary public receives a:
   A. license.
   B. commission.
   C. permit.
   D. certificate of official character.

9. A law established by an act of the state legislature is a(n):
   A. ordinance.
   B. statute.
   C. rule.
   D. bylaw.

10. The formal declaration made by a subscribing witness to the execution of a document is a:
   A. subscribing witness.
   B. testificandum.

C. proof of execution.
D. certificate of official character.

11. A notary public is appointed and commissioned by the:
    A. governor.
    B. attorney general.
    C. state comptroller.
    D. secretary of state.

12. Which official act incorporates the use of the statement: "You do solemnly, sincerely and truly, declare and affirm, that the statements made by you are true and correct?"
    A. Acknowledgment.
    B. Proof of execution.
    C. Affirmation.
    D. Oath.

13. While all are recommended and customary, which item is statutorily required to lawfully complete an official certification by a notary public?
    A. Statement of authority rubber stamp.
    B. Embossing official seal.
    C. Black ink pen.
    D. Gold foil seal for embossment.

14. The statute requiring that certain contracts be in writing or partially complied with in order to be legally enforceable at law is the:
    A. statute of limitations.
    B. statute of frauds.
    C. statute of instruments.
    D. statute of execution.

15. A duplicate identification card may be issued to a notary public for one lost, destroyed or damaged upon application therefor on a form prescribed by the secretary of state and upon payment of a nonrefundable fee of:
    A. $10.
    B. $5.
    C. $2.
    D. $3.

16. After successful completion of the state examination and favorable review of the application for appointment, the term of office of a notary public expires:
    A. four years after the examination date.
    B. four years after the appointment date.
    C. four years after the next March 30.
    D. four years after the applicant's birthday.

17. A notary public is presented with a conveyance for real property by a grantee. In addition to taking and certifying the acknowledgment of the execution, the notary must mark the accurate venue of the acknowledgment act. The venue designates:
    A. the home or business address of the grantor.
    B. the home or business address of the grantee.
    C. the legal jurisdiction at which the act transpired.
    D. the physical situs of the real property.

18. According to banking law, any documents, letters or other papers of a private nature and any property or articles of no apparent value among the contents of any such abandoned safe deposit box shall not be sold, but shall be retained by the lessor for a period of at least:
    A. one year.
    B. two years.
    C. three years.
    D. ten years.

19. If a person has stated or given testimony (either orally or in writing), when under oath or affirmation, and knew the statement or testimony to be false and willfully made, he has committed the crime of:
    A. perjury.
    B. fraud.
    C. coercion.
    D. subversion.

20. Change of residence and mailing address status is legally required to be communicated, in writing, to the department of state within how many days after such change?
    A. 5.
    B. 10.

C. 15.
D. 30.

21. For a class d felony, the prison term shall be fixed by the court, and shall not exceed:
A. ten years.
B. seven years.
C. four years.
D. one year.

22. If a notary public asks for, or receives more than the statutory allowance in connection with administering and certifying an oath for an affidavit, he subjects himself to:
A. criminal prosecution by the district attorney.
B. civil law suit by the affiant.
C. monetary fine/suspension/revocation of commission by the secretary of state.
D. all of these penalties.

23. The secretary of state is empowered to appoint and remove notaries public under which volume of state statute?
A. Executive law.
B. Public officers law.
C. Judiciary law.
D. Penal law.

24. According to executive law section 130, an applicant is granted an extension for the purposes of re-appointment to the office of notary public, provided such application for re-appointment is made within . . . after the military discharge of the applicant under conditions other than dishonorable.
A. 30 days.
B. six months.
C. one year.
D. two years.

25. The particular state, county and/or city where a court has legal jurisdiction and a notarial act is performed is the:
A. jurat.
B. venue.
C. territory.
D. district.

26. According to executive law section 135-a, a notary public or commissioner of deeds, who in the exercise of the powers, or in the performance of the duties of such office shall practice any fraud or deceit, the punishment for which is not otherwise provided for by this act, shall be guilty of a:
   A. felony.
   B. misdemeanor.
   C. infraction.
   D. violation.

27. In performing the protest of a dishonored negotiable instrument, a notary public is permitted to collect which fee for (each) notice of protest?
   A. $.10.
   B. $.75.
   C. $1.
   D. $5.

28. The jurisdiction for a notary public consists of:
   A. the county in which he qualified.
   B. the entire state, except New York City, unless he qualified in one of the five boroughs.
   C. the entire state, including New York City, regardless of the county of qualification.
   D. the entire state, except Long Island, unless he qualified in Nassau or Suffolk counties.

29. To witness the execution of a written instrument, at the request of the person who makes it, and subscribe the same as witness is to:
   A. affirm it.
   B. acknowledge it.
   C. attest it.
   D. annul it.

30. In order to qualify for office, the oath of office and specimen signature for a duly commissioned notary public is filed with the:
   A. attorney general.
   B. secretary of state.
   C. county clerk.
   D. court of appeals clerk.

31. By state statute, the criteria for appointment as a notary public is:
    A. 18 years of age.
    B. United States citizenship.
    C. residence or office or place of employment.
    D. satisfaction of all of these criteria.

32. According to executive law section 135, for any misconduct by a notary public in performance of any of his powers such notary shall be liable to the parties injured for:
    A. treble damages sustained by the parties.
    B. double damages sustained by the parties.
    C. actual damages sustained by the parties.
    D. any fee paid to the notary.

33. A person presents an affidavit to a notary public. The affiant is known to the notary. He executes the affidavit. In the event that the affiant commits perjury, which action by the notary is the most critical to the successful criminal prosecution of the affiant?
    A. Taking the express assent of the affiant to an oral oath or affirmation.
    B. Taking the oral acknowledgment of the affiant.
    C. Asking the affiant if the signature on the affidavit is his own.
    D. Marking the correct venue at the top of the affidavit.

34. The certification by the secretary of state verifying the legitimacy of a county clerk's certificate of the authenticity of the act of a notary public is an:
    A. annotation.
    B. codicil.
    C. apostille.
    D. certified copy.

35. The legally required ceremony to be orally recited by a notary public taking an acknowledgment is:
    A. "Do you acknowledge that this is your signature, and that you [freely and willfully] executed this document for the purposes contained in it?"
    B. "Do you solemnly swear that you executed this document?"
    C. "Do you solemnly affirm that you executed this document for the purposes contained in it?"
    D. "Do you acknowledge that this is your signature?"

36. A notary public may not perform which act?
    A. Administer an oath for a U.S. Coast Guard officer.
    B. Take and certify an acknowledgment of paternity.
    C. Take and certify an affidavit of execution for a will.
    D. Take and certify a standard acknowledgment of a will.

37. Conviction of all of the following criminal acts will disqualify an applicant for a notary public commission, except:
    A. loitering and soliciting men for the purpose of committing a crime against nature.
    B. loitering involving deviate sexual behavior.
    C. engaged in some illegal occupation or bearing an evil reputation and with an unlawful purpose consorting with thieves and criminals or frequenting unlawful resorts.
    D. none; all will bar an applicant from appointment.

38. A clause which permits the placing of a mortgage at a later date which takes priority over an existing mortgage is:
    A. a chattel clause.
    B. res judicata.
    C. a subordination clause.
    D. lis pendens.

39. A person is guilty of . . . when, being a public servant authorized by law to make or issues official certificates or other official written instruments, and with intent to defraud, deceive or injure another person, he issue such an instrument, or makes the same with intent that it be issued, knowing that it contains a false statement or false information.
    A. issuing a false certificate.
    B. forgery in the second degree.
    C. forgery in the third degree.
    D. obstructing governmental administration.

40. The maximum prison sentence for the felonious crime described in question number 39 is:
    A. two years.
    B. three years.
    C. four years.
    D. five years.

SAMPLE EXAMINATION C

1. According to the New York State Supreme Court case, *People ex. rel. Kenyon v. Sutherland,* 81 N.Y. 1, which of the following is the simplest form in which an affirmation may be administered?
   A. "Do you solemnly swear that the contents of this affidavit subscribed by you is correct and true?"
   B. "Do you solemnly, sincerely and truly, declare and affirm, that these statements made by you are true and correct?"
   C. "Do you acknowledge that the contents of this document are known to you?"
   D. "Do you acknowledge that this is your signature?"

2. A legal right or claim upon specific property which attaches to the property until a debt is satisfied is a:
   A. chattel paper.
   B. lien.
   C. lis pendens.
   D. judgment.

3. The sentence of imprisonment for a class e felony shall not exceed:
   A. seven years.
   B. five years.
   C. six years.
   D. four years.

4. The public officers law provides that a person who executes any of the functions of a public office without having taken and duly filed the required oath of office, as prescribed by law, is guilty of:
   A. a felony.
   B. an infraction.
   C. a violation.
   D. a misdemeanor.

5. A written instrument given to pass title of personal property from vendor to vendee is a:
   A. conveyance.
   B. chattel paper.

C. bill of sale.
D. codicil.

6. A handwritten or typewritten statement of facts, made voluntarily, and confirmed by the sworn oath of the party making such statment is a(n):
A. affidavit.
B. deposition.
C. acknowledgment.
D. testamentum.

7. The placing of an instrument in the hands of a person as a depository who, on the happening of a designated event, is to deliver the instrument to a third person is described as:
A. laches.
B. fiduciary.
C. escrow.
D. trust.

8. Forgery in the second degree is a:
A. class b felony.
B. class c felony.
C. class d felony.
D. class e felony.

9. Which of the following acts may not be performed by a non-resident notary public while he is in New York state?
A. Take and certify an acknowledgment.
B. Administer an oath of office.
C. Protest a dishonored negotiable instrument.
D. None; he possesses the same power as a resident notary.

10. Unlawful constraint exercised upon a person whereby he is forced to do some act against his will is:
A. coercion.
B. duress.
C. influence.
D. conspiracy.

11. In order to receive a notary public commission, an attorney and counsellor at law duly admitted to the New York state bar:

A. must follow the same procedure as any other person.
B. must take and pass a special written examination.
C. must submit a standard application for appointment with fee and a certificate of good standing from the appellate department of admission.
D. may proceed to exercise the powers immediately upon admission to practice law.

12. The written testimony of a witness taken out of a court or hearing proceeding under oath before a notary public or other authorized officer is a(n):
A. affidavit.
B. deposition.
C. testamentum.
D. covenant.

13. A person is guilty of . . . when, with intent to harass, annoy, threaten or alarm another person, he: (1) communicates, or causes a communication to be initiated by mechanical or electronic means or otherwise, with a person, anonymously or otherwise, by telephone, or by telegraph, mail or any other form of written communication, in a manner likely to cause annoyance or alarm; or (2) makes a telephone call, whether or not a conversation ensues, with no purpose or legitimate communication; or (3) strikes, shoves, kicks, or otherwise subjects another person to physical contact, or attempts or threatens to do the same because of the race, color, religion or natural origin of such person.
A. aggravated harassment in the first degree.
B. aggravated harassment in the second degree.
C. aggravated harassment in the third degree.
D. aggravated harassment in the fourth degree.

14. A public officer authorized to take and certify an acknowledgment or proof of an instrument is civilly liable in damages sustained by the parties if he is guilty of:
A. misfeasance.
B. nonfeasance.
C. malfeasance.
D. negligence.

15. All of the following criteria are required when taking and certifying an acknowledgment, except:
    A. personal appearance of the signatory.
    B. known or proven personal identity of the signatory.
    C. actually making the signature before the officer.
    D. oral admission of free and willful execution.

16. What length of time must pass before a safe deposit lessor must inform the lessee of its intent to sell the contents of an abandoned safe deposit box?
    A. Six months.
    B. One year.
    C. Two years.
    D. Ten years.

17. According to judiciary law section 484, "No natural person shall ask for or receive compensation for appearing for a person other than himself as attorney . . . preparing instruments . . . or pleadings . . . brought before any court . . . unless he has been regularly admitted to practice, as an attorney or counselor; but nothing in this section shall apply to all except which of the following?
    A. Officers of societies for the prevention of cruelty.
    B. Law students who have completed at least two semesters.
    C. Law school graduates who have not failed the bar examination more than once.
    D. Law school graduates who have not failed the bar examination more than twice.

18. Anything opposed to justice, modesty or good morals is called:
    A. integrity.
    B. subversion.
    C. misfeasance.
    D. moral turpitude.

19. A clause which permits the placing of a mortgage at a later date which takes priority over an existing mortgage is a(n):
    A. mortgage clause.
    B. note clause.
    C. commercial clause.
    D. subordination clause.

20. One is guilty of . . . if he has stated or given testimony on a material matter, under oath, as to the truth thereof, when he knew the statement or testimony to be false and willfully made:
   A. fraud.
   B. suborning perjury.
   C. perjury.
   D. peculation.

21. A notary public or other authorized officer may not lawfully take and certify an acknowledgment in each instance except:
   A. where the officer is the mortgagor in a conveyance.
   B. where the officer is the grantee in a conveyance.
   C. where the officer is president and sole shareholder, and the treasurer executes a ten-year lease on behalf of the corporation.
   D. where the officer is the named attorney-in-fact in a corporation power of attorney.

22. A formal written statement by a notary public under seal that a specific bill of exchange or promissory note was presented on a certain day for payment or acceptance and was refused is a:
   A. negotiable instrument.
   B. draft.
   C. canceled check.
   D. protest.

23. A man appointed by the court to manage the estate of a deceased person who left no will is a(n):
   A. executor.
   B. administrator.
   C. executrix.
   D. administratrix.

24. Unauthorized notarial practice includes:
   A. giving advice to others on the law.
   B. drawing certain legal documents.
   C. making arrangements to split attorney fees.
   D. all of these.

25. The fee for a certificate of authentication issued by a county clerk:

A. $1.
B. $3.
C. $5.
D. $10.

26. Banking law provides special remedies to safe box depositories, if the amount due for the rental of any safe deposit box let by any lessor shall not have been paid for one year, or:
    A. if the lessee thereof shall not have removed the contents within 10 days from the termination of the lease.
    B. if the lessee thereof shall not have removed the contents within 30 days from the termination of the lease.
    C. if the lessee thereof shall not have removed the contents within 45 days from the termination of the lease.
    D. if the lessee thereof shall not have removed the contents within 60 days from the termination of the lease.

27. A non-resident who accepts an appointment to the office of notary public in New York, thereby appoints which state officer as the person upon whom civil process can be served on his behalf?
    A. Secretary of state.
    B. Attorney general.
    C. State comptroller.
    D. Governor.

28. Provided a person remains eligible, the number of terms that a notary public may be commissioned is:
    A. eight.
    B. twelve.
    C. twenty-four.
    D. not limited.

29. If a notary public commits an act relating to his office which is an unauthorized exercise of his official functions, or if he knowingly refrains from performing a duty which is legally imposed upon him or is clearly inherent in the nature of his office, he is guilty of the crime of official misconduct. Official misconduct is which class crime?
    A. Class a misdemeanor.
    B. Class b misdemeanor.
    C. Unclassified misdemeanor.

D. Class e felony.

30. A law that limits the time within which a criminal prosecution or a civil action must be started is the:
    A. statute of frauds.
    B. statute of limitations.
    C. statute of litigation.
    D. statute of mitigation.

31. Which activity may be lawfully performed by a notary public?
    A. Draw the bill of sale for the boat of his priest.
    B. Take an acknowledgment for a marriage contract.
    C. Take an acknowledgment for a will execution.
    D. Administer an oath of office to a sheriff.

32. In a forced safe deposit box situation, the lessor must retain documents, letters, personal papers and articles of no apparent value for:
    A. three years from the forced box entry.
    B. three years from the public auction.
    C. ten years from the public auction.
    D. ten years from the forced box entry.

33. When taking and certifying the proof of execution of an instrument, which duties are imposed upon a notary public or other authorized officer?
    A. Personal appearance of the subscribing witness/s.
    B. Personal acquaintance with the subscribing witness/s.
    C. Administering an oath to the subscribing witness/s.
    D. All of these duties are legally mandatory.

34. A written instrument given to pass title of personal property from vendor to vendee is a:
    A. bill of sale.
    B. conveyance.
    C. chattel paper.
    D. contract.

35. State law regarding the use of an embossing seal by a notary public stipulates that its use is:
    A. required for all acts.

B. required for only court documents.
C. required for certain acts.
D. required only if a notary possesses an embossing seal.

36. When a notary public is called upon to attend a forced safe deposit box opening, which role is chiefly performed by the notary?
   A. Appraisal of the box contents.
   B. Inspection of the box contents.
   C. Inventory of the box contents.
   D. All of these roles are performed.

37. Which criminal conviction might not bar a person from being commissioned a notary public?
   A. Issuing a bad check.
   B. Aiding escape from a prison.
   C. Entering hospital to negotiate settlement or obtain release or statement.
   D. Purchase of claims by corporations or collection agencies.

38. Which legal term is often interchanged, although technically incorrect, with the term "affiant"?
   A. Appellant.
   B. Claimant.
   C. Deponent.
   D. Respondent.

39. Which is not legally required of a notary public when marking his statement of authority onto documents?
   A. Registration number printed on his notary public state identification card.
   B. Strict use of black ink for his official signature.
   C. Strict use of black ink for marking his statement of authority information.
   D. The county name in which he qualified.

40. When a notary public files a certificate of official character with a county clerk or recorder, the filing fee is:
   A. $5.
   B. $10.
   C. $15.
   D. $25.

SAMPLE EXAMINATION D

1. A felony is best defined by which of the following characteristics?
   A. Damages exceed $50,000.
   B. Federal law has been violated.
   C. The sentence is confinement in a city or county jail.
   D. The sentence is confinement in a state or U.S. prison.

2. Which of the following describes the minimum time for imprisonment on a felony conviction?
   A. Three hundred and sixty four days.
   B. Three hundred and sixty five days.
   C. Two thousand days.
   D. Three thousand and six hundred and fifty days.

3. When a married woman is reappointed to the office of notary public, which surname may she choose?
   A. Only her maiden name.
   B. Only her husband's name.
   C. Either her maiden name or husband's name.
   D. Only the name provided in her initial application.

4. Of the following sources, which is the best source for an official-certified copy of a document?
   A. Notary public.
   B. Attorney.
   C. Public records office with custody of the original.
   D. Public reference librarian.

5. One advantage of a document that has been acknowledged is that it can be presented in a court of law as:
   A. presumptive evidence.
   B. conclusive evidence.
   C. oral evidence.
   D. prima facie evidence.

6. The clause "subscribed and sworn to before me this [day] in the year of our Lord [year]" is termed:
   A. repondez s'il vous plait.
   B. jurat.

C. fleur-de-lis.
D. tamponner.

7. Evidence which, if uncontradicted or unexplained, is sufficient to sustain a judgment in favor of the issue it supports, but which may be contradicted by other evidence is:
   A. prima facie evidence.
   B. parol evidence.
   C. second-hand evidence.
   D. extrajudicial evidence.

8. The secretary of state may assess a fine not to exceed . . . against a notary public for official misconduct.
   A. $100.
   B. $250.
   C. $500.
   D. $1,000.

9. A woman appointed by a testator to carry out the directions and requests in his will and to dispose of the property according to his testamentary provisions after his death is an:
   A. executrix.
   B. exempli gratia.
   C. exemplum.
   D. executioner.

10. Executive law section 135-a provides that a notary public or commissioner of deeds, who in the exercise of the powers, or in the performance of the duties of such office shall practice any fraud or deceit, the punishment for which is not otherwise provided for by this act, shall be guilty of a:
    A. misdemeanor.
    B. class c felony.
    C. class d felony.
    D. class e felony.

11. A public officer is entitled to collect a fee for administering an oath to a:
    A. county clerk.
    B. notary public.
    C. deputy sheriff.
    D. none of the above.

12. Executive law provides three categories of exceptions to the general maxim of conflict of interest except:
    A. a bank stockholder, director, officer, employee, or agent.
    B. a corporation stockholder, director, officer, employee, or agent.
    C. a partnership partner, employee, or agent.
    D. an attorney and counsellor at law.

13. In exercising his powers pursuant to executive law, a notary public, in addition to the venue of his act and his signature, shall print, typewrite, or stamp beneath his signature in black ink:
    A. his name, the words "Notary Public State of New York," the state registration number, the name of the county in which he originally qualified, and the date upon which his commission expires.
    B. his name, the words "Notary Public State of New York," the name of the county in which he originally qualified, and the date upon which his commission was issued.
    C. his name, the words "Notary Public State of New York," the name of the county in which he originally qualified, and the date upon which his commission expires.
    D. his name, the words "Notary Public State of New York," the name of the county in which he originally qualified, and the date upon which his commission was issued and expires.

14. The certification by the secretary of state verifying the legitimacy of a county clerk's certificate of the authenticity of a notary public act is an:
    A. apostille.
    B. appurtenance.
    C. attachiamenta.
    D. attachiamentum.

15. Prior to the public auction of the contents of an abandoned safe deposit box, the lessor must publish an advertisement in the legal notices of the newspaper situated in the locale of the auction. Upon publication, the newspaper is then required to prepare:
    A. a sworn affidavit of publication containing a specimen of the actual advertisement in the legal notices to the lessee.

B. a sworn affidavit of publication containing a specimen of the actual advertisement in the legal notices to the state comptroller.
C. a sworn affidavit of publication containing a specimen of the actual advertisement in the legal notices to the lessor.
D. a sworn affidavit of publication containing a specimen of the actual advertisement in the legal notices to the secretary of state.

16. In New York notarial practice, when a person has taken all of the steps necessary for holding office, including taking and filing the oath of office, the incumbent has:
A. registered.
B. applied.
C. qualified.
D. nominated.

17. In civil litigation, the party who commences the action is referred to as the:
A. defendant.
B. plaintiff.
C. bailiff.
D. appellator.

18. The fee to file a certificate of official character in a county clerk's office is:
A. $5.
B. $10.
C. $15.
D. $25.

19. The fee to secure a certificate of official character issued by the department of state is:
A. $5.
B. $10.
C. $15.
D. $25.

20. Anything of value given to induce entering into a contract, including money, personal services, and even love and affection, is:
A. consent.

B. collateral.
C. conscription.
D. consideration.

21. Any method used by the court to get or use its jurisdiction over a person or a specific property; the summons, writ, warrant, or mandate from a court is:
A. dictum.
B. process.
C. litura
D. abetment.

22. An article of personal, movable property, as distinguished from real property, is (a):
A. fixture.
B. chattel.
C. replevin.
D. corpus.

23. A person appointed by a court to manage the affairs of an incompetent or liquidate a business is a:
A. conservator.
B. comptroller.
C. special surrogate.
D. attorney-in-fact.

24. A notary public is a:
A. state official.
B. state employee.
C. public officer.
D. officer of the court.

25. Fees collected by a notary public for official services rendered are legally payable to the:
A. notary.
B. employer.
C. county treasurer.
D. state comptroller.

26. A notary public shall not:
A. share office space with an attorney.

B. administer an oath to a person in bankruptcy.
C. split fees with an attorney.
D. advertise services.

27. Where a person whose commission as a notary public has expired, what is the maximum period of time that is allowed to pass before the applicant must take the state written examination again?
A. Thirty days.
B. Sixty days.
C. Six months.
D. One year.

28. A writing or writings which evidence both a monetary obligation and a security interest in or a lease of specific goods is a:
A. mortgage.
B. chattel paper.
C. bill of exchange.
D. judgment.

29. If a notary public continues to serve after his commission expires, or willfully submits false information on his application for appointment, he is guilty of a:
A. misdemeanor.
B. felony.
C. violation.
D. infraction.

30. Banking law section 335 designates that the lessor of a safe deposit box, which is subject to forced opening, must give proper notice to the last known address of the lessee by certified, return-receipt mail, at least . . . days prior to opening.
A. ten.
B. thirty.
C. sixty.
D. ninety.

31. An oath for a deposition may be orally administered over the telephone:
A. in the event of physical handicap of the deponent.

B. if a special oath is administered to the deponent.
C. only if a proof of execution is not indicated.
D. never.

32. If a notary public is not available to provide official services, his powers may be delegated to:
A. his spouse.
B. his employee.
C. his attorney-in-fact.
D. no one.

33. The acknowledgment of a legal instrument:
A. makes it legal.
B. permits it to be recorded in a county clerk's office.
C. eliminates the necessity of subscribing witnesses.
D. all of the above.

34. Judiciary law section 750 provides for the power of courts to punish for criminal contempt and a proceeding under this subdivision may be instituted on all of the following except:
A. the court's own motion.
B. on the motion of any officer charged with the duty of investigating or prosecuting unlawful practice of law.
C. by any bar association incorporated under the laws of New York.
D. a complaint by the secretary of state.

35. A will or deed written entirely by the testator or grantor with his own hand and not witnessed or attested is:
A. holographic.
B. hologramic.
C. nudum pactum.
D. cartulary.

36. The state or condition of dying without having made a valid will, or without having disposed by will of a part of his property is:
A. inter vivos.
B. intervenor.
C. causa mortis.
D. intestacy.

37. A supplement or an addition to a will is a:
    A. conveyance.
    B. codicil.
    C. collateral covenant.
    D. copyright.

38. In New York, all of the following elections matters may involve the action of a notary public except a:
    A. nominating petition.
    B. designating petition.
    C. absentee ballot for a military voter.
    D. declination of nomination.

39. The instrument by which authority of one person to act in place of another is a(n):
    A. power of attorney.
    B. attorney's lien.
    C. pro se.
    D. mechanic's lien.

40. A court process, initiated by a party in litigation, compelling production of certain specific documents and other items, material and relevant to facts in issue in a pending judicial proceeding is a:
    A. subpoena ad testificandum.
    B. subpoena duces tecum.
    C. subordination agreement.
    D. subscribing witness affidavit.

Examination Answer Keys with Rationale

Answer Key—A

1. B. Executive law section 130 provides that a notary public shall have been served with a copy of the charges against him and have an opportunity of being heard. The quasi-judicial hearing will be held before an administrative law judge of the department of state.

2. A. Banking law section 335 designates that a lessor may force open a safe deposit box if the lessee does not remove the contents within 30 days of the termination of the lease.

3. B. The state or federal legislature pass laws called statutes. Municipal governments (city, town or village) pass local laws called ordinances. Private or quasi-private organizations create internal rules called bylaws.

4. A. Executive law section 130 states that no person shall be appointed as a notary public who has been convicted of a felony or certain misdemeanors, and who has not received an executive pardon or a certificate of good conduct from the state parole board. A certificate of relief from (civil) disabilities is insufficient to restore eligibility to hold any public office.

5. A. Real property law section 309 specifically in the language of the corporation acknowledgment certificate, requires the person executing the instrument to swear to the truth of his affiliation denoted in the certificate. It is unreasonable to require a notary to request or require corporation identification credentials.

6. B. An oath is a form of attestation by which a person signifies that he is bound to perform an act faithfully and truthfully. An acknowledgment does not involve the administration of an oath (except in a corporation acknowledgment).

7. A. Real property law section 298 provides that an acknowledgment or proof (of execution) may be made at any place in New York state before a supreme court justice (SCJ), an official examiner of title or referee, or a notary public.

8. D. Executive law section 131 designates the term of a commission to the office of a notary public is four years.

9. B. In *Bookman v. City of New York,* 200 N.Y.53, the trial court judge decided that the simplest form in which an oath may be administered is "Do you solemnly swear that the content of this (affidavit) subscribed by you is true and correct?" Court judicial decisions, often called "judge-made" law, are legally equivalent to statutes passed by a legislature. The collection of these decisions is referred to as the common law.

10. D. Penal law section 175.40 classifies the crime of issuing a false certificate as a class e felony.

11. B. Executive law section 130 provides that the secretary of state may fine, suspend or remove any notary public from office for misconduct. However, the accused notary must have been served with a copy of the charges against him and have an opportunity to respond to the charges made against him.

12. D. Although an applicant must either be a resident, or have a place of business or an office in New York state, no specific length of "residency" is required for consideration of a commission applicant.

13. B. According to executive law section 130, the secretary of state may appoint and commission notaries public whose jurisdiction shall be co-extensive with the boundaries of the state.

14. D. Penal law section 195.00 provides that an officer before whom an oath or affidavit may be taken is bound to administer it when requested. Refusal is a misdemeanor crime, carrying a maximum penalty of a one year jail sentence and a fine up to $1,000.

15. C. The state attorney general has issued an opinion warning notaries not to take the acknowledgment of a paper which is executed "entirely in blank."

16. A. Judiciary law section 485 designates that the practice of law without a license is a misdemeanor crime.

17. B. Since the notary public has personal knowledge of the identity of the affiant, identification credentials from the affiant are not required. Although positive identity is legally required for taking acknowledgments and proofs, it is not legally required for affiants or deponents in New York State. However, it would be considered good notarial practice to request identification from a party who is unknown to the notary.

18. C. New York state constitution section 13 declares that a sheriff is not eligible to hold any other public office at the same time he holds the civil office of sheriff.

19. A. Executive law section 137 requires a notary public to mark the venue of his act when exercising his powers upon a document. Failure to comply with the law may result in discipline by the secretary of state.

20. C. The concluding phrase is an acknowledgment certificate form which indicates to the notary public that he shall take and certify the acknowledgment of the person before him.

21. B. Penal law section 170.10 declares that a person is guilty of forgery in the second degree when, with intent to defraud, deceive or injure another, he falsely makes, completes or alters a written instrument which is or purports to be, or which is calculated to become or represent if completed a written instrument officially issued or created by a public officer, public servant or government instrumentality.

22. D. Banking law section 335 requires that a notary public must be present at a forced opening of an abandoned safe deposit box. The notary may be an employee of the lessor. It is customary that a lessor representative, typically an officer, is present at the opening and during the inventory process.

23. C. Executive law section 130 states that a notary public who is a resident of the state and who moves out of the state, but still maintains an office or place of business in New York state, does not vacate his office.

24. B or D. A woman can add (or remove) her husband's name after her maiden name, if she chooses to do so. If desired, at the time of application for appointment to another term, she can register her change of name by providing a written request to the department of state. Instead of waiting until the commission expires before registering a name change, a notary may change her name at any time during her term. Effective September 30, 1999, the fee to change a name on a "license, permit, registration or other identifying document", because of a change of marital status, was abolished under New York civil rights law. However, the New York legislature neglected to also amend New York executive law concerning the name change fee charged to holders of notary commissions. As of the publication of this edition, executive law was still conflicting with civil rights law. Therefore, if an examinee encounters an examination question on this

topic, he should select an answer which is in agreement with existing executive law. This also corresponds with the printed notary public examination study material provided by the NYS department of state. He would not be expected to be aware of this obscure section of civil rights law, nor to have access to such a law.

25. A. Real property law section 303 requires that an acknowledgment must not be taken by any officer unless he knows or has satisfactory evidence, that the person making it is the person described in and who executed such instrument.

26. B. Banking law section 335 requires that a legal notice be published by the lessor in the local newspaper ten days prior to the public auction of the contents of an abandoned safe deposit box.

27. D. The New York environment is filled with numerous inconsistencies regarding the raised seal requirement for a notary public. There is not one valid reason why a notary should not possess and impress an embossing-type official seal on all documents. As a standard of customary practice for all of the reasons outlined, a notary is strongly urged to emboss his official seal impression (plus the required statement of authority) under his official signature.

28. B. An apostille may be obtained from the New York department of state upon the payment of a $10 fee each.

29. B. A criminal act is differentiated into either of two categories: felony (sentence of one year or more in a prison); misdemeanor (sentence of up to, but not including, one year in a jail).

30. C. Executive law section 135 permits a notary public to collect a fee of $.75 for protesting a dishonored negotiable instrument and issuing a certificate of protest.

31. B. Contempt is any behavior disrespectful of the authority of a court which disrupts the execution of court orders.

32. D. Civil practice law and rules number 3113 authorizes a deposition to be taken before a notary public in a civil proceeding.

33. A. Civil practice law and rules section 2309(b) requires an oral oath to be administered to an affiant, regardless of whether or not the affiant is personally known to the officer.

34. D. Public officers law section 534 directs each county clerk to designate from among the members of his staff at least one notary public to be available to serve the public in his office during normal business hours free of charge.

35. C. A birth certificate is not satisfactory for positive identification purposes because it contains no descriptive information.

36. A. The state attorney general has issued an opinion declaring that a notary public may administer an oath, take an affidavit, acknowledgment or a deposition in a criminal matter on Sunday; however, a deposition in a civil judicial proceeding may not be taken on Sunday. 1964, Op.Atty.Gen. (Inf.) 103.

37. B. Executive law section 130 requires that any applicant for a commission as notary public, unless he be an attorney and counsellor at law duly admitted to practice in New York shall satisfy the secretary of state that the applicant is of good moral character, has the equivalent of a common school education and is familiar with the duties and responsibilities of a notary public. A common school education is provided by a free elementary school.

38. D. Civil practice law and rules section 2309 is the source of the official state forms of ceremonies for oaths and affirmations.

39. B. Executive law section 132 designates the fee to obtain a certificate of official character for a notary public from a county clerk as $5.

40. C. An authentication is the certificate subjoined (attached) by a county clerk to any certificate of acknowledgment, certificate of proof or oath certificate signed by a notary public.

Answer Key—B

1. B. Civil practice law and rules (rule number 3113) authorizes a deposition to be taken before a notary public in a civil proceeding.

2. C. Executive law section 136 permits a notary public to collect a maximum of $2.00 to swear a witness in connection with a deposition; the affixing of the jurat and official signature is part of the swearing procedure. Thus, all of the individual parts constitute a single notarial act.

3. A. Penal law section 70.15 establishes the maximum term or sentence for class a misdemeanors shall be fixed by the court and not exceed one year in jail.

4. D. Domestic relations law section 11 prohibits a notary public for solemnizing marriages, nor may he take the acknowledgment of parties and witnesses to a written contract of marriage.

5. A. Notaries public, county clerks, court clerks, chamberlains, registers and recorders are often classified as ministerial-type officers. An official's duty is ministerial when it is absolute, certain and imperative, involving merely execution of a specific duty arising from fixed and designated facts.

6. D. Penal law section 195.00 establishes official misconduct a class a misdemeanor. A notary public is a public servant. Public servants should not be narrowly viewed as applying to only New York state employees, but also at every person specifically retained to perform some government purposes. *Matter of Onondaga County District Attorney's Office to File a Sealed Grand Jury Report as a Public Record* (4 Dept. 1983) 92 A.D. 2d 32, 459 N.Y.S. 2d 507. In determining whether a person is a public officer, the court must consider nature of office, function and duties of office with regard to the manner in which they concern and affect the public, and whether such duties

involve some portion of sovereign power. *People v. Confoy,* 1981, 110 Misc.2d 252, 441 N.Y.S.2d 941. The officers before whom oaths and affidavits may by law be taken are bound to administer the same, when requested. Thus, a notary public may not refuse to perform an act, upon request. He has no discretion or right to decline. *People v. Brooks,* 1 Denio 457, 43 A.Dec. 704.

7. D. Executive law section 136 allows a notary public to collect $2.00 for taking and certifying the acknowledgment of a written instrument, by one person, and by each additional person, an additional $2.00.

8. B. Under executive law section 131, the notary public receives a grant of authority called a commission, as a constitutional officer of the state of New York. Although the commission paperwork is processed by the department of state division of licensing services, the secretary of state grants a commission, not a license.

9. B. A law established by an act of the state legislature is commonly called a statute. Although a statute can be a formal written enactment of a legislative body at the federal, state, county or municipal level, it is often referred to in a state or federal context.

10. C. Real property law section 304 authorizes a proof of execution. A proof of execution of a document is performed in very special cases where a person has signed a document, but is unable to personally appear before an authorized officer (e.g.: notary public) to acknowledge the execution (i.e. due to death, coma, communicable disease). Instead, the witness of the execution (subscribing witness) appears before the officer and, under oath, swears he knew the person described in and who executed the document, and that he personally saw such person execute the document.

11. D. Executive law section 130 empowers the secretary of state to appoint and commission "as many notaries pub-

lic for the state of New York as in his judgment may be deemed best."

12. C. An affirmation is a solemn and formal declaration that an affidavit or deposition is true or that a witness will testify truthfully. It is utilized in certain cases instead of an oath which refers to swearing before God. It is legally equivalent to an oath.

13. C. Executive law section 137 outlines the essential "statement of authority" information required to be marked beneath the official signature of a notary public. While the other items listed are customary and recommended, the law requires that only the official signature (of the notary public or other officer) and statement of authority be printed, typewritten or stamped in black ink.

14. B. Originally called the "statute of frauds and perjuries", the contemporary "statute of frauds" is the law which requires that certain contracts be in writing in order to be legally enforceable. The object of the law is to reduce the potential temptation for fraud, perjury and deception by forcing contracting parties to make the agreement in writing at the time that the deal is transacted.

15. A. Executive law section 131 provides that a duplicate identification card may be issued to a notary public for one lost, destroyed or damaged upon application therefor on a form prescribed by the secretary of state and upon payment of a nonrefundable fee of $10.00.

16. B. Executive law section 131 designates that the term of office for a notary public extends four years after the date of appointment by the secretary of state.

17. C. The venue designates the legal, territorial jurisdiction (i.e. country, state, county, city) where an official legal act was performed or took place. Executive law section 137 requires a notary public to mark the venue each time he exercises his powers.

18. D. Banking law section 335 requires that documents, letters or other papers of a private nature, and property or articles of no apparent value among the contents of abandoned safe deposit boxes shall not be sold, but shall be retained by the lessor for a period of at least ten years.

19. A. Penal law section 210 provides that perjury has been committed if a person has made a statement or given testimony when under oath, and knew the statement or testimony to be false and willfully made.

20. A. Executive law section 130 requires a notary public to notify the department of state within five days of change of residence and/or post office address.

21. B. Penal law section 70 provides that the prison sentence for a class D felony shall be fixed by the court, and shall not exceed seven years.

22. D. A notary public may suffer all of these penalties if he asks for or receives more than the statutory allowance. Public officers law section 67, penal law section 200.35, and an attorney general opinion condemn such acts. 12 State Department Reports 507 (1917).

23. A. Executive law section 130 empowers the secretary of state to sanction a notary public by assessing a fine, suspending him or removing him from office.

24. C. Executive law section 130 grants a military extension for one year after the military discharge of the applicant under conditions other than dishonorable.

25. B. Venue indicates the legal jurisdiction in which a notarial act is performed.

26. B. Executive law section 135-a provides that a notary public or commissioner of deeds, who in the exercise of the powers, or in the performance of the duties of such office shall practice any fraud or deceit, the punishment for

which is not otherwise provided for by this act, shall be guilty of a misdemeanor.

27. A. Executive law section 135 stipulates the fee for additional notices of protest is $.10 for each notice, not collecting a fee for more than five notices. A notary may issue more than five notices, but the maximum fee for such notices is $.50.

28. C. Executive law section 130 establishes the legal jurisdiction of a notary public as "co-extensive with the boundaries of the state."

29. C. Attestation is the act of witnessing the actual execution of a written document, at the request of the party executing it. The witness signs his name in formal testimony of such an act.

30. C. Executive law section 131 requires a person appointed as a notary public to "qualify" for the public office by filing his sworn and signed oath of office and specimen signature in the county clerk's office in the county in which he resides. A non-New York resident who is appointed as a notary public follows the same protocol, except he files his sworn oath of office and specimen signature in the county clerk's office in which he maintains a place of business or has an office.

31. D. Executive law section 130 states "Every person appointed as a notary public must, at the time of his appointment, be a citizen of the United States and either a resident of the state of New York or have an office or place of business in New York state." Public officers law section three requires a minimum age of 18 years in order to be capable of holding a civil office. In *Bernal v. Fainter* (1984), the U.S. Supreme Court held that it is unconstitutional for a state to deny a notary public commission to a person strictly based on non-U.S. citizenship. Although New York statute currently requires citizenship, for all practical purposes, the secretary of state has disregarded the New York law. No citizenship question is made

whatsoever on the application for appointment blank, nor is there any other citizenship investigation or inquiry undertaken. Thus, a properly registered, resident U.S. alien residing or working in New York state is eligible for an appointment. However, for the purposes of taking the state examination, the author recommends that the examinee approach such a question by selecting an answer choice that agrees with the actual state statute, until the law is properly and formally revised by the New York legislature. It is not reasonable to expect that the average examinee would be familiar with this complex, obscure legal case.

32. A. Executive law section 135 states that for any misconduct by a notary public in performance of any of his powers, such notary shall be liable to the parties injured for treble (triple) damages sustained by the parties.

33. A. In order for the government to successfully prosecute a person for the crime of perjury, the alleged perjurer (the affiant) must have made an "unequivocal and present act by which he consciously took upon himself the obligation of an oath; silent delivery is insufficient."

34. C. An apostille is a certificate attached to a notarized and county clerk certified document. The apostille is certification by the New York secretary of state that the underlying certification by the county clerk (who certified to the legitimacy of the notary public) is bonafide. Such "compound" certifications are routinely incorporated with matters involving the filing of the document with another nation.

35. A. In order for a notary public to properly take an acknowledgment he must orally recite "Do you acknowledge that this is your signature, and that you freely and willfully executed this document for the purposes contained in it?" If the document is signed in the presence of the notary, he may omit the "Do you acknowledge that this is your signature" language; however, he must then ask

"Do you acknowledge that you freely and willfully executed this document for the purposes contained in it?".

36. D. In *Matter of Flynn,* 142 Misc. 7, a notary public is warned against taking the acknowledgment of a will (which is different than the typical acknowledgment) because it may be potentially misleading to the general public, ". . . in effect acting as a lawyer."

37. D. Executive law section 130 states that conviction of any of these offenses will permanently disqualify an applicant for a commission as a notary public.

38. C. A subordination clause permits the placing of a mortgage at a later date which takes priority over an existing mortgage.

39. A. Penal law section 70.00 designates the crime of issuing a false certificate a class e felony.

40. C. Penal law section 70.00 establishes the maximum prison term for a class e felony as four years.

Answer Key—C

1. B. In *People ex rel. Kenyon v. Sutherland,* 81 N.Y. 1, the simplest form in which an affirmation may be administered is "Do you solemnly, sincerely and truly, declare and affirm that the statements made by you are true and correct?"

2. B. A lien is a legal right or claim upon specific property which attaches to the property until a debt is satisfied.

3. D. Penal law section 70.00 establishes the maximum term or sentence for class e felonies shall be fixed by the court and not exceed four years.

4. D. Public officers law section 15 provides that a person who executes any of the functions of a public office without having taken and duly filed the required oath of office, as prescribed by law, is guilty of a misdemeanor.

5. C. A bill of sale is a written instrument given to pass title of personal property from vendor to vendee.

6. A. An affidavit is a statement of facts (either hand-written or typed), made voluntarily, and confirmed or "verified" by the oath of the party making it, before a notary public or other authorized officer.

7. C. Escrow is the placing of an instrument in the hands of a trusted person as a depository who, on the happening of a designated event, is to deliver the instrument to a third person.

8. C. Penal law section 170.10 designates the crime of forgery in the second degree as a class d felony.

9. D. Executive law section 130 does not specifically distinguish between the powers granted to notaries public who are New York residents and those granted to non-New York residents. Therefore, non-resident notaries are au-

thorized to perform the same range of legal acts equal to resident notaries. The only caveat is that any New York notary must actually be physically situated in New York state territory to perform any authorized act.

10. A. Coercion is the unlawful constraint exercised upon a person whereby he is forced to do some act against his will.

11. C. Executive law section 130 designates that an attorney who has taken and passed the state bar examination does not have to take the pre-appointment examination required for notaries public. However, New York admitted attorneys are not automatically appointed notaries public. A New York attorney seeking a commission must submit an standard application for appointment with a fee and a certificate of good standing from the appropriate appellate department of the state supreme court of admission.

12. B. A deposition is the written testimony of a witness taken out of a court or hearing proceeding under oath before a notary public or other authorized officer. It may be voluntary. However, if a witness refuses to voluntarily comply with a request to make a deposition, the request may become involuntary and the recalcitrant witness compelled to testify in a summons or subpoena.

13. B. Penal law section 240.30 classifies this illegal act as the crime of aggravated harassment in the second degree. Aggravated harassment in the second degree is a class a misdemeanor. Executive law section 130 includes this offense among the crimes which automatically render, for life, an applicant disqualified from consideration for appointment as a notary public.

14. C. Real property law section 330 states, "an officer, authorized to take the acknowledgment or proof of a conveyance or other instrument, or to certify such proof or acknowledgment, or to record the same, who is guilty of malfeasance or fraudulent practice in the execution of any duty. . ., is liable in damages to the person injured."

15. C. In New York case law, *People v. Kempner,* 49 App. Div. 121, the court declared "it is not essential that the person who executed the instrument sign his name in the presence of the officer." However, the three remaining criteria are all mandatory.

16. C. Banking law section 335 requires the lessor (safe deposit box owner) to allow two years (from the time of mailing the original certificate of opening) to pass before the lessor may notify the lessee (safe deposit box renter) of the intent to sell the contents of the safe deposit box.

17. C. Judiciary law section 484, *permits* law school graduates who have not failed the bar examination more than *twice* to practice law in limited situations. The selection of *once* is not correct.

18. D. Moral turpitude describes offenses which are classified *malum in se* (Latin for "wrong in itself"), based upon principles of nature, morals and public law. An example is the crime of bribery. These offenses are contrasted with *malum prohibita* offenses (Latin for "prohibited wrong . . ."). An example is the crime of lobstering without a license. Conviction of *malum in se* offenses will likely cause the secretary of state to deny approval of an appointment to the office of notary public.

19. D. A subordination clause permits the placing of a mortgage at a later date which takes priority (in terms of repayment) over an existing mortgage.

20. C. Perjury is committed if a person has stated or given testimony on a material matter, under oath, as to the truth thereof, when he knew the statement or testimony to be false and willfully made.

21. C. Executive law section 138 clarifies that a notary public (or other authorized officer) who is a stockholder, officer, director or employee of a corporation *may* lawfully take and certify an acknowledgment or proof, or administer an oath, . . . on behalf of such corporation, provided that

such officer is *not* actually executing the document, either individually or as a representative of such corporation. In *Armstrong v. Combs,* 15 App. Div. 246, the court declared "a notary public should not take an acknowledgment to a legal instrument to which the notary is a party in interest."

22. D. A protest is a formal written statement by a notary public under seal that a specific bill of exchange or promissory note was presented on a certain day for payment or acceptance and was refused. In New York state, a notarial protest is routinely utilized in connection with criminal and civil actions regarding bad check prosecutions.

23. B. An administrator is a man appointed by the county surrogate to manage the estate of a deceased person who failed to make a will. An administrator may also be appointed if the decedent left a will, but neglected to name an executor in it, or if he named an executor who then refused to accept the appointment.

24. D. Judiciary law section 484 states "no natural person shall ask or receive, directly or indirectly, compensation for appearing for a person other than himself in any court or before any magistrate, or for preparing deeds, mortgages, . . . wills, . . . pleadings of any kind in any action brought before any court of record. Judiciary law section 479 (soliciting business on behalf of any attorney), section 480 (entering hospital to negotiate settlement or obtain release or statement), section 481 (aiding, assisting or abetting the solicitation of persons or the procurement of a retainer for or on behalf of any attorney), section 489 (purchase of claims by corporations or collection agencies) and section 491 (sharing of compensation by attorneys prohibited) are also applicable.

25. B. Executive law section 133 fixes the fee for a certificate of authentication issued by a county clerk at $3 each.

26. B. Banking law section 335 provides special remedies to safe box depositories under two conditions: (1) if the box

rent is overdue for one year, or (2) if the box "tenant" doesn't vacate the premises within 30 days after the lease expires. As a practical matter, since most safe box depositories lease boxes for annual periods, it won't be necessary for the "landlord" to wait for a year to seek remedies. Rather, if it elects to pursue the matter, the safe box depository need wait only 30 days to commence the "eviction" process.

27. A. Executive law section 130 designates the secretary of state as the person upon whom civil process can be served on behalf of a non-resident notary public. In order to be "served" process (i.e.: summons or subpoena), the party must be physically in New York state. Since it might be very difficult to actually locate a non-resident notary public in New York state, the law permits the process server to deliver the summons or subpoena on the secretary of state in Albany. The process server must actually hand-deliver the summons or subpoena; under certain circumstances, the law allows him to tack one copy up on the front door of the person's home and place another copy in the U.S. mail (called "nail and mail"). In this special case, upon his receipt of the summons or subpoena, the secretary of state places it in the U.S. mail, certified service, return-receipt requested, to the post office address on file of the non-resident notary public.

28. D. The number of terms that a notary public may be commissioned is not limited by statute at this time. He may be re-appointed provided he continues to meet the eligibility criteria required for initial appointment.

29. A. Penal law section 195.00 classifies the crime of official misconduct as a class a misdemeanor.

30. B. The statute of limitations limits the time within which a criminal prosecution or a civil action must be started. Generally speaking, the statute of limitations for most criminal matters is seven years, except for murder, income tax evasion and a few other crimes.

31. D. Public officers law section 10 designates that an oath of office may be administered by any officer authorized (within the state) to take the acknowledgment of a real property deed. Therefore, a notary public may "swear in" any elected or appointed public officer or public employee — municipal, county, state or federal.

32. D. Executive law section 335 requires that the safe deposit box lessor retain all documents, letters, personal papers and articles of no apparent value for ten years from the box opening.

33. D. Real property law section 304 requires that the proof not be taken unless the officer is personally acquainted with such witness, or has satisfactory evidence that he is the same person, who was the subscribing witness to the conveyance. The officer must also administer an oath to the witness, which requires personal appearance.

34. A. A bill of sale is a written instrument given to pass title of personal property, called personalty or chattel, from vendor (seller) to vendee (buyer). Bills of sale are usually presented to notaries public to take an acknowledgment for the sale of automobiles, trucks, boats, mobile homes and other personal property.

35. C. Although the secretary of state doesn't directly order all notaries public to acquire official, embossing seal presses, there are a number of other requirements (i.e. for matters connected with the Uniform Commercial Code, federal law matters, interstate and international matters, etc.) which necessitate the use of a seal. Since there will *never* be a case where the use of a seal is improper, a prudent notary should utilize both the statement of authority rubber stamp and embossing seal in his routine protocol.

36. C. Banking law section 335 designates that a notary public will be present at the forced safe deposit box opening to supervise and certify the inventory process of the box container contents.

37. A. Executive law section 130 designates that a person may not be appointed as a notary public who has been convicted of a felony or certain listed offenses. The crime of issuing a bad check is a misdemeanor and not listed in the law as a disqualifying offense. Therefore, conviction of this crime might not automatically disqualify an applicant.

38. C. Deponent is the term interchanged, although technically incorrect, with the term "affiant". A deponent is a person who make a deposition. An affiant is a person who makes an affidavit. Due to haste or carelessness, some drafters of affidavits often are guilty of improper use of the incorrect terminology. A contributing factor to the confusion is that both types of documents are sworn, written testimony. However, some drafters are not fully aware of the real distinction between the two types of sworn testimony.

39. A. Executive law section 137 prescribes the required information. The state registration number is not legally required. Some county clerk's offices pressure notaries to put their number in their statement of authority. However, the state attorney general has issued several opinions, 1960 Op. Atty. Gen (Inf.) 115, Op. Atty. Gen. (Inf.) No. 92-55, and Op. Atty. Gen. (Inf.) No. 97-15, which clarify that matters of state concern are not subject to regulation by local law. A notary public is a matter of state concern. Therefore, a county clerk or register of deeds cannot impose additional requirements, not specifically authorized by state statute, on any notary public. Application of varying local standards would not be appropriate.

40. B. Executive law section 132 establishes the fee which may be charged by the county clerk for receiving, filing and indexing a certificate of official character as $10.

ANSWER KEY—D

1. D. A felony is a crime of more serious nature than a misdemeanor. Under New York and United States law, a felony is any offense punishable by death or imprisonment for a term of one year or more in a prison. Felonies and misdemeanors are found in both state and federal systems.

2. B. Penal law article 55 defines a felony as a crime with imprisonment for a term of three hundred and sixty five days or one year or more.

3. C. Executive law section 131 discusses name changes. A married woman who is reappointed to the office of notary public, may choose either her maiden surname or husband's surname.

4. C. The best source for an official-certified copy of a document is the public records office with custody of the original. Examples are the municipal registrar of vital records (birth, death, and marriage certificates), court clerk (change of name order, divorce decree), county clerk (discharge of mortgage, veteran's discharge, power of attorney, or deed).

5. A. or D. Executive law section 137 stipulates that all New York courts shall receive a certificate of a notary public as presumptive evidence of the facts contained in it. Presumptive evidence, also called *prima facie* evidence (Latin for "on the face of it"), is evidence which must be received by the court and treated as true and sufficient, until and unless rebutted by other evidence.

6. B. A jurat is the certificate of a notary public before whom a document was sworn to. It is the clause written at the foot of an affidavit, deposition or pleading stating when, where and before whom such document was sworn to. When a notary administers an oath, he then documents

such fact in a jurat. Thus, an officer *never* "performs a jurat."

7. A. Prima facie evidence is evidence which, if uncontradicted or unexplained, is sufficient to sustain a judgment in favor of the issue it supports, but which may be contradicted by other evidence.

8. C. Executive law Section 130 grants the secretary of state the authority to levy a fine against a notary public for official misconduct of up to $500.

9. A. An executrix is a woman appointed by a testator to carry out the directions and requests in his will and to dispose of the property according to his testamentary provisions after his death; an executor is a man appointed by the testator. Personal representative is a term that is sometimes substituted for executrix or executor.

10. A. Executive law section 135-a states that when a notary public exercises his powers or performs his duties and practices any fraud or deceit, not specifically defined in state law, he is guilty of a misdemeanor. Since this section does not specify the classification of misdemeanor, this is an unclassified misdemeanor. Penal law section 55.05(2) clarifies that, if an offense fails to state a classification (class a, class b) or jail sentence, it is a class a misdemeanor. Thus, the sentence is up to one year in jail and a fine up to $1,000, both to be fixed by the trial court.

11. D. Public officers law section 69 prohibits a fee being collected in connection with the administration of an oath of office to any public officer or employee.

12. C. Executive law section 135 and 138 specially exempt three categories of notaries public: banks, corporations and attorneys and counselors at law. Traditional partnership firms, unless law firms, are not included. Newer business organizations such as limited liability compa-

nies and limited liability partnerships are also *not* included.

13. C. Executive law section 137 declares the specific data that a notary public must place beneath his signature in his statement of authority. The commission number printed on the state notary public identification card and oath and signature card is not required by state law in any situation. Thus, a notary should not include the number on his statement of authority rubber stamp.

14. A. In French law, an apostille means an addition, annotation or note made upon a document. Since the secretary of state certification verifying the county clerk's certificate is an addition to the underlying notarial certificate, it's called an authentication, or apostille.

15. C. Abandoned property law requires the newspaper to prepare a sworn affidavit of publication containing a specimen of the actual advertisement in the legal notices to the lessor.

16. C. When an appointed person has taken all of the steps necessary for holding a public office, including taking the oath of office and filing the sworn, signed oath of office, he has qualified.

17. B. In civil litigation, the party who commences the action is the plaintiff. Other terms which may be substituted are complainant, appellant and petitioner, depending on the actual judicial forum. In criminal prosecution, the corresponding party to the plaintiff is the prosecution (i.e. people, state, commonwealth, or United States).

18. B. Executive law section 132 authorizes a county clerk to charge a fee of $10 to file and index a certificate of official character.

19. B. Executive law section 132 authorizes the secretary of state to charge a fee of $10 to issue a certificate of official character.

20. D. Consideration is anything of value given by one person to another in order to induce them to enter into a contract.

21. B. Process is any method used by the court to get or use its power over a person or a specific property. In legal practice, the term is used to describe the actual summons, subpoena, writ, or warrant issued by a court or other judicial or quasi-judicial authority.

22. B. Chattel is an article of personal property, also called personalty. Some examples are automobiles, farm animals, clothing, lobsters, and even pets.

23. A. A conservator is a person appointed by a county surrogate to manage the affairs of an incompetent person or ward (i.e. due to infancy, infirmity, illness or injury). Other terms which may be substituted include guardian, special guardian, and guardian *ad litem* (Latin for "the lawsuit").

24. C. In *People v. Rathbone,* 145 N.Y. 434, 40 N.E. 395 (1895), New York's highest court declared that a notary public is a public officer. This case decision is probably one of the most important cases in New York concerning notaries public. As of publication, no court has challenged the ruling made over one hundred years ago. Thus, this common law decision is still "good law".

25. A. All fees collected by a notary public for official services rendered are legally payable to the notary. While the law clearly states the position, the practical matter is more complex. (*Kress v. Manufacturers Trust Co.,* 250 A.D. 93, 293 N.Y.S 646). For example, in the private sector, an employer is not entitled to the fee revenue, even if the employer has sponsored costs and expenses for the employee notary including class tuition, textbook, examination fee, application and appointment fees, official seal and stamp, register, etc. However, due to the often fragile nature of employer-employee relationships, it will be very difficult for a notary to convince his employer to adopt such an arrangement. In the public sector, a gov-

ernment employer may or may not be legally entitled to notary fee revenue. For example, a town officer may be appointed a notary public. The state comptroller has stated that a town officer may retain for his own use any fees received while active as a notary, but the expense of his appointment is not a proper town charge. (1947) *Ops. St. Compt.* 405 Thus, if the town *does* sponsor all costs for the notary to maintain his official duties, the town, not the notary, is entitled to keep any fees. Many elected and appointed officials provide notary service as a courtesy to their constituents.

26. C. Judiciary law chapter 30, article 15, section 491 makes it unlawful for any person or organization to share fees (or even agree to) with or receive from any attorney. The prohibition is *not* limited to notaries public, but applies to all non-attorneys. Attorneys can agree to divide fees with other attorneys. The crime of sharing of compensation by attorneys is a misdemeanor.

27. C. Executive law section 140 states that where a person whose term as a notary public has expired and he applies within six months of the expiration for reappointment with the county clerk, the qualifying requirements (namely taking and passing the written examination) may be waived by the secretary of state.

28. B. Chattel paper is a document which evidences both a monetary obligation and a security interest in or a lease of specific goods.

29. A. Executive law section 135-a states if a notary public continues to serve after his commission expires, or willfully submits false information on his application for appointment, he is guilty of a misdemeanor.

30. B. Banking law section 335 requires that the lessor must give proper notice to the last known address of the lessee by certified, return-receipt mail, at least 30 days prior to opening the safe deposit box.

31. D. An oath ceremony is a personal experience. It requires both the oath administrator and oath taker to be in the physical presence of each other at the same time. There are no exceptions, whatsoever. *People v. Semonite,* 18 Misc.2d 427, 189 N.Y.S.2d 256. *Matter of Napolis,* 169 App. Div. 469.

32. D. The powers of a notary public are personal. The powers are non-delegable.

33. B. The acknowledgment of a legal instrument permits it to be recorded in a county clerk's office. Hence, the association of the acknowledgment with deeds, mortgages, certain leases, business certificates, etc., all of which are filed in a county clerk's office.

34. D. The power of the state supreme court to conduct a hearing for and also punish for criminal contempt may not be instituted by the secretary of state.

35. A. A holographic will or deed is handwritten entirely by the testator or grantor and not witnessed or attested. These wills and deeds are contestable and are useful only in limited circumstances: military personnel (hence, the common name of "soldier's will") and civilian support personnel during active combat or armed conflict; also naval and merchant mariners while at sea.

36. D. Intestacy is the state or condition of dying without having made a valid will, or without having disposed by will of a part of his property. In order to protect the deceased and the estate beneficiaries, each state has instituted a "default will" by virtue of enacting intestacy statutes in the probate code. Thus, even though a person may die without crafting his own will, he actually has, even unwittingly, chosen the state statutory will.

37. B. A codicil is a supplement or an addition to a will. With the widespread use of personal computers in law offices today, along with the virtual abandonment of the conventional typewriter, use of the codicil has declined.

Rather than prepare a separate codicil and then attach the codicil to the original will, many attorneys simply amend the original will (stored on a computer based file), print an amended will and then execute the fully up-to-date version. The codicil had its heyday during the reign of the typewriter. Instead of typing the entire will over again from the beginning, the codicil allowed minor revisions to the original will.

38. C. Election law involves the action of a notary public except for an absentee ballot for a military voter. Nominating petitions, designating petitions and declinations of nominations involve a notary public.

39. A. A power of attorney is the instrument by which authority of one person is granted to act in place of another. The power of attorney is the actual legal instrument. The person granting his power of attorney is the principal. The attorney in fact is the recipient of the power of attorney. An attorney in fact is not required to be an attorney at law. Although it is frequently the case, powers of attorney are not always required to be acknowledged before a notary public. However, even if not legally required, a prudent person is strongly advised to acknowledge his power of attorney before a notary public, record it at a county clerk's office, and then have the clerk issue a certified copy of the recorded power of attorney.

40. B. A subpoena duces tecum is a court process, on a summons, which compels production of certain specific documents and items, and material relevant to facts in issue in a pending judicial proceeding.

Appendix A: New York State Department of State Directory

The nine offices of the department of state are listed to assist prospective notaries public in obtaining applications for appointment, filing their applications, and follow up on their testing and appointment. Completed applications for initial appointment should be directed to the *Albany* office.

Commissioned notaries public will find the information helpful when required for notifying the department of state regarding change of address or name information, filing resignation letters, or any other questions in reference to official duties and responsibilities.

For updates to this directory, please consult the following web pages via the internet: http://www.dos.state.ny.us

NYS Department of State
Division of Licensing Services
84 Holland Avenue
Albany, New York 12208-3490
(518) 474-4429

Notary Public Unit
(518) 474-2643

State Office Building Annex
164 Hawley Street
Binghamton, New York 13901
(607) 773-7722

65 Court Street
Buffalo, New York 14202
(716) 847-7110

State Office Building
Veterans Memorial Highway
Hauppauge, New York 11788
(516) 360-6579

114 Old Country Road
Mineola, New York 11501
(516) 747-0700

270 Broadway
New York, New York 10007
(212) 417-5740

One Marine Midland Plaza
Rochester, New York 14604
(716) 454-3094

Hughes State Office Building
333 East Washington Street
Syracuse, New York 13202
(315) 428-4258

State Office Building
207 Genesee Street
Utica, New York 13501
(315) 793-2533

Appendix B: New York State County Clerks Directory

The office addresses and telephone numbers of the 62 New York county clerks are provided to assist notaries public in: filing their oaths of office; obtaining and filing certificates of official character; assisting constituents in obtaining certification of notarial signatures (county clerk's certificate of authentication); and filing public documents.

For updates to this directory, please consult the following web pages via the internet: http://www.dos.state.ny.us/lists/coclerks.html or http://www.albanycounty.com/elected/clerk/veterans.html

ADDRESS ALL CORRESPONDENCE TO "THE . . . COUNTY CLERK"

Albany	County Court House Room 128 Albany, 12207 (518) 487-5110 Fax: (518) 487-5099
Allegany	Courthouse Belmont, 14813 (716) 268-9270 Fax: (716) 268-9446

Bronx	851 Grand Concourse Bronx, 10451 (718) 590-3650 Fax: (718) 590-8122
Broome	44 Hawley Street P.O. Box 2062 Binghamton, 13902 (607) 778-2451 Fax: (607) 778-2243
Cattaraugus	303 Court Street County Center Little Valley, 14755 (716) 938-9111 x293 Fax: (716) 938-9438
Cayuga	County Office Bldg. 160 Genesee Street Auburn, 13021 (315) 253-1271 Fax: (315) 253-1006
Chautauqua	County Court House P.O. Box 170 Mayville, 14757 (716) 753-4331 Fax: (716) 753-4310
Chemung	210 Lake Street P.O. Box 588 Elmira, 14902 (607) 737-2920 Fax: (607) 737-2897
Chenango	County Office Building 5 Court Street Norwich, 13815 (607) 337-1450 Fax: (607) 337-1455

Clinton | 137 Margaret Street
Plattsburgh, 12901
(518) 565-4700
Fax: (518) 565-4780

Columbia | 560 Warren Street
Hudson, 12534
(518) 828-3339
Fax: (518) 828-5299

Cortland | Court House
P.O. Box 5590
Cortland, 13045
(607) 753-5021
Fax: (607) 758-5500

Delaware | P. O. Box 426
Delhi, 13753
(607) 746-2123
Fax: (607) 746-6924

Dutchess | County Office Bldg.
22 Market Street
Poughkeepsie, 12601
(914) 486-2132
Fax: (914) 486-2138

Erie | 25 Delaware Avenue
Buffalo, 14202
(716) 858-8865
Fax: (716) 858-6550

Essex | Court Street
Elizabethtown, 12932
(518) 873-3600
Fax: (518) 873-3548

Franklin | 63 W. Main Street
P.O. Box 70
Malone, 12953
(518) 481-1684
Fax: (518) 483-9143

Fulton	P.O. Box 485 Johnstown, 12095 (518) 762-0556 Fax: (518) 762-3839
Genesee	County Bldg. #1 P.O. Box 379 Batavia, 14021 (716) 344-2550 x2242 Fax: (716) 344-8521
Greene	Court House P.O. Box 446 Catskill, 12414 (518) 943-2050 Fax: (518) 943-2146
Hamilton	P.O. Box 204 Lake Pleasant, 12108 (518) 548-7111 Fax: (518) 548-7608
Herkimer	109 Mary Street Suite 111 Herkimer, 13350 (315) 867-1129 Fax: (315) 866-4396
Jefferson	175 Arsenal Street County Building Watertown, 13601 (315) 785-3081 Fax: (315) 785-5048
Kings	360 Adams Street Room 190 Brooklyn, 11201 (718) 643-7037 Fax: (718) 643-8187
Lewis	P. O. Box 232 Lowville, 13367 (315) 376-5333 x334 Fax: (315) 376-3768

Livingston	County Gov't Center Room 201 Geneseo, 14454 (716) 243-7010 Fax: (716) 243-7159
Madison	County Office Building P.O. Box 668 Wampsville, 13163 (315) 366-2260 Fax: (315) 366-2615
Monroe	39 West Main Street Rochester, 14614 (716) 428-5177 Fax: (716) 428-5447
Montgomery	County Office Building Fonda, 12068 (518) 853-8115 Fax: (518) 853-8171
Nassau	240 Old Country Road Mineola, 11501 (516) 571-2661 Fax: (516) 742-4099
New York	60 Centre Street Room 161 New York, 10007 (212) 374-8360 Fax: (212) 374-5970
Niagara	175 Hawley Street P. O. Box 461 Lockport, 14094 (716) 439-7022 Fax: (716) 439-7066

NYC Register	31 Chambers Street Room 201 New York, 10007 (212) 788-8512 Fax: (212) 788-8521
Oneida	800 Park Avenue Utica, 13501 (315) 798-5775 Fax: (315) 798-6440
Onondaga	Court House 401 Montgomery Street Syracuse, 13202 (315) 435-2227 Fax: (315) 435-3455
Ontario	20 Ontario Street Canandaigua, 14424 (716) 396-4200 Fax: (716) 396-4245
Orange	255 Main Street Goshen, 10924 (914) 291-2690 Fax: (914) 291-2691
Orleans	Court House Square 3 South Main Street Albion, 14411 (716) 589-5334 Fax: (716) 589-0181
Oswego	46 East Bridge Street Oswego, 13126 (315) 349-8385 Fax: (315) 349-8383
Otsego	197 Main Street P.O. Box 710 Cooperstown, 13326 (607) 547-4276 Fax: (607) 547-7544

Putnam	40 Gleneida Avenue Carmel, 10512 (914) 225-3641 x302 Fax: (914) 228-0231
Queens	88-11 Sutphin Blvd. Jamaica, 11435 (718) 520-3135 Fax: (718) 520-4731
Rensselaer	Court House Congress & Second Street Troy, 12180 (518) 270-4080 Fax: (518) 271-7998
Richmond	18 Richmond Terrace Staten Island, 10301 (718) 390-5396 Fax: (718) 390-5269
Rockland	27 New Hempstead Road New City, 10956 (914) 638-5221 Fax: (914) 638-5647
Saratoga	40 McMaster Street Ballston Spa, 12020 (518) 885-2213 Fax: (518) 884-4726
Schenectady	620 State Street Schenectady, 12305 (518) 388-4222 Fax: 518) 388-4224
Schoharie	300 Main Street P. O. Box 549 Schoharie, 12157 (518) 295-8316 Fax: 518) 295-8338

Schuyler	105 Ninth Street P.O. Box 8 Watkins Glen, 14891 (607) 535-8133 Fax: (607) 535-8130
Seneca	1 DiPronio Drive Waterloo, 13165 (315) 539-5655 x2040 Fax: (315) 539-9479
St. Lawrence	County Court House Canton, 13617 (315) 379-2237 Fax: (315) 379-2302
Steuben	3 Pulteney Square, East Bath, 14810 (607) 776-9631 x3204 Fax: 607) 776-7158
Suffolk	310 Center Drive Riverhead, 11901 (631) 852-2001 Fax: (631) 852-2004
Sullivan	Government Center 100 North Street Monticello, 12701 (914) 794-3000 x3150 Fax: (914) 794-3459
Tioga	16 Court Street P.O. Box 307 Owego, 13827 (607) 687-8660 Fax: 607) 687-4612
Tompkins	320 N. Tioga Street Ithaca, 14850 (607) 274-5431 Fax: 607) 274-5445

Ulster	Fair Street Kingston, 12402 (914) 340-3040 Fax: (914) 340-3299
Warren	Municipal Center Lake George, 12845 (518) 761-6427 Fax: (518) 761-6551
Washington	Municipal Center Upper Broadway Fort Edward, 12828 (518) 746-2171 Fax: (518) 746-2166
Wayne	9 Pearl Street P.O. Box 608 Lyons, 14489 (315) 946-7470 Fax: 315) 946-5978
Westchester	110 Dr. Martin Luther King Jr. Blvd. White Plains, 10601 (914) 285-3114 Fax: 914) 285-9005
Wyoming	143 N. Main Street P. O. Box 70 Warsaw, 14569 (716) 786-8810 Fax: (716) 786-3703
Yates	110 Court Street Penn Yan, 14527 (315) 536-5528 Fax: (315) 536-5545

Appendix C: New York State Department of State Examination Study Material

Editor's Note: The information contained in this appendix is transcribed verbatim from the information provided by the New York State Department of State. The author and publisher assume no responsibility for any errors, inaccuracies, omissions or inconsistencies. It is provided solely as a service and convenience to readers, and in no way implies an endorsement of the material contained within the appendix.

For updates to this appendix, please consult the following web pages via the internet: http://www.dos.state.ny.us

Introduction

Notaries are commissioned by the Secretary of State after they pass the walk-in examination and their applications are reviewed. The written examination is based on material contained in this booklet, and may also include questions pertaining to general knowledge and reasoning ability.

Upon request, county clerks will authenticate the signature of the notary on a document and will attest to the notary's authority to sign. This is normally obtained when the documents will be used outside the State. Notaries who expect to sign documents regularly in counties other than that of their residence may elect to file a certificate of official character with other New York State county clerks.

Out-of-State Residents. Attorneys, residing out of State, who are admitted to practice in the State and who maintain a law office within the State are deemed to be residents of the county where the office is maintained.

Nonresidents other than attorneys who have offices or places of business in New York State may also become notaries. The oath of office and signature of the notary must be filed in the office of the county clerk of the county in which the office or place of business is located.

NOTARY PUBLIC LICENSE LAW

Section	
	Professional conduct
	APPOINTMENT AND QUALIFICATIONS
	EXECUTIVE LAW
130	Appointment of notaries public
131	Procedure of appointment; fees and commissions
132	Certificates of official character of notaries public
133	Certification of notarial signatures
140	Executive Law (14) and (15)
3-200 and 3-400	Election Law
	PUBLIC OFFICERS LAW
3	Qualifications for holding office, provides that:
534	County clerk; appointment of notaries public
	MISCELLANEOUS
	Member of legislature
	Sheriffs
	Notary public—disqualifications
	POWERS AND DUTIES EXECUTIVE LAW
134	Signature and seal of county clerk
135	Powers and duties; in general; of notaries public who are attorneys at law
135-a	Notary public or commissioner of deeds; acting without appointment; fraud in office
136	Notarial fees
137	Statement as to authority of notaries public
138	Powers of notaries public or other officers who are stockholders, directors, officers or employees of a corporation
142-a	Validity of facts of notaries public and commissioners of deeds notwithstanding certain defects
	REAL PROPERTY LAW
290	Definitions; effect of article
298	Acknowledgments and proofs within the state
302	Acknowledgments and proofs by married women

PROFESSIONAL CONDUCT

Use of the office of notary in other than the specific, step-by-step procedure required is viewed as a serious offense by the Secretary of State. The practice of taking acknowledgments and affidavits over the telephone, or otherwise, without the actual, personal appearance of the individual making the acknowledgment or affidavit before the officiating notary, is illegal.

The attention of all notaries public is called to the following judicial declarations concerning such misconduct:

> "The court again wishes to express its condemnation of the acts of notaries taking acknowledgments or affidavits without the presence of the party whose acknowledgment is taken for the affiant, and that it will treat serious professional misconduct the act of any notary thus violating his official duty." (*Matter of Napolis,* 169 App. Div. 469, 472.)

> "Upon the faith of these acknowledgments rests the title of real property, and the only security to such titles is the fidelity with which notaries and commissioners of deeds perform their duty in requiring the appearance of parties to such instruments before them and always refusing to execute a certificate unless the parties are actually knows to them or the identity of the parties executing the instruments is satisfactorily proved." (*Matter of Gottheim,* 153 App. Div. 779, 782.)

Equally unacceptable to the Secretary of State is slipshod administration of oaths. The simplest form in which an oath may be lawfully administered is:

"Do you solemnly swear that the contents of this affidavit subscribed by you is correct and true?" (*Bookman v. City of New York,* 200 N.Y. 53, 56.)

Alternatively, the following affirmation may be used for persons who conscientiously decline taking an oath. This affirmation is legally equivalent to an oath and is just as binding:

"Do you solemnly, sincerely and truly declare and affirm that the statements made by you are true and correct?"

Whatever the form adopted, it must be in the presence of an officer authorized to administer it, and it must be an unequivocal and present act by which the affiant consciously takes upon himself the obligation of an oath. (Idem, citing People ex rel. *Kenyon v. Sutherland,* 81 N.Y. 1; *O'Reilly v. People,* 86 N.Y. 154, 158, 161.)

Unless a lawyer, the notary public may not engage directly or indirectly in the practice of law. Listed below are some of the activities involving the practice of law which are prohibited, and which subject the notary public to removal from office by the Secretary of State, and possible imprisonment, fine or both. A notary:

1. **May not give advice on the law.** The notary may not draw any kind of legal papers, such as wills, deeds, bills of sale, mortgages, chattel mortgages, contracts, leases, offers, options, incorporation papers, releases, mechanics liens, power of attorney, complaints and all legal pleadings, papers in summary proceedings to evict a tenant, or in bankruptcy, affidavits, or any papers which our courts have said are legal documents or papers.

2. **May not ask for and get legal** business to send to a lawyer or lawyers with whom he has any business connection or from whom he receives any money or other consideration for sending the business.

3. **May not divide or agree to divide** his fees with a lawyer, or accept any part of a lawyer's fee on any legal business.

4. **May not advertise in, or circulate** in any manner, any paper or advertisement, or say to anyone that he has any powers or rights not given to the notary by the laws under which the notary was appointed.

A notary public is cautioned not to execute an acknowledgment of the execution of a will. Such acknowledgment cannot be deemed equivalent to an attestation clause accompanying a will. (*See definition of Attestation Clause*)

Appointment and Qualifications

Index

Law	Sec	Subject
Executive Law	130	Appointment of Notaries Public
Executive Law	131	Procedure of Appointment; Fees
Executive Law	132	Certificates of Official Character

Executive Law	133	Certification of Notarial Signatures
Executive Law	140	Commissioner of Deeds, NYC
Election Law	3-200 3-400	Commissioner of Elections
Public Officers Law	3	Qualifications for Holding Office
Public Officers Law	534	County Clerk; Appointment of Notaries
NYS Constitution	Art. II Sec. 7	Member of Legislature
NYS Constitution	Art. XIII Sec. 13a	Sheriffs
Miscellaneous		Disqualifications

EXECUTIVE LAW

§130. Appointment of notaries public.

The Secretary of State may appoint and commission as many notaries public for the State of New York as in his judgment may be deemed best, whose jurisdiction shall be co-extensive with the boundaries of the state. The appointment of a notary public shall be for a term of 4 years. An application for an appointment as notary public shall be in form and set forth such matters as the Secretary of State shall prescribe. Every person appointed as notary public must, at the time of his appointment, be a citizen of the United States and either a resident of the State of New York or have an office or place of business in New York State. A notary public who is a resident of the State and who moves out of the state but still maintains a place of business or an office in New York State does not vacate his office as a notary public. A notary public who is a nonresident and who ceases to have an office or place of business in this state, vacates his office as a notary public. A notary public who is a resident of New York State and moves out of the state and who does not retain an office or place of business in this State shall vacate his office as a notary public. A non-resident who accepts the office of notary public in this State thereby appoints the Secretary of State as the person upon whom process can be served on his behalf. Before issuing to any applicant a commission as notary public, unless he be an attorney and counselor at law duly admitted to practice in this state, the Secretary of State shall satisfy himself that the applicant is of good moral character, has the equivalent of a common school education and is familiar with the duties and responsibilities of a notary public; provided, however, that where a notary public applies, before the expiration of his term, for reappointment with the county clerk or where a person whose term as notary public shall have expired applies within 6 months thereafter for reappointment as a notary public with the county clerk, such qualifying requirements may be waived by the Secretary of State, and further, where an application for reappointment is filed with the county clerk after the expiration of the aforementioned renewal period by a person who failed or was unable to reapply by reason of his induction or enlistment in the armed forces of the United States, such qualifying requirements may also be waived by the Secretary of State, provided such application for reappointment is made within a period of 1 year after the military discharge of the applicant under conditions other than dishonorable. In any case, the appointment or reappointment of any applicant is in the discretion of the Secretary of State. The Secretary of State may suspend or remove from office, for misconduct, any notary public appointed by him but no such removal shall be made unless the person who is sought to be removed shall have been served with a copy of the charges against him and have an opportunity of being heard. No person shall be appointed as a notary public under this article who has been convicted, in this State or any other state or territory, of a felony or any of the following offenses, to wit:

(a) illegally using, carrying or possessing a pistol or other dangerous weapon;
(b) making or possessing burglar's instruments;
(c) buying or receiving or criminally possessing stolen property;
(d) unlawful entry of a building;
(e) aiding escape from prison;
(f) unlawfully possessing or distributing habit forming narcotic drugs;
(g) violating §§270, 270-a, 270-b, 270-c, 271, 275, 276, 550, 551, 551-a and subdivisions 6, 8, 10 or 11 of § 722 of the former Penal Law as in force and effect immediately prior to September 1, 1967, or violating §§ 165.25, 165.30, subdivision 1 of § 240.30, subdivision 3 of § 40.35 of the Penal Law, or violating §§478, 479, 480, 481, 484, 489 and 491 of the Judiciary Law; or

(h) vagrancy or prostitution, and who has not subsequent to such conviction received an executive pardon therefor or a certificate of good conduct from the parole board to remove the disability under this section because of such conviction. A person regularly admitted to practice as an attorney and counselor in the courts of record of this state, whose office for the practice of law is within the State, may be appointed a notary public and retain his office as such notary public although he resides in or removes to an adjoining state. For the purpose of this and the following sections of this article such person shall be deemed a resident of the county where he maintains such office.

§131. Procedure of appointment; fees and commissions.

1. Applicants for a notary public commission shall submit to the Secretary of State with their application the oath of office, duly executed before any person authorized to administer an oath, together with their signature.

2. Upon being satisfied of the competency and good character of applicants for appointment as notaries public, the Secretary of State shall issue a commission to such persons; and the official signature of the applicants and the oath of office filed with such applications shall take effect.

3. The Secretary of State shall receive a non-refundable application fee of $60 from applicants for appointment, which fee shall be submitted together with the application. No further fee shall be paid for the issuance of the commission.

4. A notary public identification card indicating the appointee's name, address, county and commission term shall be transmitted to the appointee.

5. The commission, duly dated, and a certified copy or the original of the oath of office and the official signature, and $20 apportioned from the application fee shall be transmitted by the Secretary of State to the county clerk in which the appointee resides by the 10th day of the following month.

6. The county clerk shall make a proper index of commissions and official signatures transmitted to that office by the Secretary of State pursuant to the provisions of this section.

7. Applicants for reappointment of a notary public commission shall submit to the county clerk with their application the oath of office, duly executed before any person authorized to administer an oath, together with their signature.

8. Upon being satisfied of the completeness of the application for reappointment, the county clerk shall issue a commission to such persons; and the official signature of the applicants and the oath of office filed with such applications shall take effect.

9. The county clerk shall receive a non-refundable application fee of $60 from each applicant for reappointment, which fee shall be submitted together with the application. No further fee shall be paid for the issuance of the commission.

10. The commission, duly dated, and a certified or original copy of the application, and $40 apportioned from the application fee plus interest as may be required by statute shall be transmitted by the county clerk to the Secretary of State by the 10th day of the following month.

11. The Secretary of State shall make a proper record of commissions transmitted to that office by the county clerk pursuant to the provisions of this section. 12. Except for changes made in an application for reappointment, the Secretary of State shall receive a non-refundable fee of $10 for changing the name or address of a notary public.

13. The Secretary of State may issue a duplicate identification card to a notary public for one lost, destroyed or damaged upon application therefor on a form prescribed by the Secretary of State and upon payment of a non-refundable fee of $10. Each such duplicate identification card shall have the word "duplicate" stamped across the face thereof, and shall bear the same number as the one it replaces.

§132. Certificates of official character of notaries public. The Secretary of State or the county clerk of the county in which the commission of a notary public is filed may certify to the official character of such notary public and any notary public may file his autograph signature and a certificate of official character in the office of any county clerk of any county in the State and in any register's office in any county having a register and thereafter such county clerk may certify as to the official character of such notary public. The Secretary of State shall collect for each certificate of official character issued by him the sum of $10. The county clerk and register of any county with whom a certificate of official character has been filed shall collect for filing the same the sum of $10. For each certificate of official character issued, with seal attached, by any county clerk, the sum of $5 shall be collected by him.

§133. Certification of notarial signatures.

The county clerk of a county in whose office any notary public has qualified or has filed his autograph signature and a certificate of his official character, shall, when so requested and upon payment of a fee of $3 affix to any certificate of proof or acknowledgment or oath signed by such notary anywhere in the State of New York, a certificate under his hand and seal, stating that a commission or a certificate of his official character with his autograph signature has been filed in his office, and that he was at the time of taking such proof or acknowledgment or oath duly authorized to take the same; that he is well acquainted with the handwriting of such notary public or has compared the signature on the certificate of proof or acknowledgment or oath with the autograph signature deposited in his office by such notary public and believes that the signature is genuine. An instrument with such certificate of authentication of the county clerk affixed thereto shall be entitled to be read in evidence or to be recorded in any of the counties of this State in respect to which a certificate of a county clerk may be necessary for either purpose.

§140. Commissioner of deeds.

14. No person who has been removed from office as a commissioner of deeds for the City of New York, as hereinbefore provided, shall thereafter be eligible again to be appointed as such commissioner nor, shall he be eligible thereafter to appoint to the office of notary public.

15. Any person who has been removed from office as aforesaid, who shall, after knowledge of such removal, sign or execute any instrument as a commissioner of deeds or notary public shall be deemed guilty of a misdemeanor.

§§3-200 and 3-400. Election Law.
A commissioner of elections or inspector of elections is eligible for the office of notary public.

PUBLIC OFFICERS LAW

§3. Qualifications for holding office, provides that:
No person is eligible for the office of notary public who has been convicted of a violation of the selective draft act of the U.S. enacted May 18, 1917, or the acts amendatory or supplemental thereto, or of the federal selective training and service act of 1940 or the acts amendatory thereof or supplemental thereto.

§534. County clerk; appointment of notaries public.
Each county clerk shall designate from among the members of his or her staff at least one notary public to be available to notarize documents for the public in each county clerk's office during normal business hours free of charge. Each individual appointed by the county clerk to be a notary public pursuant to this section shall be exempt from the examination fee and application fee required by §131 of the Executive Law.

MISCELLANEOUS

Member of legislature.
"If a member of the legislature be *** appointed to any office, civil *** under the government *** the State of New York *** his or her acceptance thereof shall vacate his or her seat in the legislature, providing, however, that a member of the legislature may be appointed *** to any office in which he or she shall receive no compensation." (§7 of Article III of the Constitution of the State of New York.) A member of the legislature may be appointed a notary public in view of transfer of power of such appointment from the governor and senate to the Secretary of State. (1927, Op. Atty. Gen. 97.)

Sheriffs.
*** Sheriffs shall hold no other office. *** (§13(a) of Article XIII of the Constitution of the State of New York.)

Notary public—disqualifications.

Though a person may be eligible to hold the office of notary the person may be disqualified to act in certain cases by reason of having an interest in the case. To state the rule broadly: if the notary is a party to or directly and pecuniarily interested in the transaction, the person is not capable of acting in that case. For example, a notary who is a grantee or mortgagee in a conveyance or mortgage is disqualified to take the acknowledgment of the grantor or mortgagor; likewise a notary who is a trustee in a deed of trust; and, of course, a notary who is the grantor could not take his own acknowledgment. A notary beneficially interested in the conveyance by way of being secured thereby is not competent to take the acknowledgment of the instrument. In New York the courts have held an acknowledgment taken by a person financially or beneficially interested in a party to conveyance or instrument of which it is a part to be a nullity; and that the acknowledgment of an assignment of a mortgage before one of the assignees is a nullity; and that an acknowledgment by one of the incorporators of the other incorporators who signed a certificate was of no legal effect.

POWERS AND DUTIES

Index

Law	Sec	Subject
Executive Law	134	Signature and Seal of County Clerk
Executive Law	135	Powers and Duties
Executive Law	135a	Acting Without Appointment, Fraud in Office
Executive Law	136	Notarial Fees
Executive Law	137	Statement as to authority
Executive Law	138	Powers of Notaries—Corporations
Executive Law	142-a	Validity of facts
Real Property Law	290	Definitions
Real Property Law	298	Acknowledgments and Proofs within the State
Real Property Law	302	Acknowledgments and Proofs By Married Women
Real Property Law	303	Requisites of Acknowledgments

Real Property Law	304	Proof by Subscribing Witness
Real Property Law	306	Certificate of Acknowledgment Or Proof
Real Property Law	309	Acknowledgment by Corporation
Real Property Law	330	Officers Guilty of Malfeasance
Real Property Law	333	When Conveyances Not to Be Recorded
Banking Law	335	Unpaid Rental of Safe Deposit Box
Civil Practice Law	3113	Taking of Deposition by and Rules Notary
Domestic Relation	S11	No Authority to Solemnize Marriage
Public Officers	10	Administering Oath of Public Officer

EXECUTIVE LAW

§134. Signature and seal of county clerk.
The signature and seal of a county clerk, upon a certificate of official character of a notary public or the signature of a county clerk upon a certificate of authentication of the signature and acts of a notary public or commissioner of deeds, may be a facsimile, printed, stamped, photographed or engraved thereon.

§135. Powers and duties; in general; of notaries public who are attorneys at law.
Every notary public duly qualified is hereby authorized and empowered within and throughout the State to administer oaths and affirmations, to take affidavits and depositions, to receive and certify acknowledgments or proof of deeds, mortgages and powers of attorney and other instruments in writing; to demand acceptance or payment of foreign and inland bills of exchange, promissory notes and obligations in writing, and to protest the same for non-acceptance or non-payment, as the case may require, and, for use in another jurisdiction, to exercise such other powers and duties as by the laws of nations and according to commercial usage, or by the laws of any other government or country may be exercised and performed by notaries public, provided that when exercising such powers he shall set forth the name of such other jurisdiction.

A notary public who is an attorney at law regularly admitted to practice in this State may, in his discretion, administer an oath or affirmation to or take the affidavit or acknowledgment of his client in respect of any matter, claim, action or proceeding.

For any misconduct by a notary public in the performance of any of his powers such notary public shall be liable to the parties injured for all damages sustained by them. A notary public shall not, directly or indirectly, demand or receive for the protest for the non-payment of any note, or for the non-acceptance or non-payment of any bill of exchange, check or draft and giving the requisite notices and certificates of such protest, including his notarial seal, if affixed thereto, any greater fee or reward than 75 cents for such protest, and 10 cents for each notice, not exceeding five, on any bill or note. Every notary public having a seal shall, except as otherwise provided, and when requested, affix his seal to such protest free of expense.

§135-a. Notary public or commissioner of deeds; acting without appointment; fraud in office.

1. Any person who holds himself out to the public as being entitled to act as a notary public or commissioner of deeds, or who assumes, uses or advertises the title of notary public or commissioner of deeds, or equivalent terms in any language, in such a manner as to convey the impression that he is a notary public or commissioner of deeds without having first been appointed as notary public or commissioner of deeds, or

2. A notary public or commissioner of deeds, who in the exercise of the powers, or in the performance of the duties of such office shall practice any fraud or deceit, the punishment for which is not otherwise provided for by this act, shall be guilty of a misdemeanor.

§136. Notarial fees.

A notary public shall be entitled to the following fees:

1. For administering an oath or affirmation, and certifying the same when required, except where another fee is specifically prescribed by statute, $2.

2. For taking and certifying the acknowledgment or proof of

execution of a written instrument, by one person, $2, and by each additional person, $2, for swearing such witness thereto, $2.

§137. Statement as to authority of notaries public.
In exercising his powers pursuant to this article, a notary public, in addition to the venue of his act and his signature, shall print, typewrite, or stamp beneath his signature in black ink, his name, the words "Notary Public State of New York," the name of the county in which he originally qualified, and the date upon which his commission expires and, in addition, wherever required, a notary public shall also include the name of any county in which his certificate of official character is filed, using the words "Certificate filed .... County." A notary public who is duly licensed as an attorney and counselor at law in this State may in his discretion, substitute the words "Attorney and Counselor at Law" for the words "Notary Public." A notary public who has qualified or who has filed a certificate of official character in the office of the clerk in a county or counties within the City of New York must also affix to each instrument his official number or numbers in black ink, as given to him by the clerk or clerks of such county or counties at the time such notary qualified in such county or counties and, if the instrument is to be recorded in an office of the register of the City of New York in any county within such city and the notary has been given a number or numbers by such register or his predecessors in any county or counties, when his autographed signature and certificate are filed in such office or offices pursuant to this chapter, he shall also affix such number or numbers. No official act of such notary public shall be held invalid on account of the failure to comply with these provisions. If any notary public shall wilfully fail to comply with any of the provisions of this section, he shall be subject to disciplinary action by the secretary of state. In all the courts within this State the certificate of a notary public, over his signature, shall be received as presumptive evidence of the facts contained in such certificate; provided, that any person interested as a party to a suit may contradict, by other evidence, the certificate of a notary public.

§138. Powers of notaries public or other officers who are stockholders, directors, officers or employees of a corporation.

A notary public, justice of the supreme court, a judge, clerk, deputy clerk, or special deputy clerk of a court, an official examiner of title, or the mayor or recorder of a city, a justice of the peace, surrogate, special surrogate, special county judge, or commissioner of deeds, who is a stockholder, director, officer or employee of a corporation may take the acknowledgment or proof of any party to a written instrument executed to or by such corporation, or administer an oath of any other stockholder, director, officer, employee or agent of such corporation, and such notary public may protest for non-acceptance or non-payment, bills of exchange, drafts, checks, notes and other negotiable instruments owned or held for collection by such corporation; but none of the officers above named shall take the acknowledgment or proof of a written instrument by or to a corporation of which he is a stockholder, director, officer or employee, if such officer taking such acknowledgment or proof to be a party executing such instrument, either individually or as representative of such corporation, nor shall a notary public protest any negotiable instruments owned or held for collection by such corporation, if such notary public be individually a party to such instrument, or have a financial interest in the subject of same. All such acknowledgments or proofs of deeds, mortgages or other written instruments, relating to real property heretofore taken before any of the officers aforesaid are confirmed. This act shall not affect any action or legal proceeding now pending.

§142-a. Validity of acts of notaries public and commissioners of deeds notwithstanding certain defects.

1. Except as provided in subdivision three of this section, the official certificates and other acts heretofore or hereafter made or performed of notaries public and commissioners of deeds heretofore or hereafter and prior to the time of their acts appointed or commissioned as such shall not be deemed invalid, impaired or in any manner defective, so far as they may be affected, impaired or questioned by reason of defects described in subdivision two of this section.

2. This section shall apply to the following defects:

(a) ineligibility of the notary public or commissioner of deeds to be appointed or commissioned as such;

(b) misnomer or misspelling of name or other error made in his appointment or commission;

(c) omission of the notary public or commissioner of deeds to take or file his official oath or otherwise qualify;

(d) expiration of his term, commission or appointment;

(e) vacating of his office by change of his residence, by acceptance of another public office, or by other action on his part;

(f) the fact that the action was taken outside the jurisdiction where the notary public or commissioner of deeds was authorized to act.

3. No person shall be entitled to assert the effect of this section to overcome a defect described in subdivision two if he knew of the defect or if the defect was apparent on the face of the certificate of the notary public or commissioner of deeds; provided however, that this subdivision shall not apply after the expiration of six months from the date of the act of the notary public or commissioner of deeds.

4. After the expiration of six months from the date of the official certificate or other act of the commissioner of deeds, subdivision one of this section shall be applicable to a defect consisting in omission of the certificate of a commissioner of deeds to state the date on which and the place in which an act was done, or consisting of an error in such statement.

5. This section does not relieve any notary public or commissioner of deeds from criminal liability imposed by reason of his act, or enlarge the actual authority of any such officer, nor limit any other statute or rule of law by reason of which the act of a notary public or commissioner of deeds, or the record thereof, is valid or is deemed valid in any case.

Real Property Law

§290. Definitions; effect of article.

***

3. The term "conveyance" includes every written instrument, by which any estate or interest in real property is created, transferred, mortgaged or assigned, or by which the title to any real

property may be affected, including an instrument in execution of power, although the power be one of revocation only, and an instrument postponing or subordinating a mortgage lien; except a will, a lease for a term not exceeding three years, an executory contract for the sale or purchase of lands, and an instrument containing a power to convey real property as the agent or attorney for the owner of such property.

***

§298. Acknowledgments and proofs within the state.
The acknowledgment or proof, within this state, of a conveyance of real property situate in this State may be made:

1. At any place within the state, before
   (a) a justice of the supreme court;
   (b) an official examiner of title;
   (c) an official referee; or
   (d) a notary public.

2. Within the district wherein such officer is authorized to perform official duties, before
   (a) a judge or clerk of any court of record;
   (b) a commissioner of deeds outside of the City of New York, or a commissioner of deeds of the City of New York within the five counties comprising the City of New York;
   (c) the mayor or recorder of a city;
   (d) a surrogate, special surrogate, or special county judge; or
   (e) the county clerk or other recording officer of a county.

3. Before a justice of the peace, town councilman, village police justice or a judge of any court of inferior local jurisdiction, anywhere within the county containing the town, village or city in which he is authorized to perform official duties.

§302. Acknowledgments and proofs by married women.
The acknowledgment or proof of a conveyance of real property, within the state, or of any other written instrument, may be made by a married woman the same as if unmarried.

§303. Requisites of acknowledgments.
An acknowledgment must not be taken by any officer unless he

knows or has satisfactory evidence, that the person making it is the person described in and who executed such instrument.

§304. Proof by subscribing witness.

When the execution of a conveyance is proved by a subscribing witness, such witness must state his own place of residence, and if his place of residence is in a city, the street and street number, if any thereof, and that he knew the person described in and who executed the conveyance. The proof must not be taken unless the officer is personally acquainted with such witness, or has satisfactory evidence that he is the same person, who was a subscribing witness to the conveyance.

§306. Certificate of acknowledgment or proof.

A person taking the acknowledgment or proof of a conveyance must endorse thereupon or attach thereto, a certificate, signed by himself, stating all the matters required to be done, known, or proved on the taking of such acknowledgment or proof; together with the name and substance of the testimony of each witness examined before him, and if a subscribing witness, his place of residence.

***

§309-a. Uniform forms of certificates of acknowledgment or proof within this state.

1. The certificate of an acknowledgment, within this State, of a conveyance or other instrument in respect to real property situate in this State, by a person, must conform substantially with the following form, the blanks being properly filled:

State of New York)
) ss.:
County of . . . .)

On the . . . . . . day of . . . . . . in the year . . . . . . before me, the undersigned, a Notary Public in and for said State, personally appeared . . . . . ., personally known to me or proved to me on the basis of satisfactory evidence to be the individual(s) whose name(s) is (are) subscribed to the within instrument and acknowledged to me that he/she/they executed the same in his/her/their capacity(ies), and that by his/her/their signature(s) on the instrument, the individual(s), or the person upon behalf of which the individual(s) acted, executed the instrument.

(*Signature and office of individual taking acknowledgment.*)

2. The certificate for a proof of execution by subscribing witness, within this state, of a conveyance or other instrument made by any person in respect to real property situate in this state, must conform substantially with the following form, the blanks being properly filled:

State of New York)
) ss.:
County of . . . .)

On the . . . . . . day of . . . . . . in the year . . . . . . before me, the undersigned, a Notary Public in and for said State, personally appeared . . . . . ., the subscribing witness to the foregoing instrument, with whom I am personally acquainted, who, being by me duly sworn, did depose and say that he/she/they reside(s) in . . . . . . (if the place of residence is in a city, include the street and street number, if any, thereof); that he/she/they know(s) . . . . . . to be the individual described in and who executed the foregoing instrument; that said subscribing witness was present and saw said . . . . . . execute the same; and that said witness at the same time subscribed his/her/their name(s) as a witness thereto.

(*Signature and office of individual taking proof*).

3. A certificate of an acknowledgment or proof taken under §300 of this article shall include the additional information required by that section.

4. For the purposes of this section, the term "person" means any corporation, joint stock company, estate, general partnership (including any registered limited liability partnership or foreign limited liability partnership), limited liability company (including a professional service limited liability company), foreign limited liability company (including a foreign professional service limited liability company), joint venture, limited partnership, natural person, attorney in fact, real estate investment trust, business trust or other trust, custodian, nominee or any other individual or entity in its own or any representative capacity.

§ 309-b. Uniform forms of certificates of acknowledgment or proof without this state.

1. The certificate of an acknowledgment, without this State of a conveyance or other instrument with respect to real property situate in this State, by a person, may conform substantially with the following form, the blanks being properly filled:

State, District of Columbia,)
Territory, Possession, or) ss.:
Foreign Country)

On the . . . . . . day of . . . . . . in the year . . . . . . before me, the undersigned, personally appeared . . . . . ., personally known to me or proved to me on the basis of satisfactory evidence to be the individual(s) whose name(s) is (are) subscribed to the within instrument and acknowledged to me that he/she/they executed the same in his/her/their capacity(ies), that by his/her/their signature(s) on the instrument, the individual(s), or the person upon behalf of which the individual(s) acted, executed the instrument, and that such individual made such appearance before the undersigned in the . . . . . . (insert the city or other political subdivision and the state or country or other place the acknowledgment was taken).

(*Signature and office of individual taking acknowledgment.*)

2. The certificate for a proof of execution by subscribing witness, without this state, of a conveyance or other instrument made by any person in respect to real property situate in this State, may conform substantially with the following form, the blanks being properly filled:

State, District of Columbia,)
Territory, Possession, or) ss.:
Foreign Country)

On the . . . . . . day of . . . . . . in the year . . . . . . before me, the undersigned, personally appeared . . . . . ., the subscribing witness to the foregoing instrument, with whom I am personally acquainted, who, being by me duly sworn, did depose and say that he/she resides in (if the place of residence is in a city, include the street and street number, if any, thereof); that he/she knows . . . . . . to be the individual described in and who executed the foregoing instrument; that said subscribing witness was present

and saw said . . . . . . execute the same; that said witness at the same time subscribed his/her name as a witness thereto; and that said subscribing witness made such appearance before the undersigned in . . . . . . (insert the city or other political subdivision and the state or country or other place in which the proof was taken.)
(*Signature and office of individual taking proof.*)

3. No provision of this section shall be construed to:
   (a) modify the choice of laws afforded by §§299-a and 301-a of this article pursuant to which an acknowledgment or proof may be taken;
   (b) modify any requirement of §307 of this article;
   (c) modify any requirement for a seal imposed by subdivision one of §308 of this article;
   (d) modify any requirement concerning a certificate of authentication imposed by §308, 311, 312, 314, or 318 of this article; or
   (e) modify any requirement imposed by any provision of this article when the certificate of acknowledgment or proof purports to be taken in the manner prescribed by the laws of another state, the District of Columbia, territory, possession, or foreign country.

4. A certificate of an acknowledgment or proof taken under §300 of this article shall include the additional information required by that section.

5. For the purposes of this section, the term "person" means a person as defined in subdivision 4 of §309-a of this article.

§330. Officers guilty of malfeasance liable for damages.
An officer authorized to take the acknowledgment or proof of a conveyance or other instrument, or to certify such proof or acknowledgment, or to record the same, who is guilty of malfeasance or fraudulent practice in the execution of any duty prescribed by law in relation thereto, is liable in damages to the person injured.

§333. When conveyances of real property not to be recorded.

***

2. A recording officer shall not record or accept for record any

conveyance of real property, unless said conveyance in its entirety and the certificate of acknowledgment or proof and the authentication thereof, other than proper names therein which may be in another language provided they are written in English letters or characters, shall be in the English language, or unless such conveyance, certificate of acknowledgment or proof, and the authentication thereof be accompanied by and have attached thereto a translation in the English language duly executed and acknowledged by the person or persons making such conveyance and proved and authenticated, if need be, in the manner required of conveyances for recording in this state, or, unless such conveyance, certificate of acknowledgment or proof, and the authentication thereof be accompanied by and have attached thereto a translation in the English language made by a person duly designated for such purpose by the county judge of the county where it is desired to record such conveyance or a justice of the supreme court and be duly signed, acknowledged and certified under oath or upon affirmation by such person before such judge, to be a true and accurate translation and contain a certification of the designation of such person by such judge.

Special Note

By reason of changes in certain provisions of the Real Property Law, any and all limitations on the authority of a notary public to act as such in any part of the State have been removed; a notary public may now, in addition to administering oaths or taking affidavits anywhere in the State, take acknowledgments and proofs of conveyances anywhere in the State. The need for a certificate of authentication of a county clerk as a prerequisite to recording or use in evidence in this State of the instrument acknowledged or proved has been abolished. The certificate of authentication may possibly be required where the instrument is to be recorted or used in evidence outside the jurisdiction of the State.

§335. Banking Law

If the rental fee of any safe deposit box is not paid, or after the termination of the lease for such box, and at least 30 days after giving proper notice to the lessee, the lessor (bank) may, in the presence of a notary public, open the safe deposit box, remove and inventory the contents. The notary public shall then file with the lessor a certificate under seal which states the date of the opening of the safe deposit box, the name of the lessee, and a list of the contents. Within 10 days of the opening of the safe deposit box, a copy of this certificate must be mailed to the lessee at his last known postal address.

Rule 3113. Civil Practice Law and Rules

This rule authorizes a deposition to be taken before a notary public in a civil proceeding.

§11. Domestic Relations Law

A notary public has no authority to solemnize marriages; nor may a notary public take the acknowledgment of parties and witnesses to a written contract of marriage.

§10. Public Officers Law

Official oaths, permits the oath of a public officer to be administered by a notary public.

Restrictions and Violations

Law	Sec	Index Subject
Judiciary Law	484	None but Attorneys to Practice
Judiciary Law	485	Misdemeanor Violations
Judiciary Law	750	Powers of Courts to Punish
Public Officers Law	15	Notary Must Not Act Before Taking/ Filing Oath
Public Officers Law	67	Fees of Public Officers
Public Officers Law	69	Fees Prohibited for Administering Certain Oaths
Executive Law	135a	Removal From Office for Misconduct
Penal Law	70.00	Sentence of Imprisonment for Felony
Penal Law	70.15	Sentences of Imprisonment for Misdemeanors
Penal Law	170.10	Forgery in the Second Degree
Penal Law	175.40	Issuing a False Certificate
Penal Law	195.00	Official Misconduct

JUDICIARY LAW

§484. None but attorneys to practice in the state.
No natural person shall ask or receive, directly or indirectly, compensation for appearing for a person other than himself as attorney in any court or before any magistrate, or for preparing deeds, mortgages, assignments, discharges, leases or any other instruments affecting real estate, wills, codicils, or any other instrument affecting the disposition of property after death, or decedents' estates, or pleadings of any kind in any action brought before any court of record in this state, or make it a business to practice for another as an attorney in any court or before any magistrate unless he has been regularly admitted to practice, as an attorney or counselor, in the courts of record in the state; but nothing in this section shall apply

(1) to officers of societies for the prevention of cruelty, duly appointed, when exercising the special powers conferred upon such corporations under §1403 of the Not-for-Profit Corporation Law; or

(2) to law students who have completed at least 2 semesters of law school or persons who have graduated from a law school, who have taken the examination for admittance to practice law in the courts of record in the state immediately available after graduation from law school, or the examination immediately available after being notified by the board of law examiners that they failed to pass said exam, and who have not been notified by the board of law examiners that they have failed to pass two such examinations, acting under the supervision of a legal aid organization, when such students and persons are acting under a program approved by the appellate division of the supreme court of the department in which the principal office of such organization is located and specifying the extent to which such students and persons may engage in activities prohibited by this statute; or

(3) to persons who have graduated from a law school approved pursuant to the rules of the court of appeals for the admission of attorneys and counselors-at-law and who have taken the examination for admission to practice as an attorney and counselor-at-law immediately available after graduation from law school or the examination immediately available after being notified by the board of law examiners that they failed to pass said exam, and who have not been notified by the board of law examiners that

they have failed to pass two such examinations, when such persons are acting under the supervision of the state or a subdivision thereof or of any officer or agency of the state or a subdivision thereof, pursuant to a program approved by the appellate division of the supreme court of the department within which such activities are taking place and specifying the extent to which they may engage in activities otherwise prohibited by this statute and those powers of the supervising governmental entity or officer in connection with which they may engage in such activities.

§485. Violation of certain preceding sections a misdemeanor.

Any person violating the provisions of §§478, 479, 480, 481, 482, 483 or 484, shall be guilty of a misdemeanor.

§750. Power of courts to punish for criminal contempts.

*** B. *** the supreme court has power under this section to punish for a criminal contempt any person who unlawfully practices or assumes to practice law; and a proceeding under this subdivision may be instituted on the court's own motion or on the motion of any officer charged with the duty of investigating or prosecuting unlawful practice of law, or by any bar association incorporated under the laws of this State.

Illegal practice of law by notary public.

To make it a business to practice as an attorney at law, not being a lawyer, is a crime. "Counsel and advice, the drawing of agreements, the organization of corporations and preparing papers connected therewith, the drafting of legal documents of all kinds, including wills, are activities which have been long classed as law practice." (*People v. Alfani,* 227 NY 334, 339.)

Wills.

The execution of wills under the supervision of a notary public acting in effect as a lawyer, "cannot be too strongly condemned, not only for the reason that it means an invasion of the legal profession, but for the fact that testators thereby run the risk of frustrating their own solemnly declared intentions and rendering worthless maturely considered plans for the disposition of estates whose creation may have been the fruit of lives of industry and self-denial." (*Matter of Flynn,* 142 Misc. 7.)

Public Officers Law

Notary must not act before taking and filing oath of office. The Public Officers Law (§15) provides that a person who executes any of the functions of a public office without having taken and duly filed the required oath of office, as prescribed by law, is guilty of a misdemeanor. A notary public is a public officer.

§67. Fees of public officers.

1. Each public officer upon whom a duty is expressly imposed by law, must execute the same without fee or reward, except where a fee or other compensation therefor is expressly allowed by law.

2. An officer or other person, to whom a fee or other compensation is allowed by law, for any service, shall not charge or receive a greater fee or reward, for that service, than is so allowed. 3. An officer, or other person, shall not demand or receive any fee or compensation, allowed to him by law for any service, unless the service was actually rendered by him; except that an officer may demand in advance his fee, where he is, by law, expressly directed or permitted to require payment thereof, before rendering the service.

4. *** An officer or other person, who violates either of the provisions contained in this section, is liable, in addition to the punishment prescribed by law for the criminal offense, to an action in behalf of the person aggrieved, in which the plaintiff is entitled to treble damages.

A notary public subjects himself to criminal prosecution, civil suit and possible removal by asking or receiving more than the statutory allowance, for administering the ordinary oath in connect with an affidavit. (Op. Atty. Gen. (1917) 12 St. Dept. Rep. 507.)

§69. Fee for administering certain official oaths prohibited. An officer is not entitled to a fee, for administering the oath of office to a member of the legislature, to any military officer, to an inspector of election, clerk of the poll, or to any other public officer or public employee.

EXECUTIVE LAW

Misconduct by a notary and removal from office.
A notary public who, in the performance of the duties of such office shall practice any fraud or deceit, is guilty of a misdemeanor (Executive Law, §135-a), and may be removed from office. The notary may be removed from office if the notary made a misstatement of a material fact in his application for appointment; for preparing and taking an oath of an affiant to a statement that the notary knew to be false or fraudulent.

PENAL LAW

§70.00 Sentence of imprisonment for felony.

***

2. Maximum term of sentence. The maximum term of an indeterminate sentence shall be at least three years and the term shall be fixed as follows:

***

(d) For a class D felony, the term shall be fixed by the court, and shall not exceed 7 years; and

(e) For a class E felony, the term shall be fixed by the court, and shall not exceed 4 years.

***

§70.15 Sentences of imprisonment for misdemeanors and violation.
1. Class A misdemeanor. A sentence of imprisonment for a class A misdemeanor shall be a definite sentence. When such a sentence is imposed the term shall be fixed by the court, and shall not exceed one year;

***

✓ **§170.10 Forgery in the second degree.**
A person is guilty of forgery in the second degree when, with intent to defraud, deceive or injure another, he falsely makes, completes or alters a written instrument which is or purports to be, or which is calculated to become or to represent if completed:

1. A deed, will, codicil, contract, assignment, commercial in-

strument, or other instrument which does or may evidence, create, transfer, terminate or otherwise affect a legal right, interest, obligation or status; or 2. A public record, or an instrument filed or required or authorized by law to be filed in or with a public office or public servant; or

3. A written instrument officially issued or created by a public office, public servant or governmental instrumentality.

***

Forgery in the second degree is a class D felony.

√§175.40 Issuing a false certificate.
A person is guilty of issuing a false certificate when, being a public servant authorized by law to make or issue official certificates or other official written instruments, and with intent to defraud, deceive or injure another person, he issues such an instrument, or makes the same with intent that it be issued, knowing that it contains a false statement or false information. Issuing a false certificate is a class E felony.

√§195.00 Official misconduct.
A public servant is guilty of official misconduct when, with intent to obtain a benefit or to injure or deprive another person of a benefit:

1. He commits an act relating to his office but constituting an unauthorized exercise of his official functions, knowing that such act is unauthorized; or

2. He knowingly refrains from performing a duty which is imposed upon him by law or is clearly inherent in the nature of his office.

Official misconduct is a class A misdemeanor.

Notary must officiate on request.
The Penal Law (§195.00) provides that an officer before whom an oath or affidavit may be taken is bound to administer the same when requested, and a refusal to do so is a misdemeanor. (*People v. Brooks,* 1 Den. 457.)

Perjury.
One is guilty of perjury if he has stated or given testimony on a

material matter, under oath or by affirmation, as to the truth thereof, when he knew the statement or testimony to be false and willfully made.

Definitions and General Terms

Acknowledgment

A formal declaration before a duly authorized officer by a person who has executed an instrument that such execution is his act and deed.

Technically, an "acknowledgment" is the declaration of a person described in and who has executed a written instrument, that he executed the same. As commonly used, the term means the certificate of an officer, duly empowered to take an acknowledgment or proof of the conveyance of real property, that on a specified date "**before me came ...., to me known to be the individual described in and who executed the foregoing instrument and acknowledged that he executed the same.**" The purposes of the law respecting acknowledgments are not only to promote the security of land titles and to prevent frauds in conveyancing, but to furnish proof of the due execution of conveyances (*Armstrong v. Combs,* 15 App. Div. 246) so as to permit the document to be given in evidence, without further proof of its execution, and make it a recordable instrument.

The Real Property Law prescribes:

"**§303. Requisites of acknowledgments.** An acknowledgment must not be taken by any officer unless he knows or has satisfactory evidence, that the person making it is the person described in and who executed such instrument."

The thing to be known is the identity of the person making the acknowledgment with the person described in the instrument and the person who executed the same. This knowledge must be possessed by the notary (*Gross v. Rowley,* 147 App. Div. 529), and a notary must not take an acknowledgment unless the notary knows or has proof that the person making it is the person described in and who executed the instrument (*People v. Kempner,* 49 App. Div. 121). It is not essential that the person who executed the instrument sign his name in the presence of the notary. Taking acknowledgments over the telephone is illegal and a notary public is guilty of a misdemeanor in so acting. **In the certificate of acknowledgment a notary public declares: "On this .... day of .... 19 ...., before me came .... to me known," etc.** Unless the person purporting to have made the acknowledgment actually and personally appeared before the notary on the day specified, the notary's certificate that he so came is palpably false and fraudulent. (*Matter of Brooklyn Bar Assoc.,* 225 App. Div. 680.)

Interest as a disqualification. A notary public should not take an acknowledgment to a legal instrument to which the notary is a party in interest. (*Armstrong v. Combs,* 15 App. Div. 246.)

Fraudulent certificates of acknowledgment. A notary public who knowingly makes a false certificate that a deed or other written instrument was acknowledged by a party thereto is guilty of forgery in the second degree, which is punishable by imprisonment for a term of not exceeding 7 years (Penal Law, §§170.10 and 70.00[2(d)]. The essence of the crime is false certification, intention to defraud. (*People v. Abeel,* 182 NY 415.) While the absence of guilty knowledge or criminal intent would absolve the notary from criminal liability, the conveyance, of which the false certification is an essential part, is a forgery and, therefore, invalid. (*Caccioppoli v. Lemmo,* 152 App. Div. 650.)

Damages recoverable from notary for false certificate. Action for damages sustained where notary certified that mortgagor had appeared and acknowledged a mortgage. (*Kainz v. Goldsmith,* 231 App. Div. 171.)

Administrator

A person appointed by the court to manage the estate of a deceased person who left no will.

Affiant

The person who makes and subscribes his signature to an affidavit.

Affidavit

An affidavit is a signed statement, duly sworn to, by the maker thereof, before a notary public or other officer authorized to administer oaths. The venue, or county wherein the affidavit was sworn to should be accurately stated. But it is of far more importance that the affiant, the person making the affidavit, should have personally appeared before the notary and have made oath to the statements contained in the affidavit as required by law. Under the Penal Law (§210.00) the wilful making of a false affidavit is perjury, but to sustain an indictment therefor, there must have been, in some form, in the presence of an officer authorized to administer an oath, an unequivocal and present act by which the affiant consciously took upon himself the obligation of an oath; his silent delivery of a signed affidavit to the notary for his certificate, is not enough. (*People v. O'Reilly,* 86 NY 154; People ex rel. *Greene v. Swasey,* 122 Misc. 388; *People v. Levitas* (1963) 40 Misc. 2d 331.) A notary public will be removed from office for preparing and taking the oath of an affiant to a statement that the notary knew to be false. (*Matter of Senft,* August 8, 1929; *Matter of Trotta,* February 20, 1930; *Matter of Kibbe,* December 24, 1931.)

The distinction between the taking of an acknowledgment and an affidavit must be clearly understood. In the case of an acknowledgment, the notary public certifies as to the identity and execution of a document; the affidavit involves the administration of an oath to the affiant. There are certain acknowledgment forms which are a combination of an acknowledgment and affidavit. It is incumbent on the notary public to scrutinize each document presented to him and to ascertain the exact nature of the notary's duty with relation thereto. An affidavit differs from a deposition in that an affidavit is an ex parte statement. (*See definition of Deposition.*)

Affirmation

A solemn declaration made by persons who conscientiously decline taking an oath; it is equivalent to an oath and is just as binding; if a person has religious or conscientious scruples against taking an oath, the notary public should have the person affirm. **The following is a form of affirmation: "Do you solemnly, sincerely, and truly, declare and affirm that the statements made by you are true and correct."**

Apostile

Department of State authentication attached to a notarized and county-certified document for possible international use.

Attest
To witness the execution of a written instrument, at the request of the person who makes it, and subscribe the same as a witness.

Attestation Clause
That clause (*e.g.* at the end of a will) wherein the witnesses certify that the instrument has been executed before them, and the manner of the execution of the same.

Authentication (Notarial)
A certificate subjoined by a county clerk to any certificate of proof or acknowledgment or oath signed by a notary; this county clerk's certificate authenticates or verifies the authority of the notary public to act as such. (See §133, Executive Law.)

Bill of Sale
A written instrument given to pass title of personal property from vendor to vendee.

Certified Copy
A copy of a public record signed and certified as a true copy by the public official having custody of the original. A notary public has no authority to issue certified copies. Notaries must not certify to the authenticity of legal documents and other papers required to be filed with foreign consular officers. Within this prohibition are certificates of the following type:

United States of America)
State of New York) ss.:
County of New York)

"I ...., a notary public of the State of New York, in and for the county of ...., duly commissioned, qualified and sworn according to the laws of the State of New York, do hereby certify and declare that I verily believe the annexed instrument executed by .... and sworn to before ...., a notary public of the State of ...., to be genuine in every respect, and that full faith and credit are and ought to be given thereto. "In testimony whereof I have hereunto set my hand and seal at the City of ...., this .... day of ...., 19 ....

(Seal) (Notarial Signature.)"

Concerning such a notarial certificate it has been held:

> "The law has made specific provisions for the manner in which papers may be certified as to authenticity and originality.

While in this individual case there may be no indication of deceiving nor any deception, nevertheless it is a practice which may become subject to deception and therefore the requirements as laid down by the law for the conduct of notaries should be most strictly enforced." (Op. Atty. Gen.)

The making of a useless certificate and the collection of a fee therefore, by a notary public, after the notary has had official warning against such practices, justifies a conclusion of misconduct which warrants the notary's removal from office. (Op. Atty. Gen., May 26, 1931.) But a notarial certificate that an attached copy of a paper is a true and exact copy of the original document is not within the ban of the last mentioned opinion, for the reason that while this form of certificate does not permit the copy of the paper to be read in evidence, it might be accepted by certain persons as sufficient proof of the correctness of the copy and, accordingly, it cannot be said to be entirely valueless. (Op. Atty. Gen., Aug. 22, 1933.)

Chattel
Personal property, such as household goods or fixtures.

Chattel Paper
A writing or writings which evidence both an obligation to pay money and a security interest in a lease or specific goods. The agreement which creates or provides for the security interest is known as a security agreement.

Codicil
An instrument made subsequent to a will and modifying it in some respects.

Consideration
Anything of value given to induce entering into a contract; it may be money, personal services, or even love and affection.

Contempt of Court
Behavior disrespectful of the authority of a court which disrupts the execution of court orders.

Contract
An agreement between competent parties to do or not to do certain things for a legal consideration, whereby each party acquires a right to what the other possesses.

Conveyance (Deed)
Every instrument, in writing, except a will, by which any estate or interest in real property is created, transferred, assigned or surrendered.

County Clerk's Certificate
See "Authentication (Notarial)."

Deponent
One who makes oath to a written statement. Technically, a person subscribing a deposition but used interchangeably with "Affiant."

Deposition
The testimony of a witness taken out of court or other hearing proceeding, under oath or by affirmation, before a notary public or other person, officer or commissioner before whom such testimony is authorized by law to be taken, which is intended to be used at the trial or hearing.

Duress
Unlawful constraint exercised upon a person whereby he is forced to do some act against his will.

Escrow
The placing of an instrument in the hands of a person as a depository who on the happening of a designated event, is to deliver the instrument to a third person. This agreement, once established, should be unalterable.

Executor
One named in a will to carry out the provisions of the will.

Ex Parte (From One Side Only)
A hearing or examination in the presence of, or on papers filed by, one party and in the absence of the other.

Felony
A crime punishable by death or imprisonment in a state prison.

Guardian
A person in charge of a minor's person or property.

Judgment
Decree of a court declaring that one individual is indebted to another and fixing the amount of such indebtedness.

Jurat
A jurat is that part of an affidavit where the officer (notary public) certifies that it was sworn to before him. It is not the affidavit.

The following is the form of jurat generally employed:

> "Sworn to before me this .... day of ...., 19 ......"
>
> Those words placed directly after the signature in the affidavit stating that the facts therein contained were sworn to or affirmed before the officer (notary public) together with his official signature and such other data as required by § 137 of the Executive Law.

Laches
The delay or negligence in asserting one's legal rights.

Lease
A contract whereby, for a consideration, usually termed rent, one who is entitled to the possession of real property transfers such right to another for life, for a term of years or at will.

Lien
A legal right or claim upon a specific property which attaches to the property until a debt is satisfied.

Litigation
The act of carrying on a lawsuit.

Misdemeanor
Any crime other than a felony.

Mortgage On Real Property
An instrument in writing, duly executed and delivered that creates a lien upon real estate as security for the payment of a specified debt, which is usually in the form of a bond.

Notary Public
A public officer who executes acknowledgments of deeds or writings in order to render them available as evidence of the facts therein contained; administers oaths and affirmation as to the truth of statements contained in papers or documents requiring the administration of an oath. The notary's general authority is defined in §135 of the Executive Law; the notary has certain other powers which can be found in the various provisions of law set forth earlier in this publication.

Oath
A verbal pledge given by the person taking it that his statements are made under an immediate sense of this responsibility to God, who will punish the affiant if the statements are false.

Notaries public must administer oaths and affirmations in manner and form as prescribed by the Civil Practice Law and Rules, namely:

> **§2309(b) Form.** An oath or affirmation shall be administered in a form calculated to awaken the conscience and impress the mind of the person taking it in accordance with his religious or ethical beliefs. An oath must be administered as required by law. The person taking the oath must personally appear before the notary; an oath cannot be administered over the telephone (*Matter of Napolis,* 169 App. Div. 469), and the oath must be administered in the form required by the statute (*Bookman v. City of New York,* 200 NY 53, 56).
>
> When an oath is administered the person taking the oath must express assent to the oath repeated by the notary by the words "I do" or some other words of like meaning.
>
> For an oath or affirmation to be valid, whatever form is adopted, it is necessary that: first, the person swearing or affirming must personally be in the presence of the notary public; secondly, that the person unequivocally swears or affirms that what he states is true; thirdly, that he swears or affirms as

of that time; and, lastly, that the person conscientiously takes upon himself the obligation of an oath.

A notary public does not fulfill his duty by merely asking a person whether the signature on a purported affidavit is his. An oath must be administered.

A corporation or a partnership cannot take an oath; an oath must be taken by an individual.

A notary public cannot administer an oath to himself.

The privileges and rights of a notary public are personal and cannot be delegated to anyone.

Plantiff

A person who starts a suit or brings an action against another.

Power of Attorney

A written statement by an individual giving another person the power to act for him.

Proof

The formal declaration made by a subscribing witness to the execution of an instrument setting forth his place of residence, that he knew the person described in and who executed the instrument and that he saw such person execute such instrument.

Protest

A formal statement in writing by a notary public, under seal, that a certain bill of exchange or promissory note was on a certain day presented for payment, or acceptance, and that such payment or acceptance was refused.

Seal

The laws of the State of New York do not require the use of seals by notaries public. If a seal is used, it should sufficiently identify the notary public, his authority and jurisdiction. It is the opinion of the Department of State that the only inscription required is the name of the notary and the words "Notary Public for the State of New York."

Signature of Notary Public

A notary public must sign the name under which he was appointed and no other. In addition to his signature and venue, the notary public shall print, typewrite or stamp beneath his signature in black ink, his name, the words "Notary Public State of New York," the name of the county in which he is qualified, and the date upon which his commission expires (§137, Executive Law).

When a woman notary marries during the term of office for which she was appointed, she may continue to use her maiden name as notary public. However, if she elects to use her marriage name, then for the balance of her term as a notary public she must continue to use her maiden name in her signature and seal when acting in her notarial capacity, adding after her signature her married name, in parentheses. When renewing her commission as a notary public, she may apply under her married name or her maiden name. She must then perform all her notarial functions under the name selected.

A member of a religious order, known therein by a name other than his secular cognomen, may be appointed and may officiate as a notary public under the name by which he is known in religious circles. (Op. Atty. Gen., Mar. 20, 1930.)

Statute
A law established by an act of the Legislature.

Statute of Frauds
State law which provides that certain contracts must be in writing or partially complied with, in order to be enforceable at law.

Statute of Limitations
A law that limits the time within which a criminal prosecution or a civil action must be started.

Subordination Clause
A clause which permits the placing of a mortgage at a later date which takes priority over an existing mortgage.

Sunday

A notary public may administer an oath or take an affidavit or acknowledgment on Sunday. However, a deposition cannot be taken on Sunday in a civil proceeding.

Swear

This term includes every mode authorized by law for administering an oath.

Taking an Acknowledgment

The act of the person named in an instrument telling the notary public that he is the person named in the instrument and acknowledging that he executed such instrument; also includes the act of the notary public in obtaining satisfactory evidence of the identity of the person whose acknowledgment is taken.

The notary public "certifies to the taking of the acknowledgment" when the notary signs his official signature to the form setting forth the fact of the taking of the acknowledgment.

Venue

The geographical place where a notary public takes an affidavit or acknowledgment. Every affidavit or certificate of acknowledgment should show on its face the venue of the notarial act. The venue is usually set forth at the beginning of the instrument or at the top of the notary's jurat, or official certification, as follows: "State of New York, County of (New York) ss.:". Section 137 of the Executive Law imposes the duty on the notary public to include the venue of his act in all certificates of acknowledgments or jurats to affidavits.

Will

The disposition of one's property to take effect after death.

Schedule of Fees

Appointment as Notary Public–	
Total Commission Fee	$60.00
($40 appointment and $20 filing of Oath of Office)	
Change of Name/Address	10.00
Duplicate Identification Card	10.00
Issuance of Certificate of Official Character	5.00

Filing Certificate of Official Character	10.00
Authentication Certificate	3.00
Protest of Note, Commercial Paper, etc.	.75
Each additional Notice of Protest (limit 5) each	.10
Oath or Affirmation	2.00
Acknowledgment (each person)	2.00
Proof of Execution (each person)	2.00
Swearing Witness	2.00

Note

Where gender pronouns appear in this booklet, they are meant to refer to both male and female persons.

INDEX

AFTERWORD

The foregoing handbook was the result of intensive research and meticulous preparation. It is the desire of both the author and the publisher to provide a handbook of the highest quality. Reader feedback is encouraged. In preparation of future editions, a key component is reader suggestion.

Have you come across an interesting newspaper, magazine of journal article or other publication concerning notaries public or a notarial matter? Have you been involved in a court case (administrative, civil or criminal) concerning a notorial matter? Have you evidence of possible notary misconduct, but are experiencing difficulty in having the matter investigated? Have you been the victim of notary misconduct? Are you experiencing some difficulty with a partivular notorial area? Are you noticing some new trends in notorial practice? Do you have any special tips that you have found helpful in your own notorial practice? Would you like to personally correspond with the author on some related legal topic? Would you like to invite the author to testify on a notorial matter, speak before your organization as a keynote speaker, or perhaps conduct an educational seminar at a confrence or other meeting?

Please direct all materials and comments to the attention of the author in care of the publisher. Please include a telephone contact number, including facsimile telephone number, if available. All correspondence will receive a written response. The postal address is:

ALFRED E. PIOMBINO
C/o ECP
P.O. Box 3539
Poughkeepsie, New York 12603

NOTARY PUBLIC HANDBOOK:
A GUIDE FOR NEW YORK, FOURTH EDITION
BY PIOMBINO

COMMENT REPLY FORM

1. What did you like about this book?

2. What did you dislike about this book?

3. How do you rate the illustrations? (Circle one)
   very good good not useful poor

4. How do you rate the readability?
   very good good not useful poor

5. How do you rate the glossary?
   very good good not useful poor

6. How do you rate the appendices?
   very good good not useful

7. How do you use this book? (check all that apply)
   ____ refrence ____ review ____study purposes

8. Who would you say this book is written for?
   ____ persons not yet appointed
   ____ presently appointed officers ____ both

9. Suggested additional topics:

10. Comments:

Signature ______________________ Date ____________________

PERMISSION IS GRANTED TO QUOTE ME.

Address ____

____

RETURN TO: EDITORIAL DEPARTMENT

P.O. BOX 2829, POUGHKEEPSIE, NEW YORK 12603

WHERE IS *YOUR* NOTARY PUBLIC REGISTER?

Why would a notary public keep records? Simple. It's affordable, legal protection. *Every* time you sign your name as a notary public, you are putting your personal credibility *and* legal liability on the line.

State law in over 35 states either mandates or strongly recommends that a notary public maintain written records and every year, more states are requiring it. Although Vermont Law does not compel a notary public to keep records, can 35 other states be wrong? In the event that a Vermont notary public is the subject of a lawsuit or indicted, the state government does not suffer from a guilty verdict—the *notary public* bears the financial loss and public humiliation.

Why should you keep records? Here are three reasons.

1. *Even careful and intelligent notaries public are human and make mistakes.* Upon realizing a mistake was made, a written transaction record makes client contact *possible* to rectify the error. Basic transaction data could help to avoid unnecessary legal costs, disciplinary action (including suspension, revocation or up to $500 fine) by the court, and even a costly damage award for negligence in your official notarial duties—not to mention lost professional credibility in the eyes of the client or your employer.

2. *People have been known to deny that they appeared before a notary public (even when they did actually appear).* This puts the notary public on the defense. Record of the client's signature, identification serial number and other legal data will help bolster the credibility of the notary public in the eyes of the law. How else do you *prove* that you *did* examine identification?

3. *Forgery of notary public signatures is increasing.* You *can't* prevent an unscrupulous person from forging your official signature (by tracing your signature from a legitimate document that you notarized onto a forged document). But you *can* defend yourself from allegations by showing your record book (with no record of this transaction) to the authorities. Simply declaring on a witness stand that it wasn't your action may *not* be enough to combat accusations against you. Protect yourself!

Selected Books By the Author

Notary Public Handbook: Principles, Practices & Cases, National Edition

Notary Public Handbook: A Guide for New York, Fourth Edition

Notary Public Handbook: A Guide for New Jersey

Notary Public Handbook: A Guide for Maine

Notary Public Handbook: A Guide for Florida

Notary Public Handbook: A Guide for Vermont Notaries, Commissioners & Justices of the Peace

Notary Public Handbook: A Guide for California Notaries & Commissioners

Notary Public Register & Recordkeeping Protocols

The Office of Alfred E. Piombino

Piombino@AlfredPiombino.com

www.NotaryPublicLaw.us